X

Theatre and Empowerment

Theatre and Empowerment examines the ability of drama, theatre, dance and performance to empower communities of very different kinds, and it does so from a multicultural perspective. The communities involved include disadvantaged children in Ethiopia and the Indian subcontinent, disenfranchised Native Americans in the USA and young black men in Britain, people caught in cycles of violence in South Africa and Northern Ireland, and a threatened agricultural town in Italy. The book asserts the value of performance as a vital agent of necessary social change, and makes its arguments through the close examination, from 'inside' practice, of the success – not always complete – of specific projects in their practical and cultural contexts. Practitioners and commentators ask how performance in its widest sense can play a part in community activism on a scale larger than the individual, 'one-off' project by helping communities find their own liberating and creative voices.

RICHARD BOON is Professor of Performance Studies at the School of Performance and Cultural Industries, University of Leeds. JANE PLASTOW is Senior Lecturer in Theatre Studies at the Workshop Theatre, School of English, University of Leeds. They are also the editors of *Theatre Matters: Performance and Culture on the World Stage* (Cambridge University Press, 1998).

CAMBRIDGE STUDIES IN MODERN THEATRE

Series editor
David Bradby, *Royal Holloway, University of London*

Advisory board
Martin Banham, *University of Leeds*
Jacky Bratton, *Royal Holloway, University of London*
Tracy Davis, *Northwestern University*
Sir Richard Eyre
Michael Robinson, *University of East Anglia*
Sheila Stowell, *University of Birmingham*

Volumes for Cambridge Studies in Modern Theatre explore the political, social and cultural functions of theatre while also paying careful attention to detailed performance analysis. The focus of the series is on political approaches to the modern theatre with attention also being paid to theatres of earlier periods and their influence on contemporary drama. Topics in the series are chosen to investigate this relationship and include both playwrights (their aims and intentions set against the effects of their work) and process (with emphasis on rehearsal and production methods, the political structure within theatre companies, and their choice of audiences or performance venues). Further topics will include devised theatre, agitprop, community theatre, para-theatre and performance art. In all cases the series will be alive to the special cultural and political factors operating in the theatres examined.

Books published
Brian Crow with Chris Banfield, *An Introduction to Post-colonial Theatre*
Mario DiCenzo, *The Politics of Alternative Theatre in Britain, 1968–1990:7:84 (Scotland)*
Jo Riley, *Chinese Theatre and the Actor in Performance*
Jonathan Kalb, *The Theatre of Heiner Müller*
Richard Boon and Jane Plastow, eds., *Theatre Matters: Performance and Culture on the World Stage*
Claude Schumacher, ed., *Staging the Holocaust: the Shoah in Drama and Performance*
Philip Roberts, *The Royal Court Theatre and the Modern Stage*
Nicholas Grene, *The Politics of Irish Drama: Plays in Context from Boucicault to Friel*
Anatoly Smeliansky, *The Russian Theatre after Stalin*
Clive Barker and Maggie B. Gale, eds., *British Theatre Between the Wars, 1918–1939*
Michael Patterson, *Strategics of Political Theatre: Post-war British Playwrights*
Gabriele Griffin, *Contemporary Black and Asian Women Playwrights in Britain*
Elaine Aston, *Feminist Views on the English Stage: Women Playwrights, 1990–2000*
Loren Kruger, *Post-Imperial Brecht: Politics and Performance, East and South*
Richard Boon and Jane Plastow, eds., *Theatre and Empowerment: Community Drama on the World Stage*

Theatre and Empowerment

Community Drama on the World Stage

Edited by
Richard Boon and Jane Plastow

 CAMBRIDGE
UNIVERSITY PRESS

PUBLISHED BY THE PRESS SYNDICATE OF THE UNIVERSITY OF CAMBRIDGE
The Pitt Building, Trumpington Street, Cambridge, United Kingdom

CAMBRIDGE UNIVERSITY PRESS
The Edinburgh Building, Cambridge, CB2 2RU, UK
40 West 20th Street, New York, NY 10011–4211, USA
477 Williamstown Road, Port Melbourne, VIC 3207, Australia
Ruiz de Alarcón 13, 28014 Madrid, Spain
Dock House, The Waterfront, Cape Town 8001, South Africa

http://www.cambridge.org

First published 2004

Printed in the United Kingdom at the University Press, Cambridge

Typefaces Trump Mediaeval 9.25/14 pt. and Schadow BT   System LaTeX 2ε [TB]

Library of Congress Cataloguing in Publication data

ISBN 0 521 81729 3 hardback

For Kitty Burrows

Contents

Contents

Notes on contributors

RICHARD ANDREWS is Emeritus Professor of Italian at the
University of Leeds, UK. He is the author of *Scripts and
Scenarios: the performance of comedy in Renaissance Italy*
(Cambridge University Press, 1993), and of articles on Italian
and European comic drama and opera. He has also been
visiting Monticchiello on an annual basis since 1985,
witnessing and monitoring rehearsals and performances,
occasionally attending script conferences, and recently
compiling performance records for the archive.

RICHARD BOON is Professor of Performance Studies in the School of
Performance and Cultural Industries at the University of
Leeds, UK. His teaching and research interests lie primarily in
political theatre of all kinds, in directing for the stage and in
multicultural theatre. He is the author of *Brenton the
Playwright* and of a number of articles mainly in the area of
British political theatre of the twentieth century, and is
co-editor, with Jane Plastow, of *Theatre Matters: Performance
and Culture on the World Stage*.

MICHAEL ETHERTON has lectured in universities in Africa and the
UK, and is the author of *The Development of African Drama*
and *Contemporary Irish Drama*, as well as articles on popular
theatre and on education. For the past twelve years he has been
working for International Non-Governmental Organisations
in Asia. He has spent three years as Field Director for VSO in
Bhutan, has been Oxfam GB's Country Representative in
Vietnam, and Education Advisor and Head of the Regional
Office for Save the Children UK in South and Central Asia.

Notes on contributors

SANJOY GANGULY was active in Communist politics as a student. Disillusioned by its centralist tendencies, he left the party to search for a political culture of dialogue and democracy. He began working in theatre in rural Bengal in the early 1980s. His encounter several years later with Augusto Boal and the Theatre of the Oppressed, coupled with his own passionate commitment to the creation of a more just and equal society, led him to found Jana Sanskriti, an independent organisation committed to the use of theatre to conscientise and empower the communities it serves. With more than thirty active theatre groups associated with the group, Jana Sanskriti is now the largest organisation of its kind in India.

MICHAEL MACMILLAN is a black British playwright and theatre practitioner. He is currently researching in the area of black British theatre at Manchester Metropolitan University, UK, and was until recently Writer-in-Residence at the School of English, University of Leeds, UK.

GERRI MORIARTY works as a community artist and arts consultant in the North West of England and in Northern Ireland. She has devised and directed community theatre projects in the British Isles and in East Africa, and has pioneered the use of the arts as a method of public consultation. She has worked with a wide variety of community groups, voluntary organisations, local authorities, statutory agencies and educational institutions, both to develop practical arts projects and to develop policy and strategy. She is currently researching evaluation methodologies appropriate for arts projects working in areas of social exclusion. She is an advisor to North West Arts and a member of the Arts Council of Northern Ireland.

STEPHANIE MARLIN-CURIEL is a Research Associate at the Sliflia Program for Intercommunal Coexistence at Brandeis University, Massachusetts, and has taught in the Department of Art and Public Policy at New York University's Tisch School of the Arts, where she received her PhD in Performance Studies. Her various publications (see, for example, her chapter in *Art and the Performance of Memory:*

Sounds and Gestures of Recollection, edited by Richard Cándida Smith) offer analyses of cultural responses to South Africa's Truth and Reconciliation Commission.

JANE PLASTOW is Senior Lecturer in Theatre Studies and Deputy Director of the Workshop Theatre, School of English, University of Leeds, UK, where she teaches primarily in the areas of African and developmental theatre. She is also Director of Leeds University Centre for African Studies. She has worked on a variety of theatre projects in Africa since the 1980s, primarily in Ethiopia, Tanzania and Zimbabwe, and is at present closely involved in developing Eritrean theatre in the post-liberation period. She has written widely on emergent Eritrean theatre and is the author of *African Theatre and Politics.*

RICARDO VILLANUEVA has acted, directed and written for Chicana/o Teatro since the mid 1970s. He earned his PhD under Martin Banham at the Workshop Theatre, Leeds, in 1994. He now teaches Theatre and Ethnic Studies at California State University, Sacramento.

1 Introduction

RICHARD BOON AND JANE PLASTOW

Several years ago we published *Theatre Matters: Performance and Culture on the World Stage* (Cambridge University Press, 1998), a collection of essays which argued – forcibly, we hope – that 'theatre, in a variety of forms and contexts, can make, and indeed has made, positive political and social interventions in a range of developing cultures across the world'. The present book rests squarely on the same conviction: to its contributors as well as to its editors, theatre *still* matters.

It matters in its power to bring together divided communities of different kinds (and in one case described here, perhaps to save a particular community from outright extinction) and to engage creatively, productively and meaningfully with a wide range of issues from extreme poverty to AIDS, violence, human rights, sexual, racial and political intolerance and the power of the state. As in the earlier book, diversity is celebrated. Material is drawn from a wide and varied geographical range: from Ethiopia and South Africa, from Bangladesh, Pakistan, India and Nepal, and from the British Isles, Italy and America. The inclusion of the three essays from the 'developed' world is important because it is our contention that the kinds of performance often referred to as 'Theatre for Development' (TfD) are by no means relevant only to the political South. It is assumed far too often that development is something which needs to be 'done' (economically and/or ideologically) to the South, whereas the West has already achieved some higher level of enlightenment. The essays in this book not only contest the notion that development can be 'done to' anyone, but also demonstrate how performance may be used in a plethora of ways to address issues of injustice,

I

prejudice and cultural and economic poverty. Compare, for example, the work practised by Gerri Moriarty in Northern Ireland and by Bongani Linda in South Africa, work exploring similarly divided communities and taking place in the most difficult and even dangerous circumstances.

The writers commissioned for this book were asked essentially to describe and discuss their own experiences *in the field*. We brought no overarching theoretical agenda to the task of gathering material; nor did we insist that our contributors locate their work within particular theoretical traditions or paradigms. We do not for a moment underestimate the importance of theory, and indeed hope that the practices discussed here will contribute to the development of theoretical understanding, but this is not a book which seeks to describe 'practice-as-example-of-theory'. There are already a number of texts which seek to fulfil that particular function.[1] This is a 'ground-up' book, and what we have discovered is that while many of 'our' contributors (like Sanjoy Ganguly) have indeed seized upon a particular practitioner/theorist such as Augusto Boal as vitally important to the way they approach their work (and Boal's ideas recur throughout this book and across a wide range of kinds of practice), what has interested us more is the diversity of motivations, ideas, perspectives and approaches, and ways of describing and accounting for them, which can be incorporated into – and debated within – practice.

For example, in terms of political orientation, Ganguly began his work from a clear socialist perspective. Similarly, the socialist heritage of the Tuscan peasants played a key informing role in how their theatrical cooperative was formed. In South Africa it was armed political struggle which had a key influence on how Linda has trained his 'cultural combatants'. However, in each case political analysis *alone* has come to be seen as insufficient for meeting the needs of those to whom the work is addressed. ANC/Inkatha rivalries are seen as only further reinforced by those in search of political power bases, and in India Ganguly moves further and further away from the kind of overbearing political dogmatism which he sees as antipathetic to inclusive 'dialectical development'.

Development theories can be similarly problematic. Sometimes this is apparently a question, as in Ethiopia, of different or competing discourses and jargons inhibiting understanding. But it is also the case that when theory is applied with insufficient understanding or, worse, when power bases – political, developmental, religious – feel themselves to be threatened, then the real problem of the subjugation of the rights and needs of already marginalised people arises: genuine participation from those whom such agencies claim to serve means that *all* involved must be open, flexible and willing continually to learn, and this can fundamentally undermine the status of the 'expert' and the authoritative institution. Ganguly expresses an understanding which we believe many in this field are feeling their way towards as a result of their participatory practice: 'Experience constantly teaches us new lessons that institutional education cannot match.'

What unites the practices explored in this book is that they are all profoundly subversive of established power. They distrust, even abhor, dogma, and have the humility to realise that they have never achieved 'truth' but are always part of the profoundly stimulating and fundamentally human process of learning from their actors, participants and spectactors.

Many of the practitioners speaking and described here did not come to community-based theatre from a theoretical, still less an academic, basis of understanding, or even from an arts background, though all have to varying extents borrowed from a range of empowerment-oriented discourses: socialism, Freierian development theory, Christianity, Schechner's ideas on the roles of the arts, black liberation theory, Hinduism, and so on. A number have had to operate for many years in relative isolation, teasing out for themselves ideas of what makes empowering arts work, before they found kindred groups or bodies of useful, established theory. This can be a weakness: progress may be slow as dead ends are explored or wheels reinvented. But it is also a great strength, insofar as practices develop that uniquely reflect and are closely tailored to the cultures and needs of the communities they serve. What seems to us vital, and what unifies the diverse practices described here, is that by working directly with the disempowered, all those involved have been forced to question their sense of their *own* expertise or authority – in that sense, willingly to disempower themselves – in favour of more open-ended, democratic and meaningful learning processes.

What we present here are, we think, some of the most exciting and empowering experiments with community-based arts that we know of. There are bound to be many more, just as there are certainly plenty of examples of bad practice. The form has already been dogmatised by many who will argue at length over whether a particular project is 'properly Boalian' or, worse, who seek to use formulae to deliver TfD, dance or video that reinforces a 'message' decided upon by a government or development agency. If this book has any importance, it lies in encouraging resistance to such doctrinaire thinking in any area purporting to support the humanisation of humanity and the empowerment of marginalised people, wherever they are, and in demonstrating that this struggle goes on simultaneously in America and Africa, in Italy and Nepal. After all, no nation has yet got anywhere near liberating the full potential of its people.

Some aspects of the work describe art forms which are expanding as tools of rights and development practice. The increasingly sophisticated use of video and other, more modern technologies in some of the projects discussed (Michael MacMillan's experiences with black youth in Britain, and Michael Etherton's work with children's rights in the Indian subcontinent, for example) reflects the use of forms which are rapidly being appropriated for community use. The use of dance as a developmental arts form is, however, still rare, at least in the context and on the scale described by Jane Plastow.

As we suggest above, this is a 'ground-up' book. We have also tried, where possible (and this is a further development of one of the themes of *Theatre Matters*), to address practice *from the inside*. Of the eight chapters which follow, five are written by practitioners who are directly involved in leading the work they describe and discuss. Their passion for the work, and the commitment they bring to it, are evident (and are shared in no small degree by those of our contributors who are not themselves practitioners). It is this which lends, at times, a deeply personal tone to the writing, a tendency we have encouraged the better to express the realities of involvement in the various projects described. What is also striking is the degree of self-questioning, self-criticism, doubt and ambivalence that characterises the way in which many of these figures practise: all, in different ways, are acutely conscious of the risks, problems and pitfalls involved in their work. Indeed, this is one of the things that makes them, we believe, *good* practitioners. It is also evident that, in many cases, engagement in performance practice which has sought in one way or another to transform the lives of individuals and their communities has also had the effect of transforming the lives of those leading that work. If TfD and its related forms are always in a real sense 'works in progress', then, for the practitioners involved, it is also true that (to borrow Michael MacMillan's words) the self, too, is a work in progress, and this casts a particular light on our understanding of what we mean by 'empowerment'.

Establishing just what *may* be meant by 'empowerment' is a – perhaps *the* – key question in this book. Who is being empowered by whom, and to what end? How can practitioners in the area prove that what they do *is* empowering? These are questions asked often, and quite legitimately, by project funders. Here arts practitioners concerned with notions of rights and empowerment can quickly find themselves in awkward, and at times confrontational, debate with both funders – government bodies, national and international non-governmental organisations (NGOs and INGOs), United Nations organisations and well-meaning individuals – and with political states. In the experience of many who have been working in this area over the past twenty years or so, what funders usually want is issue-based theatre (preferably concerned with an issue of their choice) which is contained within closely defined parameters.

Theatre informing people about HIV/AIDS, for example, has been widely used in recent years in Africa. It is obviously essential that people understand the nature of the disease and the means of its transmission, and are urged to modify their lifestyles in order to stay healthy and inhibit its currently relentless progress. Stephanie Marlin-Curiel's essay on the work of Bongani Linda demonstrates for any who may yet need convincing how important this educational work is in places like South Africa, and Linda has been able to attract considerable funding for his AIDS plays. But Marlin-Curiel also makes it clear that the problem of HIV/AIDS is related to the massive incidence of rape and the pressure for young people to appear sexually active and attractive in the South African townships. This is in turn linked to the need to acquire status in material terms, in a context where South Africa's current economic conditions and political history militate against black rural and township youth having the opportunity to improve their lot through conventional means, and therefore turning to drugs and crime. Sex becomes a means for girls to acquire material goods in return for their favours, and for boys to assert their manhood. (The latter point finds an echo in Michael MacMillan's essay on young black British men who have swallowed the colonially induced myth that black men have especial sexual prowess, and who then feel that this becomes the only area where they can assert a sense of self-worth.)

The point is that 'issues' never exist in isolation. Yet this is how funders and governments appear to want to tackle them. Why?

First, because it is easier for accountancy purposes. We can count how many condoms are given out and demonstrate that 'x' number of people are therefore moving towards safe-sex practices; we can list how many wells have been dug, and tell the publics and states which back an aid programme that so many more thousand people now have access to clean water. This is increasingly a path being followed by NGOs and INGOs, which neatly categorise and delimit their particular areas of concern – health, gender, good governance, the environment and so on – because they do not wish to make themselves vulnerable to charges of woolly do-goodery, or being vague and 'scattergun' in approach. The perceived risk is that politicians and the public will not tolerate work that does not quickly show unambiguously quantifiable and concrete results. But we would argue that such a policy will only ever have limited impact. It may ameliorate dire living conditions, but it can never truly transform lives. The clearest example of the limitations of such an approach comes in Michael Etherton's essay on his work with Save the Children in the Indian subcontinent. Etherton is the only contributor who has worked as both practitioner and aid worker, but we see a beautiful illustration of the limited perspectives of even some of the most progressive agencies in the programme manager who throws up her hands in horror when a children's rights workshop identifies drug abuse as a key source of oppression in the children's lives. 'Oh no!' she says, 'Not drugs! Please not drugs! Save the Children won't allow us to tackle the drugs problem!' Yet drugs are key to a whole range of problems experienced by those whom Save the Children specifically dedicates itself to helping. The single-issue approach is exposed as an absurdity.

The second reason for the desire to ring-fence areas of concern and to fund only immediately and obviously related arts activities, is, we fear, to do with 'domestication': the desire to control people rather than to liberate communities and individuals. The process behind much of the arts work described in this book necessarily pushes people to think and to analyse. It also encourages the taking of space (literal and metaphorical) and the raising of self-esteem, so that participants come both to question the root causes of their problems and oppressions – a process that leads from the micro to the macro, and from the particular community to the wider polity – and to believe that they can take centre stage to give voice and expression to their understandings. In Jane Plastow's essay on the Adugna Community Dance Theatre in Ethiopia, a five-year project with street children is described wherein the young people concerned move from being huddled in corners, effectively obliterating themselves from view, to the point where one of them says he feels 'like God', creating art on stage in front of an audience. Gods are not notably humble. They believe they have a right to create, and what they seek to create may well conflict with the (at best) paternal and (at worst) dictatorial regimes run by organisations ranging from governments to the World Bank to churches and to (I)NGOs. Empowerment is to do not with the amelioration of oppression and poverty *per se*, but with the liberation of the human mind and spirit, and with the transformation of participants who see themselves – and are often seen by others – as subhuman, operating only at the level of seeking merely to exist, into conscious beings aware of and claiming voices and choices in how their lives will be lived.

Such empowerment is challenging, difficult to quantify, and an ongoing process affecting facilitators, participants and audiences to varying degrees at various times. In many of the projects we see, it has resulted in improved material conditions for participants: for the people of Monticchiello in Italy, for the South African actors who have gained training and subsequent employment, for the Adugna dancers who now have a regular income (though the facilitators – Royston Muldoom in Ethiopia and Sanjoy Ganguly in India – often lose potential income themselves in pursuing community arts objectives). But instead of taking the usual economics-led line on development programmes, arts practitioners here find themselves following avenues of discovery which mean that they are searching ever more intently to understand the communities with which they work in ways that combine the personal, the political and the spiritual. Ganguly's movement from disaffected left-wing political activist to a man eschewing all absolute, doctrinaire ideologies and calling on not only political thought but also the Hindu scriptures he had scorned as reactionary when a young man is the clearest, yet not the only, example of this. Ultimately it seems to us that the various practitioners whose work is discussed in this book all have in common one central idea: that by enabling people to discover and value their own humanity, both individually and in relation to others, they seek to empower those involved to claim the status of creative, thinking beings who have agency over the shaping of their lives and those of their families and communities.

None of which is to suggest that practitioners always get it right. Not only are most projects dependent on external funders, they are also led by facilitators who are on their own journeys of exploration. We feel that one of the most fascinating and useful aspects of this book is the transparency offered by the writer-practitioners regarding the learning processes – processes which include failure – they experienced themselves through the work. The project Gerri Moriarty describes in Northern Ireland led to a cross-community play widely acclaimed by audiences and critics. But from her viewpoint as an insider and key participant, Moriarty criticises the varying perspectives of some of the writers and directors employed on the project who, she feels, compromised the confidence of the participants, and thus the potential achievement of the play, through their sometimes unsympathetic relations with aspects of the community theatre groups involved. She also wonders whether the group took enough risks, or whether it pulled back through fear of repercussions from pursuing some of the most difficult but real questions dividing Protestant and Catholic communities in sectarian Belfast. Moriarty concludes by suggesting that she would not again involve herself in a similar project, for all its ostensible success.

The Wedding was a one-off play, but in Italy and India we are given stories of theatrical ventures covering decades. The people of Monticchiello are certainly the theatre activists in this book who have evolved most 'organically', working exclusively from within their own extended community and for the most part without external subsidy. Yet even here we see the people of the village, after a number of years being led by an expatriate son, gently moving him aside as their increasing self-confidence allows them to challenge his apparently over-rosy view of their peasant heritage. Ganguly meanwhile offers a meditative essay that shows him continually reinventing himself in response to the challenges thrown up by those with whom he works and whom he seeks to serve. The theatre, and the humanity here, is always in a process of *becoming*. The process is dynamic, never static or 'achieved'.

Moreover, this kind of theatre is inherently not 'safe'. A number of contributors wrestle with what seem to us very interesting – and difficult – questions of what is 'safe' or 'unsafe' in this sort of work. At the literal level there are moments of absolute unsafety for the theatremakers. Linda sees members of his group shot at when they challenge the divide between ANC and Zulu Inkatha identities. Villanueva describes how marchers in the American Day of Mourning Procession clash with Pilgrim enactors in America. Etherton has to withdraw from a village where the sons of the ruling class threaten low-caste children who dare to question the status quo. Theatre that challenges power bases and identities founded on bigotry is never going to be allowed to develop without resistance. It asks questions that are too unsettling for those who only want old certainties reinforced, or those who see with horror that the poor might be about to claim their human rights. As Fanon and Freire, Boal and Brecht all argued, such direct action is at least a rehearsal for revolution.

There is another issue, however. Those of us involved in theatre that seeks to empower are often aware that even from the inside it is not always safe. When people start to explore and test their histories, their experiences, their beliefs and their emotions, they can become very vulnerable. In Northern Ireland Moriarty describes how pushing the boundaries between Protestant and Catholic identities led to violence between women participants. Linda has to ask his young actors to negotiate whether they feel 'safe' enough in themselves to declare their HIV status to audiences, and Ganguly describes how an actor is devastated when he finds that he has himself relapsed into the wife-beating practices that his theatre denounces. For all of us this theatre is likely to provoke inner turmoil, and for all of us there are likely to be moments when we have to decide how far such theatre is going to venture in challenging participants, audiences and the authorities. Even more problematically, we may have to decide who makes the decision. Claiming human rights is a very unsafe business; in the words of MacMillan, 'letting go of existing structures, however oppressive, is a risk'.

There is no one way, form or kind of content that is 'right' in making theatre for empowerment, though there are a host of 'wrong' ways. This book is written partly in the hope that someone in an aid or funding agency may read it, realise that to keep commissioning work of banal simplicity from undertrained young theatre groups is not good enough, and start agitating for an understanding of the potential and methodologies of arts in development and rights contexts. It also comes out of a rather rueful sense of despair we felt when a student from a 'developing' country recently solemnly recited to us the eight steps necessary in making effective theatre for development. Any arts process reducible to a simple and repeatable formula has to be wrong.

However, it is fascinating to note how much of the work described has the claiming of space as a central aspect of the form of the theatre. The dancers Royston Muldoom and Adam Benjamin and playwright and multi arts creator Michael MacMillan all talk about the need for confidence in a physical taking of space, and inscribe the body as a powerful site of empowerment. Moreover, much of the theatre discussed takes place in spaces – prisons, village squares, the town that embodies the hegemony of the white Anglo-Saxon American identity – which are traditionally associated with the power of ruling classes. There are a number of interesting discussions of how community-based arts projects try to negotiate with the large theatres usually controlled by 'high art' establishments. MacMillan and Linda, operating from the UK and South Africa respectively, both experience difficulties in having their work valued by formal arts spaces, while in Ethiopia the Gemini Trust, a local NGO which supports the Adugna Community Dance Theatre, turns the problem on its head by hiring a major city theatre and then filling it with street children who are given free tickets to see their peers perform. Control of space, personal and public, is often used as a challenging means of assertion in theatre-for-rights practice.

Control of history is similarly linked with the claiming of identity. The work described by Villanueva in America, Andrews in Italy, Moriarty in Ireland and MacMillan in England is all centrally about the marginalised reclaiming their identities by performing their usually ignored histories. It is interesting that this trope seems more central in 'first' than in 'third' world practice; in the latter, where there is more absolute oppression and less available information, the need to discuss social and political rights seems to drive most of the work described. Whatever its particular focus or inflection, community arts work leads inevitably into the realm of the political. Will the Italian state support rural villages? Can Inkatha and ANC activists learn to work together in South Africa with the help of Linda's 'cultural combatants'? When will Native American histories be properly recognised in America? Time and again we see how the micro and the macro are inextricably entwined in this theatre practice.

There is one more crucial tool that must not be overlooked in a study of the transformational power of performance. Reading these essays, we were repeatedly struck by the power of *joy* as an agent of transformation. Villanueva chronicles a conflict in Plymouth Town between upholders of two versions of American history, enacted in two public parades. Yet the interviews with both sides are filled with love and joy for the performances, and there are enough openings offered up by the marchers for the essay to end in a hope expressed by a leading pilgrim descendant that in the future both may be able to parade together. In Italy and India, in England and Ethiopia, writers with intimate knowledge of the processes they describe speak of the fun and joy of creative activity as a galvanising factor and a major reason for sustaining the work, even through times of crisis and conflict. Plastow's essay begins with a description of a dance class held for elderly citizens in one of the poorest areas of Addis Ababa. The joy they express in their dance was exactly the same as that seen on the faces of the kindergarten dance class, the disabled dance group and even the head of the Ethiopian police as he took part in a piece of Forum Theatre. As one of the children with whom Etherton has worked exclaims: 'I didn't know we could do this! I didn't know I had this in me!' Creativity *is* joyous, and many of the communities and individuals described in these pages generally have far too little joy in their lives. The pursuit of happiness is likely to be a human right which, once glimpsed, will not be lightly discarded.

NOTE

1. Suggested texts that review the history of the growth of Theatre for Development include: David Kerr's *African Popular Theatre* (London: James Currey, 1995); Zakes Mda's *When People Play People: Development Communication through Theatre* (Johannesburg: University of the Witwatersrand Press and London: Zed Books, 1993); and Penina Muhando Mlama's *Culture and Development: The Popular Theatre Approach* (Uppsala: Nordiska Afrikainstitutet, 1991).

2 *The Wedding* Community Play Project: a cross-community production in Northern Ireland

GERRI MORIARTY

My name is Geraldine Moriarty. My father's family is from Kerry in the South of Ireland; they were Catholic, became Protestant. My mother's family are Protestant and Catholic, 'mixed' marriages through several generations. I was brought up in a small Nationalist town on the coast between Ireland and Scotland; my family was pro-Unionist and lower middle class. I left Ireland to study and stayed in England for eighteen years to live and work as a community artist.

I left shortly after the beginning of 'The Troubles' (usually reckoned from the year 1969).[1] The political struggle for civil rights by Catholics living in the North of Ireland had been drowned in sectarian violence. British troops were on the streets and the strength and violent response of the IRA and Protestant paramilitaries was on the increase. I left very specifically because a friend was shot dead in the streets of Belfast.

I came back twelve years ago when the confusion and hurt I felt living away from home outweighed the confusion, hurt and fear that had driven me away in the first place. I came back in the hope that I could make a contribution, however small, to what had begun to be understood as a process that might enable all the people of Ireland to live, thrive and build a future together. When I came back I spent time working as a drama worker and community theatre director in Nationalist and Loyalist communities in North and East Belfast.

These details are important. In the North of Ireland we know that there are few neutral spaces and even fewer neutral individuals.

We carry baggage, we make contracts and allegiances, we make our own choices and endure the choices that are made for us. We know that we can be located within a political, social, emotional and spiritual landscape and we think that we can locate others.

From my particular location in that landscape, I undertook an epic journey as a contributor to *The Wedding* Community Play Project in Belfast in 1999. This was a metaphoric and literal journey undertaken by 150 community participants (ranging in age from ten to sixty-five), a number of professional arts workers, an audience of 700 and a very much wider audience who read about the project in their newspapers, saw extracts on television programmes and at conferences, and heard about it from their friends. Its production style ensured that no two people travelled exactly the same theatrical journey; its confrontational genesis ensured that no two versions of its history completely agree.

So this is my version of that journey: flawed, partisan, partial. Other voices will weave in and out of the story, but I am the narrator and I have selected, judged, shaped, edited these other voices to meet my purposes. I am a player in the narrative, not a detached observer.

The programme for the performance of *The Wedding* Community Play announces that it is:

> an invitation to the real homes of Geordie and Jean Marshall (Templemore Avenue) and Margaret and Sammy Todd (Short Strand). You will board a bus in downtown Belfast and travel to both homes to eavesdrop on the happenings, tensions and joys on the day of a mixed marriage. The audience will then travel to the wedding ceremony and then on to The Edge for the climax of the story at the wedding reception.[2]

As with a real wedding, the plans and preparation for this performance event had gone on for a long time: over a year, in fact, from September 1998 to October 1999. The second IRA ceasefire was in place; political parties, paramilitaries, the people of Northern Ireland and Senator John Mitchell were wearily and warily considering the potential reality of signed agreements, power-sharing and a devolved Assembly. A community drama worker, Jo Egan, had come up with a visionary idea – a collaborative project with the major community theatre groups in Belfast to produce a play that would take as its central point a marriage between a young Protestant and a young Catholic. It would push the concept of promenade theatre to its extremes, taking the audience by bus into real homes in the terraced streets of East Belfast (which is a predominantly Protestant area, but which contains within it a small Catholic area called the Short Strand), into a church in the city centre and into a newly developed riverside pub for the wedding reception. With her partner, Martin Lynch (a well-known Irish playwright), she began discussions with the groups to gauge interest in the proposal.

Many of the community theatre groups in Belfast developed in the 1980s and 1990s in poor working-class areas where the violence and struggle has been most deeply experienced: the Shankill and Ardoyne, Ballybeen, New Lodge and Short Strand. Some of their theatre work has directly explored that experience: for example, *Conor's Story* (Dock Ward, 1992), which was set in the seconds after a lethal bomb has exploded, and *The Mourning Ring* (Ballybeen, 1995), which explored Protestant culture and tradition. Their membership was and is cross-generational, and women tend to be important driving forces within the organisations. Although supportive of each other's development, the community theatre groups had never worked together. It is fair to say that, until the ceasefire, it would not have been safe for them to do so.

As discussions continued, the project's development aims came into focus. They were:

- to create a safe space in which participants from Protestant and Catholic backgrounds could explore difficult issues and emotions, differences and similarities through drama;
- to create a powerful piece of theatre that raised questions about 'mixed marriage', encouraging insight and debate. More people than would commonly be realised live in, or have direct experience of, the pressures and problems of mixed marriages between Protestants and Catholics in Northern Ireland; some people

have died because of them. The metaphor allowed for exploration of larger political questions at the level of the domestic and the personal;

- to create a piece of theatre that would raise awareness of the quality of community theatre practice in Belfast and give it a much higher profile;
- to create opportunities for participants to develop their theatre skills.

The project was therefore aiming to provide opportunities for individual development, as well as for development of political and social discourse and cultural growth. Although there were all kinds of questions and concerns in the initial stages, the response of the community theatre groups to the idea was generally enthusiastic. For some, like Maureen Harkins, this was a conscious political act: 'How can we develop as a people, as a community, if we ignore the issues that concern us?'[3] For others, like Jo McDowall, 'the whole idea of the play, the way it was going to work with the different locations, was the thing that really appealed to me'.[4] And for some, who shall be nameless, the major motivation was whether or not there were any interesting members of the opposite sex in the other community theatre groups!

I was asked to work with Jo Egan to facilitate the series of workshops and the residential which would begin the process of creating the play. We decided to work separately with the community groups from Catholic areas and the groups from Protestant areas before bringing them together. We believed it was important to create safe space for the groups to explore 'single identity' ideas, thoughts and feelings; we also believed this should be kept to a minimum (two workshops), so that things did not become rigid and undynamic. In these early workshops one exercise we used was to form a wedding arch made up of workshop participants for two of the young people, and to ask the human wedding arch to verbalise the kinds of warnings, questions and threats which come from relatives, friends and the wider society to people who decide to marry across tribal boundaries.

The workshop in which the two groups first came together was, I think, the most electric and voluble I have experienced in twenty-five years of drama work. It was as if a dam had burst. Jo McDowall describes an exercise we used in this period, which was focused on the worst kind of sectarian abuse people could think of or had themselves experienced: 'It wasn't embarrassing, but it was really scary. To hear what they were saying as well – it was like, is that what they really think of us? . . . It was a strange exercise but it really did work to loosen us up.'

I went to the pub after the first joint workshop with some of the very experienced community theatre group members; I wanted to check things out with them. I share Richard Schechner's belief that '[s]ecurity is needed at the outset of play more than later on . . . performance workshops need to commence in an atmosphere of "safety and trust" but once underway, are places where very risky business can be explored'.[5] The view of participants then, and in discussion with an independent evaluator later, was that this kind of atmosphere was being achieved.

However, I remain less certain of this. A weekend residential was organised for the group, to enable more indepth exploration of the issues. Towards the end of the weekend, it became clear to Jo Egan and me that a small group of Protestant women had got to the point where they were teetering on the brink of bringing some very difficult issues and feelings back into the group. In the canteen during the lunch break, in an apparently unrelated incident (in my experience these kinds of incidents never are unrelated), one of the Catholic women slapped one of the Protestant women in the face. The group overall regained cohesion after this incident, but the small Protestant group of women within it did not feel able to take the step it had been contemplating. We moved back from the edge.

I am not sure whether we did so for very wise reasons. Had we gone as far as we could at that point in time, reached our collective limits? Or, if we had been able to summon up more courage, could we have taken the exploratory process to a new level? For me, this has been a frequent and challenging question within the context of a

Belfast which is often referred to as a city 'emerging from conflict'. Do
we disempower ourselves through self-censorship, or are we making
delicate judgements about what is and is not possible at any given
moment in time?

At this point, my attention was also distracted in another direction, as difficulties both among the professionals working on the
project and between them and the participants became more and
more apparent. The workshop facilitators, Jo Egan and I, had worked
together before and had a model for creating performance which was
highly collaborative. It was becoming clear that the writers (Martin
Lynch and Marie Jones), who had also worked together before, did
not share this model. Participants noticed that, although the writers came to some workshops, they spent a great deal of time talking to each other outside the workshop area, rather than watching
the improvisation process. Participants reported in the final evaluation that they 'believed more of this [improvisation] material could
have been reflected in the script. They were disappointed that there
was little feedback from the writers during the [residential] weekend and would have welcomed opportunities for discussion with
them.'[6]

There was also disquiet among some of the Protestant members of the cast at the choice of Marie Jones as writer for the script.
Although Marie comes from a working-class Protestant background,
and is a playwright of international standing, she has described herself as Nationalist, and would be perceived by many in the Protestant
community as supporting the Republican cause. As I explained in my
introduction, these alliances (real or perceived) *matter* in Northern
Ireland.

To make matters worse, although the Project Management
Committee had agreed that Jo and I should direct the performances
in the Catholic and Protestant houses, there were considerable difficulties in identifying two additional directors for the wedding and
the reception. There were many reasons for this: we were unable to
offer professional levels of pay, some directors' schedules were already
full, some were wary of working with community theatre groups, and
there were some directors with whom the community groups were

wary of working. Perhaps there was also some anxiety about some of the other implications of the project (for example, having to rehearse late at night in areas of inner East Belfast). Finally, Martin and Jo's personal relationship had become very difficult, and this, too, was having its effects.

The micro mirrors the macro; as a mini-society we were in the middle of a draining, frustrating, 'head-banging' political negotiation. Jo Egan writes:

> I look back and think it was still a dangerous time. We didn't even have an Assembly then. Perceived normality was still an aspiration. If nothing was happening, it was symbolic of confusion, not just an ordinary day. The air was full of potential energy and that was scary given what was in the immediate past. The bottom line on this for me is that people gave what they could. When they didn't a lot of the time it was because for them it wasn't safe to go there. That included the professionals (specifically the playwrights) and participants.[7]

In a project that specialised in extremes, what happened next was a nightmare. The script, which had been contracted to arrive in June 1999, was not delivered in its entirety until the very end of September, with preview performances scheduled for the end of October (four weeks away). In a professional theatre context, this would have been inexcusable. In the context of a community theatre project which was aiming to build a sense of collective ownership and was logistically immensely complicated (remember the buses carrying audiences across Belfast, the four performance venues, the four different directors), it had hugely negative consequences. Argument erupted spectacularly and immediately, rumbling all through September as parts of the script arrived. A major (but by no means the only) contentious issue was the representation of Protestants and by implication, the Protestant community, in the script. Detailed written comments were submitted by participants and by me, and several discussions were held with the writers. Nothing changed. At the time, Maureen Harkins (Ballybeen Community Theatre) described elements of the script as resembling a 'Jimmy Young' scenario (Jimmy Young being a

Northern Irish comedian of the 1950s and 1960s). I, too, believed the representation of Protestants to be clichéd, dated and stereotyped. Jo Egan writes:

> For me, I felt that Martin Lynch had a genuine love of the community he was writing for. I think you feel that even if you disagree with artistic device or storyline or even depth. Not so in the Protestant house. I felt Marie Jones was still processing stuff about her own community and was coming from a 'guilty prod' perspective, not as accepting or loving. I didn't feel a love for her people . . . therefore the world I wanted to enter was a little barred to me. Coming from a Catholic background, I felt I wanted to see more.[8]

By this stage, therefore, some Protestant members of the group were actively considering leaving the project.

I spent a long time wondering whether I, too, should leave. I felt that participants had been betrayed, and that the principles of community theatre, at least as I understood them, had been betrayed. However, given the volatility and fragility of the project and the closeness to performance dates, I also felt that my departure might well act as a last straw for others considering leaving and hence might contribute to total collapse. I felt that there were some people in the communities, in the media and in the arts world, who would regard this as a small but telling metaphor for the inevitable failure of the wider 'peace process'.

I talked through the situation with those Protestant members who were most concerned about it. I told them that I believed it was possible for us, through an ensemble approach to acting and through sensitive direction, to develop characters who were not stereotypes but complex individuals living and responding to a changing social and political context. They had lost any sense of trust in the script; I asked them to trust me. They agreed. I am still not certain that we made the right decision.

My view now is that deeply entangled within *The Wedding Community Play Project* were two fundamentally different models of community theatre. One model sees community theatre as a collaborative creative process, owned by all those who agree to participate in it, striving to give voice to different perspectives (sometimes colliding, sometimes contradictory). This model was the one explicitly proposed in the project's written objectives: 'to provide an opportunity for individuals and groups to involve themselves in a creative process over which they had ownership and the parameters of which they could influence'. It is a non-hierarchical model and a difficult model to sustain, particularly in a tradition of (Western) theatre which privileges the writer and the director. If individuals who normally work as professionals in the theatre are to be involved, it asks them to use their creative skills and expertise *and* understand, value, encourage and work with the creativity and experience of others.

The second model is predicated more on creating theatre *about* communities, using material such as testimony and research; it is in some senses rather like a television documentary. The outcomes can more easily be predicted; for professionals, it feels less risky.

It would be satisfyingly simple to say that these are completely separate creative models and that all those involved should sign up to one or the other at the beginning of the process. In reality there are community participants who want the excitement of performing a good script in front of large audiences and are relatively unconcerned about how deeply they are involved in the creative process. There are professional writers and directors who are able to put the experience and knowledge they have gained as '*auteur*' completely at the service of a group (a good example of this would be the way in which playwright Jimmy McGovern worked with Liverpool dockers and their families to create the television play *Dockers*). But in *The Wedding Community Play Project*, the clash of the two models, exacerbated by the failure to adhere to the timetable for delivery of the script, undoubtedly caused damage; I am left with a sense of curiosity as to what we might have achieved if the level of trust between us had been more profound.

In September 1999 there was very little time for such soul-searching. The late arrival of the script was also causing very practical problems for participants. The independent evaluator, Maureen Mackin, explains:

It was quickly realised that the amount of time available to the directors and cast required a hectic rehearsal schedule . . . The fact that certain key cast members were needed for a number of scenes gave rise to a very demanding schedule for some of the participants . . . and resulted in some exhausted cast members.[9]

The final scene of the play, the wedding reception, was flawed dramatically, and this became clearer to participants, writers and directors as rehearsals proceeded. At the very last moment, there was a major rewrite; several cast members had to relearn lines and action in the very last days before the first performance. The four directors had no time to meet together to establish approaches to the performance or to discuss working methods – their 'heads were down', trying to deliver 'their' section with 'their' cast. Tempers were frayed, and it was hard to maintain any sense of whole-group cohesion when rehearsals were taking place in four different venues on different nights of the week.

Remarkably, the scales, which seemed to be weighted towards disaster, slowly began to balance. Paula McFetridge, an experienced theatre professional, came on board as production manager. Working closely with Jo Egan, she began to resolve the mass of logistical detail – getting the cast from one venue to the next in the right order and wearing the right costume, co-ordinating the stage managers' mobile phones, working out at what point in the journey audience members could go to the toilet! Key members of the group (workers and participants) dug deep into stamina, patience, dedication and determination, and the ensemble approach which Jo Egan and I had tried to encourage during the workshop process and in directing the house scenes paid high dividends. Rehearsals of the church scene, which had been written by Martin Lynch and Marie Jones as a non-naturalistic series of musical numbers, acted as a kind of hilarious release for some of the tensions the cast were experiencing. And we began to hear, first in the community previews, then in the press reviews, and finally in audience responses and evaluations how very positively others viewed the outcome of our stormy journey together.

As part of the project evaluation, audiences were asked to complete questionnaires. Approximately half did so; the evaluator points out that this high response rate is an indication of their wish to comment on what they had seen. Their responses to the performance were thoughtful and encouraging, as these comments illustrate:

> I believe that we still live in a climate that is still quite volatile in relation to mixed marriages. To address the issue in this way is a very good way of reducing tensions.

> Brilliant – so much is tied up with this issue, e.g. way of life, feelings, sectarianism, choice.

> Anything that raises the issue of diversity and allows space to have the arguments is well worth while.

> Realistic, believable, upsetting, shocking, emotional.

> Should be performed for every school and community group in Ireland.[10]

Theatre reviewers were equally impressed. Hugh Linehan, for the *Irish Times*, wrote:

> *The Wedding* Community Play Project is an ingeniously crafted, thought-provoking and highly enjoyable piece of work . . . it appropriates the most familiar and popular form of drama of the late 20th century – soap opera – and brings it to life by setting its story in the homes, streets and public spaces of the city . . . The experience is slightly disconcerting – like being physically transported into a soap opera where you can really wake up and smell the coffee.[11]

In the *Financial Times*, Ian Shuttleworth described it as 'utterly wondrous',[12] while Mic Moroney, in the *Guardian*, wrote: 'Community Theatre is very often derided, but this production, about a mixed Protestant-Catholic marriage in Belfast, is one of the most affecting pieces I have ever seen . . . the show takes up a full afternoon, but it will remain in your mind a whole lot longer.'[13] The project would go on to win the Drama award and the Arts Partnership award in the annual Belfast Arts Awards.

It was not that audiences failed to spot weaknesses: 'The ending sort of "fizzled" out' . . . 'Possible cuts – a degree of repetition' . . . 'Actors could have more quiet/reflective moments' . . . 'Slightly stereotyped' . . . 'Female characters were all very strong – some of the male ones could be improved.'[14]

Likewise, reviewers were ready to offer criticism: 'If the church and reception segments are less successful than what has gone before, then that's due to the sheer effectiveness of those intimate domestic dramas, after which the return to more conventional theatrical techniques seems something of a let-down . . .'[15] But, in general, they had been moved, entertained, challenged; they had entered into the dialogue we had hoped to create.

It is my belief that their strongly positive reactions were rooted in that holistic experience of performance described by Schechner as: 'the whole constellation of events . . . that take place in/among performers and audience from the time the first spectator enters the field of performance – the precinct where the theatre takes place – to the time the last spectator leaves'.[16] As audiences they had begun a theatrical journey as individuals, or perhaps in small groups of family and friends. They had squeezed into real kitchens, bedrooms and sitting rooms in terraced houses in both Loyalist and Republican territories, and eavesdropped on ten minutes of life on the morning of a wedding. Moving from room to room, they saw the same ten minutes of nervous anxiety and tension reenacted from three different perspectives. Back on the coach, they travelled to an inner-city church for a wedding service which abandoned heightened naturalism for exuberant high camp, using 1960's songs to underscore how key players felt about the events taking place. Then they had become the wedding guests, travelling to the wedding reception. The cabaret-style seating and the somewhat terrifying waitress who emerged to show them to their places encouraged them to feel part of the action, as the actors revealed more of their true motivations and events moved to an upbeat, if tentative, conclusion.

For many in the audience, the unconventional staging increased their sense of delight and engagement, of being part of something 'totally different':

> 'I couldn't wait to get up to the bedroom to find out what happened next' . . . 'The reception appealed to my wife Wilma, because you got to hear all the conversations that you didn't get to hear at real weddings' . . . 'It was wild in the church – and we were taught that you shouldn't speak in a good Presbyterian church!' . . . 'I enjoyed looking at the décor. At the end, their wee houses are just like ours.'[17]

Some of the audience were making an internal emotional journey, as the play stirred up their own experiences. Ann, a Protestant audience member, describes feelings of loss and separation: 'I got away with thinking of people I'd used to know in the Short Strand (the area in which the Catholic house was situated), people I used to chum with. It brought me back to them.'[18] Alan, a community worker who came to see the play, records: 'I remember being anxious about where it was leading to . . . my own experience in my family of bringing two communities together is unresolved, both socially and politically.'[19] Erica, an audience member from outside Northern Ireland, comments:

> At the bottom of the road, there was a wall with barbed wire and a slogan 'INLA – Not a Bullet, Not an Ounce, Not a Chance'.[20] That wasn't written for the benefit of an audience. Walking down the street, I felt – 'I'm from this little tight neighbourhood, where I get really frightened' – when you live in the midst of a small enclave surrounded by something else, it's in your face when you go to get your milk.'[21]

Most pointedly of all, after all those months of political negotiations, the Ulster Unionist party met at the Waterfront Hall on the day of the last performance of *The Wedding* Community Play, to decide whether or not they would enter into a power-sharing Executive with members of Sinn Fein. As we travelled on the buses from site to site, the radio kept a running commentary on the political situation. Jo Egan recalls 'how cataclysmic was that meeting on the last day with David Trimble and hearing of it just as we came out of the church'.[22]

Our feeling of a strong connection, for better or worse, with the shift in political realities, was acute.

I think there was a sense in which many in the audience (both those who watched the play and the wider audience who read about it in the press or heard about it in the media) desperately wanted the metaphor *The Wedding* Community Play Project came to represent to succeed. They wanted to believe that groups from 'frontline' Protestant and Catholic communities could work together to succeed in a common task because they wanted that to be a symbol of new and changing times.

But there was also something even deeper, more immediate, going on. I experienced the whole performance as a member of the audience on that very last day. I stood with twelve people in the kitchen in Madrid Street, became one of the thirty-six people travelling to the reception, joined the group of about a hundred in Rosemary Street Presbyterian Church, travelled on the bus to the wedding reception. I saw how this group of people had taken the script by the scruff of the neck, inhabited it with a huge collective spirit, and taken ownership of it in spite of all the problems they had experienced. And I could feel the huge part the audience were playing in that dynamic. In their level of attention in the houses, in their exuberant good humour in the church, in their willingness to enter into the role of guests at the wedding reception, they were feeding the transformational energy which is one of the greatest gifts of theatre. All things may, after all, be possible.

The impact of the performance was not ephemeral. Three years after it took place, the audience members I interviewed for this essay could remember clearly what they had observed and how it had affected them. But the impact was not as great as it might have been. We were not able to link our work into the kind of progressive framework for community and political development which could have made good use of the opportunities for discussion and dialogue we had provided. This remains, for me, a major weakness of the project. David Smith, a member of the Ballyoran Training and Support Group, comments that *The Wedding* Community Play Project 'was one of the best pieces of work in community relations and reconciliation there has been in East Belfast. But the bridge built between the two communities stopped at the end of the play, which is where the real work should have started.'[23] I agree with his criticism.

There are clear reasons for this failure. Those of us who would have been interested in a 'next phase' were physically, emotionally and spiritually exhausted. There was no obvious partner or partners for such an endeavour. The whole enterprise had been a risk, with no guarantee of outcome, so we had not planned for a programme of follow-up activities. The process and the final product had been so flawed that the flaws could have been carried into and further marred any second phase of cultural work. But the argument is more important than whether or not *The Wedding* Community Play Project could and should have been developed further. My view is that without a solid, administrative and artistic infrastructure for community theatre in Belfast, without a sustainable programme of activity, such opportunities will always be lost, as community theatre groups lurch from new project to new project. Jo Egan, commenting on the fact that the project was financially under-resourced (leading to an inability to pay the expenses incurred by cast members because of the punishing rehearsal schedule, the employment of a skeleton administrative and production team, and the underpayment of some professional workers) says: 'The real under-resourcing for me is in the attitude of funders. They have such power as potential supporters of good quality community arts practice. They could generate so much knowledge. With proper planning and a desire to help and network, money could be used much more effectively.'[24]

In the immediate aftermath of the production, arguments for developing a sustainable cultural infrastructure for community theatre in Belfast were made, but were difficult to hear. Many members of the group were in a state of understandable euphoria. There was talk of taking the play to America, there was talk of a sequel – *The Christening* perhaps, or *The Divorce* (*The Wake* was favoured by those of us who were not affected by amnesia, and could remember all the difficulties we had encountered along the way), there was bizarre talk of developing it into an attraction for Troubles tourists. I was among those counselling against all these kinds of revival, in part because of my belief that the reception the play had received was connected to its unique geographical setting in the terraced streets and city centre of Belfast and to the specific socio-political context of 1999, that these factors could not be replicated elsewhere, and that the weaknesses of the project would be easily exposed in other circumstances. Slowly these ideas receded, as people realised that they would involve at least as much preparation, planning, fundraising and dedication as *The Wedding* Community Play Project itself.

What remained was a very strong feeling that the project had created a platform on which community theatre groups in Belfast could build. At a seminar in the spring of 2000, the groups involved in *The Wedding* Community Play Project agreed to work together to form the Community Theatre Association of Belfast (CTAB), a cross-community cultural organisation which would develop a sustainable infrastructure for the future. And there, I suppose, the story of a fairytale wedding might end – 'they married and lived happily ever after'.

But, as I warned you, I am the narrator of this story, and in my view it now takes a distinct turn for the worse. It was proposed to the groups that they should take part in yet another large-scale city-centre cross-community play, *Football Mad*. This was scheduled to take place in spring 2001 as part of a major citywide community arts initiative.

By their very nature, large-scale community plays consume huge amounts of resources, resources of time, energy and money. They are usually 'set pieces', presented as part of an Arts Festival, or a civic celebration; there is therefore little opportunity for flexibility to allow additional time to explore unexpected directions or to deal with unanticipated needs or aspirations. Although considerable numbers of people participate, a much smaller number are able to play significant acting or technical parts; there is little time for serious development of skills with participants. I would argue that, in Belfast at least, large-scale community plays have had the effect of distancing groups from their communities. It is significant that since *The Wedding* Community Play Project, only one of the community theatre groups involved has created new small- to medium-scale work with and for its 'home' community. I agree with Jo Egan when she comments: 'there's a kind of "large scale community play is good for your health" attitude. This is an untruth. They are actually terminal if taken in regular doses.'[25]

These disadvantages do need to be weighed against the opportunities offered by large-scale performances. In Belfast these include the opportunity to perform in 'neutral' city-centre venues which attract a wider cross-section of audiences, to work with others across geographical and territorial divides, and to work with a range of theatrical disciplines and professional artists. For small community groups, it also means that the heavy workload associated with fundraising and production can be shared with others and delegated to paid workers.

Maureen Harkins (Ballybeen Community Theatre), commenting on the decision taken at that time, says: 'I think we needed to let success settle. The groups didn't get an opportunity to reflect. They went on down the road to another big play.'[26] But *Football Mad* (or *Playing for Time*, as it eventually became) caused specific difficulties for the newly formed CTAB. First, it was not nearly as well received by theatre reviewers as *The Wedding* Community Play Project had been; although audiences were more supportive than the critics, they were not as volubly enthusiastic as they had been about *The Wedding*. Those who held old prejudices against the validity and quality of community cultural expression were quick to use this as new ammunition against community theatre.

Second, and more crucial, it diverted the time and attention of the CTAB away from its declared aim of fundraising for a worker who could support them in making a move away from a project-to-project existence. Only now, in 2002, two-and-a-half years after *The Wedding* Community Play Project, has CTAB made a successful funding application through the Arts Council of Northern Ireland's Lottery scheme, for a one-year developmental pilot scheme. It remains to be seen whether the momentum created by *The Wedding* Community Play Project can be regained and whether the community theatre sector and its major funders can work together to devise a medium- to long-term plan to support community-based cultural production in the city. It is a very interesting moment. I wonder whether, in ten or twenty years' time, cultural activists or researchers will note *The Wedding* Community Play Project as marking the end of a certain phase of community cultural production, a phase which was shaped and fed by the political and social context of pre-ceasefire Belfast, or as marking the birth of a different kind of cultural response to social conditions?

It would be easy to stop at this point in my narrative – at the stage reached by the wider group. By doing so I could avoid going back to my starting-point, my personal and artistic journey. How much did the experience of *The Wedding* Community Play Project empower or disempower *me*?

Since 1999 most of my contribution to cultural development in Northern Ireland has been to policy development. I have played a very small part in the development of the CTAB and have been serving as a member of the Arts Council of Northern Ireland, where I have been helping to define a new five-year strategy. In part this has been my response to what I perceive as a real need for long-term sustainability. My creative activity has taken place in Ethiopia, where I have been working with Adugna Community Dance Theatre (see Jane Plastow's account of the group in chapter 6). This has been demanding, but I have been collaborating with supportive colleagues.

I am working on options for my own projects for the next three years, in Ireland and elsewhere, and I notice that I have become more selective in my planning. I aim to pay far more attention to what I need to function effectively than I have done in the past. For example, I will be working with professional artists who respect and value the collaborative model of theatremaking which I practise, even if their own practice is different. I intend to work in contexts where it is possible to make fruitful links with other development networks, whether these be health networks, environmental networks or political networks.

In some cultures there is a belief that, in life, you will go on encountering the same type of individual until you learn the lesson that he/she has been sent to teach you. For all its undoubted achievements and successes, I do not want to meet *The Wedding* Community Play Project again.

NOTES

1. Any attempt to define the conflict in Northern Ireland will be an oversimplification. Very broadly, however, the Protestant Unionist community (which is in a small and diminishing majority in Northern Ireland) wishes to be regarded as British and part of the UK. The Catholic Nationalist and Republican community wishes to be part of the Republic of Ireland. In addition, everyday life in the North has been marred for many years by discriminatory practices by those in positions of power and authority and by high levels of sectarianism and violence.

2. *The Wedding* Community Play programme, October 1999.

3. Quoted in *The Wedding* Community Play programme, *ibid.*

4. Interviewed in Claire Cochrane, 'Playing the Community', *irishtheatremagazine*, vol. 2, no. 5 (2000), p. 38. All subsequent comments by McDowall are from this source.

5. Richard Schechner, *The Future of Ritual* (London: Routledge, 1993), p. 27.

6. Maureen Mackin, unpublished independent evaluation of *The Wedding* Community Play Project, 2000.

7. Jo Egan, facilitator, director and project manager of *The Wedding* Community Play, letter to the present writer, February 2002.

8. *Ibid.*

9. Mackin, unpublished independent evaluation.

10. Mackin, *ibid.* Audience quotations are taken from questionnaires distributed and completed immediately after the performance.

11. Hugh Linehan, *Irish Times*, 10 November 1999, p. 12.

12. Ian Shuttleworth, *Financial Times*, 9 November 1999, p. 24.

13. Mic Moroney, *Guardian*, 10 November 1999, p. 17.

14. Mackin, unpublished independent evaluation, extracts from audience questionnaires.

15. Linehan, *Irish Times*.

16. Richard Schechner, *Performance Theory* (London: Routledge, 1988), p. 39.

17. Quotations are taken from interviews undertaken by the present writer in 2002 as part of the research for this essay with members of Ballyoran Training and Support Group, who attended a community preview.

18. *Ibid.*

19. *Ibid.*

20. A reference to the refusal in Republican areas of the call for arms decommissioning as part of the 'peace process'.

21. From the interviews with members of Ballyoran Training and Support Group.

22. Egan, letter.

23. From the interviews with members of Ballyoran Training and Support Group.

24. Egan, letter.

25. *Ibid.*

26. Maureen Harkins, telephone interview conducted by the present writer in February 2002 as part of the research for this essay.

3   The Poor Theatre of Monticchiello, Italy

RICHARD ANDREWS

Let us take, as an example, an evening in July 1995. The theatre is a small central square in a Tuscan village, with a bank of raked seats holding around two hundred spectators. The scenery, for the most part, is just the houses which happen to front the square, including one with a small balcony garden with a mixture of herbs and decorative bushes: together with various alleyways, it will be exploited for entrances and exits. This year (unlike some) there is also a scenic construction in the middle of the square, a mound of cubes decorated with intriguing cryptic signs. There is a quite complex lighting rig erected on gantries (so performances do not start until after dark); and the sound system will turn out to be equally sophisticated, offering at different moments either background music or some sonic interplay with the onstage dialogue.

There is no programme or cast list: as a community enterprise this presents itself as determinedly anonymous, even though many of the regular spectators (and all the journalists) do in fact know most of the main actors by name and reputation. If you are here for the first time, the impression of a seamless collectivity is marked and impressive. At the end, for the final applause, more than fifty people will gather in the square, applauding the audience back; and you will have to make an effort to spot the appearance of the man who has been directing the production, and his collaborators in the script-writing team. You may have bought a recently printed copy of the script when you picked up your ticket, but there are no helpful credits here either, just *autodramma* of the people of Monticchiello; and you don't know whether the names of characters in the text are also the names of the people playing them. (Sometimes they are, sometimes not.) It will be

33

apparent that the version you read, rushed out a few days before the first night, has been superseded in performance by a lot of last-minute rewritings.

The opening sequence of the play seems just to show ordinary people from the village, of all ages, casually dressed, reacting with some perplexity to the structure of cubes which has appeared in their square. Their reactions range from wishful thinking ('Is it my wedding present?') to fear ('Is it going to explode?'). What it actually contains is a person: a smoothly grinning television-style presenter, full of relentlessly cheerful mottoes and catchphrases, who proceeds to take over the village in the name of an all-pervading game show. In strongly satirical, deliberately exaggerated style, the whole population is subjected to a system of points, which they win or lose on their ability to answer quiz questions. People tear across the square in jubilation or despair; they become frozen, when they want to move to someone's aid, by being unable to answer a question about the Pope's trousers. Eventually a major character is pronounced 'game dead' (subject to *morte ludica*), enclosed in a cage and subjected to interrogative scrutiny. However, his personality is too strong to tolerate this for long. He turns the tables on the crowd with an agenda and a story of his own – first the story of his early life as a sharecropping peasant, then that of a character named Alizzardo, who was an all-time sucker. Maybe, he suggests to indignant protests, some of the villagers are related to him . . .? The play is actually entitled *Alizzardo*.

The story slides into a different mode and a different time. Now all the characters belong to a peasant society, around 1950, and they are all pausing at a wayside fountain on the way home from a fair. Various cameo sequences entertain, and give food for thought. One bravura performance relates to a small energetic man with the gift of the gab, who has just made a late marriage to a completely silent wife. Regulars know that Alpo has built up a fan club by playing parts like this over the years, whereas Graziella (who is not Alpo's wife) is only just released from caring full-time for a sick relative, and is appearing on stage for the first time. A newcomer in the audience remarks afterwards that the younger actors, mainly in the 'modern' part, were energetic and effective, but that the older generation, in the 'peasant' part, have an astonishing extra stage presence and relaxed sense of timing.

We eventually hear about Alizzardo again, though we never see him. He has fled in despair, after losing everything he possessed to a card sharp, at the three-card trick. The discussion about this, full of fury as well as sympathy, deals with the need we all have, perhaps, to believe that one day we are going to win something in life. It is focused by a man with a bicycle, who is an official of the Lega dei Mezzadri, the peasants' trade union which is fighting for a fair deal with the bosses, even for ownership of the land. He makes a parallel between Alizzardo's situation and that of all the peasants:

> Christ Almighty! It always happens this way. You realise that things aren't going the way they should, and it's already too late! [. . .] You know . . . when I first came to these parts, I used to stop sometimes down in a field, and think how right and proper it would be if every peasant were to become his own boss. And now I realise that they've been leading us up the garden path. That's why we needed more conviction. They've had us playing on a table with not three cards, but three hundred, and all marked. Just one swindle after another.[1]

The finale of the play shifts back to the modern, or futuristic, game show, with imperious slogans on the soundtrack, repeated sentences of *morte ludica*, and small cubes mushrooming out of the large ones. All the audience will understand the satirical presentation of a manipulative aspect of modern media culture. Only some, perhaps, will know why a link has been forced with an older world, and a long-dead political campaign. But in fact the union official's speeches were regarded as so important that they were being anxiously rewritten on the church steps at midnight, only a week before the first performance.

After the show the cast can be found winding down alongside the spectators over plates of pasta in the temporary taverna opened in the church crypt. The atmosphere is expansive, voluble and welcoming. The July heat has finally taken hold, here at an altitude of 500 metres, and the night is warm and comfortable. No one really wants to go to bed.

The present collection of essays deals, in words from Michael Etherton's chapter title, with cases where theatre has made a difference to the lives of 'marginalised, disadvantaged and excluded' sections of society. Readers will perhaps be expecting to learn about communities inside Western industrialised cultures which suffer discrimination on grounds of race, religion or ethnicity; about groups suffering extreme deprivation within 'Third World' countries; or about the desire of a whole 'developing' nation or culture to make its voice heard in the face of economic exploitation from outside. A country such as Italy – now part of the industrialised world, and probably perceived as relatively homogenous racially and culturally – might seem less of a candidate for a volume of this kind. Yet it is still within living memory that whole sections of Italian society, often the majority of the population within a given region, lived in conditions, and under economic systems, which can now only be described either as 'Third World' or as 'medieval', depending on the angle of perception adopted. Until the Second World War, peasant attitudes and means of expression were as much despised and ignored within Italy as subordinate cultures can be within more mixed and complex societies. The passage of Italian peasant communities into the modern Western system then took place as rapidly, and with as much trauma, as has happened and is still happening in many parts of Africa and Asia.

One identifiable block of people which has suffered this trauma is the rural population of Tuscany. This essay is an account of how just one small village found a way, from the late 1960s, of using theatre activity to speak on behalf of all the hundreds of other such centres which had gone through the same transformation. The empowerment which came about through envoicement has by now been achieved, and the tension and sense of struggle which originally invested the enterprise may have diminished. Nevertheless, annual productions continue into the new millennium, acting as a badge for a community which, along with simply celebrating a life-enhancing *festa*, insists on keeping faith with its past.

The defining characteristics of peasant culture within Tuscany were dictated by the particular system of landholding and farming which was predominant in the region. In the provinces of Pisa,

Florence, Arezzo and Siena, there was an overwhelming majority of cultivated land which operated under the system of sharecropping (*mezzadria* in Italian). Sharecroppers also existed in other parts of Italy, but they operated more on the margins of systems which were largely given over to other types of agricultural economy – struggling small proprietors in the Alpine region, tenants on large semi-industrialised estates in the fertile north, tenants paying rent to absentee landlords in the *latifundia* of the south. Peasants in all these varied circumstances would have had some aspects of their mentality in common – not least a shared feeling of being oppressed by a system which barely allowed them a decent living, and which seemed to put bread in other people's mouths at the expense of the peasants' own labour. At the same time, the particular economic relationships by which each form of peasantry was controlled tended to lead, in the twentieth century, to different formulations of how their oppression was constituted. This led in turn to substantially differing political agendas, addressing how that oppression could be fought and what kind of more liberating system should replace it. The pursuit of these various goals created equally varied political cultures, ingrained in the two or three generations of peasants who lived and struggled through the first half of the century, until after the Second World War. For this reason it is not enough to refer to recent generations of Tuscans as 'former peasants' (*ex-contadini*), although that is what they are: they have to be characterised more specifically as 'former sharecroppers' (*ex-mezzadri*).

The beauty of the Tuscan countryside, now enjoyed by so many incomers both temporary and permanent, is largely man made; and in particular its characteristic distribution of land use and buildings (however radically modified since the late 1960s) was a product of the sharecropping system. The idyllic relaxing 'villas' which dot the landscape, and are now owned as second homes or rented out to tourists, were once centres of backbreaking subsistence farming, carried out under oppressive and sometimes desperate conditions.[2] They were each occupied by an extended family,[3] to which was leased (on an annual, revocable, basis) a patch of surrounding land calculated as sufficient to keep such a family alive – after 50 per cent of the produce had first been turned over to the landlord who owned it. The enchanting aesthetic variety of a traditional Tuscan panorama, with its intense mixtures of colour and vegetation, was produced by the need to cultivate everything essential for survival within a small space, so that cereals, beans or flax were grown in between the olives, fruit trees or rows of vines. (Now that such a need has passed, fields are being swept bare to produce swathes of single crops, or even open pasture land: the landscape is slowly but inexorably changing.) Such dense planting severely reduced the possibility of mechanising the work, even if the landlord had been prepared to spend money on the machinery, so nearly all the labour of a sharecropper was manual.

On top of this, most landlords adopted various strategies to keep their tenants in a subordinate position: the ever-threatened sanction was that of being evicted at the year's end, which meant being deprived overnight both of a livelihood and of a home. A number of prohibitions, which now seem preposterous but which could actually be written into the sharecropping contract, regulated the peasants' lifestyles, their means of transport and even their dress. Landlords had informal power to control their workforce by permitting or forbidding marriages. A whole culture of deference was reinforced by extra duties, involving unpaid work for the landlord's personal benefit, and contracted tributes or gifts of extra produce in addition to the notional 50 per cent. Economically, the system was manipulated through the account books to ensure that peasants were constantly registered as being in debt to their masters. Many family heads were illiterate, and unable to read those account books: landlords discouraged peasant children from going to school where they might have remedied this situation, although with the rise of military conscription an increasing number of younger men gained a certain level of education in the army.

The cultural strategies which peasants built up to cope with their predicament, and the worldview created by their oral culture, were systematically despised by the rest of Italian society; even within a small rural community, those who lived in the village rather than on the farms were not only markedly better off than the sharecroppers but perceived as being socially and culturally superior. The peasants were living in a medieval economy, in which monetary values played a controlling part in their subordination but in which they themselves made limited use of money: they operated still to a great extent in terms of goods and barter rather than cash.

This system was still fully in play in the years just after the Second World War. A consciousness of its injustice had motivated peasants since they were put in contact with socialist ideas at the beginning of the century; but their first campaigns had been violently crushed by fascism. After 1945 they found themselves in a new republic which repudiated fascism, having been created by a Resistance in which Socialists and Communists had played a substantial part. There seemed to be hope therefore (at least until a backlash in 1948) for radical and even revolutionary programmes of land reform. Nevertheless, to begin with, the very energetic political actions of sharecropping leagues had limited objectives. For most of the older generation, the idea of not farming the land at all was inconceivable: they simply wanted to do so for themselves, on their own terms, without landlords, and to have full use of the produce for which they worked so hard. But during the 1950s their sons and daughters realised that the whole economy of Italy was changing, and that instead of facing a long, wearisome struggle against their bosses they had the chance simply of leaving the land altogether for better-paid work in new industries and services. Then, perhaps unexpectedly, the landlords themselves perceived that they had no chance, either, of maintaining their status and lifestyle in this new economic world – and the majority of them sold up, even in many cases giving first refusal on the land to their own tenants. In an astonishingly short space of time, during the early 1960s, the sharecropping system disappeared.[4] Those who had been born and raised in the medieval economy had to learn to live in a new one – whether they chose (as a minority did) to stay on and farm differently, or moved away from agriculture once and for all.

Tuscany is now populated, in all sectors of the economy and of society, by people who were raised on sharecropping farms, and who have brought into quite different walks of life some particular characteristics. They are enterprising, energetic, willing and able to turn their hands to anything, in love with self-sufficiency. But they are also community-spirited, wedded to notions of collective action and mutual support, which they learnt from the particular version of left-wing politics which was stamped on their minds during the dramatic campaigns of 1945–60. (The political vote in Tuscany still clings obstinately to the left – even, or especially, in the age of Berlusconi.) In addition, the collective memory of the old world – its harshness, its solidarity, its dramas and its disappointments – provides a psychological substratum for at least two generations of Tuscans. They know that they lived through a particularly gripping story, and have unique experiences to recount; but they also know that published academic history has not recounted it, or analysed it, enough.

One small hilltop village in the province of Siena – Monticchiello, in the *comune* of Pienza – has taken the initiative to recount and to analyse both the peasant experience as such and the way it came to an end – and it has done so through the medium of theatre. The community which supports this whole project consists by now of around 300 people, and had no more than 400 to 500 at the time when it all began.[5]

Those acquainted with community plays in the English-speaking world[6] will know that the first and simplest motivation for putting on such a show is a desire to tell one's story to a larger audience. The 'empowerment' involved is that of knowing that one has acquired an image, and therefore more of a presence, in other people's minds. At the same time, the process of formulating a version of one's experience, and of discovering a way of presenting it coherently on stage, both strengthens and alters the image one has of oneself. (I say 'one', but we are of course speaking of 'many': it is possible to be solipsistic when writing an individual autobiography, but the choice of community theatre as a medium for such an exercise forces the whole operation on to the level of the collective.) It is hard to say whether a community play exists more for the benefit of the audience who will come to see it, or for the community which explores itself while creating it. The audience in any case will consist partly of those members of the same community who have chosen not to participate, and whose presence as the other half of a virtual dialogue will be anticipated throughout the creative process.

When the villagers of Monticchiello began their unbroken cycle of community plays, they may not have been conscious of all these motivations, but they discovered and recognised them with extraordinary rapidity. Within a couple of years of their starting, all of the above generalisations can be said to have applied. In 1967 and 1968 the first dramatic productions were hardly 'community plays' at all. They were historical dramas, composed according to an antiquarian folkoristic formula copied from elsewhere.[7] They were offered as part of a general summer village festival, attempting to fit into a general pattern whereby the medieval and Renaissance heritage of Tuscan towns and villages was, and still is, exploited partly as an image of local autonomy obstinately clung to, and partly because it is picturesque enough to attract tourists. (The massive overbearing model for all this is the Palio of Siena – the terrifying twice-yearly horserace around the main square, introduced by a long procession in medieval costume and supported fanatically by the seventeen city districts [contrade] which compete in it. This is a phenomenon actually impossible to rival or copy, although many local communities have tried: nowhere other than in Siena itself can one find the necessary underlying social structure, whereby the contrade nurture and control social life throughout the year, for people of all ages and all classes.)[8]

In 1969, however, the proposition accepted by the village entailed rehearsal on an entirely different scale, and a dramatic content much closer to home in every sense. Twenty-five years before, there had been a small battle in and around Monticchiello between Italian partisans and Italian Fascists. The next day the German SS arrived. They had most of the village population lined up against the medieval wall, and were prepared to shoot them all in reprisal for their support of the partisans. The Nazis were talked out of the project, partly by the parish priest, but mostly by the wife of the local landowner, who herself was German and from the same hometown as the SS commander. The proposal in 1969 was to dramatise this whole story – both the battle (from the partisan point of view) and the barely avoided massacre. The villagers who took part might in some cases actually be playing themselves, reenacting the terror of that time. Certainly all the major Italian participants in the episode, including the commander of the partisan brigade and the former landowner's wife, acted as informants and advisors to the script and to the performance. The play was entitled *Quel 6 aprile del '44* (*That 6th April of 1944*).

The therapeutic value of such an exercise is so obvious that it hardly needs elaborating. In retrospect, though, it now seems as if the villagers simply needed to get that particular experience out of their system, before moving on to dramatise something else. An entirely different spectacle was mounted the following year, 1970: a head-on confrontation with the audience, speaking directly about the economic traumas and uncertainties which followed the collapse of sharecropping, and making a plea for the predicament of tiny rural communities to be taken seriously within the national agenda.[9] One villager has since described it to me as a substitute for a political demonstration – in paraphrase, he said: 'If we'd gone to Siena or Rome to march and protest, we'd have looked like a lot of other people, and no one would have known who we were. By mounting the show in the village square, we made the audience come to us, and see us in the place where we lived. It was more effective, and more memorable.' One could add that it was also more fun. The internationally known Italian theatre director Giorgio Strehler has been credited with describing Monticchiello's productions as '*autodrammi*' ('self-dramas'), and the word he coined has now stuck. The company quickly took on the title of 'Teatro Povero', 'Poor Theatre', the name being inspired by a current fashion for Grotowski but soon acquiring implications specific to this particular enterprise.

The next few years saw a succession of historical *autodrammi* which were always scripted so as to have a link with contemporary issues and a polemical bite. In 1974 the play *Contadini o no* (*Peasants or Not*) confronted directly a series of questions about the village's agricultural past, and whether it had an agricultural future.[10] It established one of the most enduring characteristics of Monticchiello's theatre: the careful, realistic depiction of the 'average' sharecropping family *(la famiglia contadina)* during the period roughly between 1920 and 1960. Plausible and typical episodes, often heavily based on memories of members of the company, were chosen and manipulated in order to dramatise the chosen theme of the year's play (which, in the earlier years, was then also debated in front of the audience in the concluding act). A whole range of villagers of all backgrounds and professions, including a number of former sharecropping peasants, discovered that 'performing themselves' *(recitare se stessi)* was a path to self-fulfilment. It led them on the one hand to a clearer view of their own lives, but it also revealed talents, personality traits, and sources of satisfaction which they would never previously have imagined. And they went on developing those talents, and gaining this satisfaction, on an annual basis, so that theatre became a permanently ingrained part of the lives of those who choose to practise it. Monticchiello has composed and mounted a new *autodramma*, only once repeating itself,[11] every summer from 1969 to 2002. A small core of older actors and actresses have appeared in practically every play, personal circumstances permitting; and a younger generation of enthusiasts was trained up from childhood. That continuous history is the major difference between this project and any other community play activity which has yet come to light.

The term 'community play' carries some implications which are not always fulfilled: the question must always arise as to how much the inspiration really comes from within the community, and how much suggestion, guidance and control has been received from outside. In Britain a pattern has arisen whereby an 'outsider' has a key role – as scriptwriter, director or general professional advisor. Monticchiello's first *autodrammi* were on the face of it prompted by, and run by, a similar outside intervention. The suggestion that they should be done at all came from a cultural journalist, Mario Guidotti, who remained as a driving force for many years afterwards and for a long time was credited as initiator and chief dramatist (although always, and justifiably, 'in collaboration with the people of Monticchiello'). The person who actually directed the plays until 1981, Arnaldo della Giovampaola, was also not technically a resident of Monticchiello. However, his mother had been born into a local sharecropping family, and he was employed in Pienza, on the next hill. Guidotti was in essence a representative of national and 'official' culture – he was based in Rome and worked partly for the Ministry of Culture. However, his family, too, originated in the village, and his personal motivation in creating the project stemmed from a desire (perhaps rather romanticised) to get back to his roots.

There are contrasting views about his artistic input into the scripts over the first thirteen years; what is indisputable is that he worked hard, with his cultural connections, to give Monticchiello's theatre a national critical profile. From 1969 on each production prompted around twenty reviews in Italian national newspapers. It was not long before radio and television took an interest as well. The first night has regularly been a news item for RAI reporters, and in some years, when the play was seen as suitable, it was actually televised and broadcast. A television director named Nico Garrone made two quirky but absorbing dramatised documentaries during the 1990s about earlier periods of Monticchiello's cultural and political life, using the village as the setting and villagers as actors and interviewees.[12]

These facts, on their own, might imply a picture of Monticchiello being entirely hijacked by the metropolitan culture industry (and thus not 'empowered' at all). The truth is considerably different. Mario Guidotti was working from the start with a team of people who demonstrated a high degree of untapped talent. The schoolmaster Aldo Nisi was an enthusiastic organiser, and functioned as president of the Teatro Povero down to the end of the century. A number of villagers at that time in their forties, and then some younger ones, discovered that they had a taste for acting; more to the point, they showed personality, stage authority, energy and timing, and could present even to an outside audience a clear, persuasive picture of the culture and attitudes they were called on to personify. And Andrea Cresti – a schoolteacher born in 1938 who was a full native resident, son of an army officer and small-scale landowner – became an indispensable presence. He could perform and lecture, but he also learnt to edit and expand Guidotti's scripts to the point of acquiring original dramaturgical skills; his visual sense (he is also a painter) made a vital contribution to outdoor stage lighting design in the village square; and eventually he showed his ability as a director as well. His more cautious and sceptical ideas, about rural life past and present, became a focus for the general restiveness of the village in relation to Guidotti's utopianism.

During the 1970s there was increasing tension – sometimes productive, but not always – between Mario Guidotti and the village as a whole. Guidotti's personal agenda seemed simplistic and unreal, and other viewpoints had to be represented in the scripts alongside his own. He could not quash such moves, because he himself had established the notion that this should be a truly representative 'community' enterprise. Around 1981 there was a major power shift in the company. Guidotti was respectfully marginalised, although his title of artistic director gave due recognition to his role in creating the Teatro Povero in the first place. At the same time, the director Arnaldo stepped down for personal reasons. Since then, Andrea Cresti has been 'coordinator' of the productions – director, designer and chief dramatist. However, in proposing ideas and creating scripts he acts as one of a team of four, and everything is subject to the vetting and approval of the Teatro Povero collective. There are cogent and influential people there who do not belong to the scriptwriting team, but who are consulted in relation to the representation of peasant life and peasant language. There are key performers whose preferences can influence both the choice and the handling of themes. Most of all, once a subject has been agreed, its dramatisation has frequently been based on episodes from individual and family memory contributed by members of the company. In a Tuscan community, as opposed to an English one, there is much less of the prejudice whereby 'cultural' activity is perceived as belonging to the affluent and the educated – here, participation has always come from every social and educational level. One might argue provocatively that the production of these 'community plays' expresses a real 'community' far better than many proclaimed examples in the English-speaking world.

From 1980, in any case, the Teatro Povero has been legally established as a non-profit-making cooperative. The official terms of its permitted activities go beyond just mounting theatre productions: they refer to general cultural projects within the village, and to unspecified 'social objectives'. Originally they may have included clauses about 'exploiting historic and environmental resources', and (even more ambitiously) 'the economic and social stabilization of the area'.[13] In a village of such small numbers, where more than one formal organisation would be senseless and wasteful, the Teatro Povero has become the umbrella under which everything happens in the village: plays, concerts, exhibitions, conferences and lectures, whether mounted internally or invited from outside. In 1996, presenting a concert of the village band, Alpo Mangiavacchi – plumber/electrician, bandmaster, and star comic actor – said publicly that even this musical body (which has a much longer and more eventful history) is indistinguishable from the theatre: 'in Monticchiello we're all the same'.

In the 1980 *autodramma* entitled *La dura terra*, a debate around the formation of the cooperative was actually dramatised as the final act. During the discussion the following speech was put into the mouth of Arturo Vignai, the postal clerk (now retired) who over the years has been one of the company's most regular and reliable performers and supporters:

> The fact is that theatre is everything in Monticchiello.
> Theatre is the show we put on, but it's also the problem, the
> question, the social condition. Theatre is everything, it's a
> practical problem as well. The theatre concerns itself with our
> neglected roads, with our people's living standards, with the
> problems of the community and of individuals. The theatre is
> there not only in the summer, when we perform in this
> square, not only at Christmas when we perform in the tavern.
> The theatre is there all the time, at all seasons of the year,
> when we meet, when we talk, when we swap speeches that
> don't come out of a script.[14]

One could be forgiven for assuming that this represents a pipe dream rather than a reality; and yet a surprising amount of it has been true, perhaps different parts of it at different times. At the very beginning, *autodrammi* allowed themselves to express considerable anxiety about Monticchiello's isolation from the new post-agricultural Italy, about the lack of proper communications and the tendency to deprive the village of facilities. When two roads to the village were asphalted, it was not absurd to suggest that this had happened because of the Teatro Povero: theatre had put the village on the map, in more senses than one, and the annual arrival of affluent spectators who included leading figures from culture and journalism may well have tipped the balance in forcing local authorities to take the place more seriously. Where facilities were concerned – in particular the closure of the village school – there was less concrete success, and the logic of the public economy has tended to prevail. Such issues were still emerging as late as 1999, when the newly privatised Italian postal services indicated that they wanted to close down the village post office. The letter written to the village about this – interestingly, addressed to the president of the Teatro Povero as being representative of Monticchiello – was read out on stage in the *autodramma* entitled *Quota 300* and subjected to rueful and ironic comment.[15] In the end services were reduced but not removed altogether – maybe the post office was shamed into this by the play, perhaps also influenced by the awkward fact that for the previous few years Poste Italiane had been listed as one of the Teatro Povero's sponsors. (More will be said about the financing of the cooperative later.)

Returning to Arturo's speech, one has to speak of the theatre as a possible saviour of the village as such. There was a real fear, expressed in the scripts of the 1970s, that agriculture was now operating with such different rules from previously, and that farming was so unattractive to the younger generation, that the community could simply fall apart and die. This might not have entailed total depopulation; but it could easily have involved takeover by entirely new inhabitants, if most of the Monticchiellesi had decided to leave. Their property could have been sold off as holiday apartments and second homes, creating a summertime population of strangers, relaxing in the midst of the medieval walls and overlooked by the keep. Or, as has happened on the other side of the valley, a new form of agriculture, even pastoralism, could have been brought in by blocks of immigrants from other regions of Italy, in particular from Sardinia. The fact that neither of these things happened – the fact that a reasonable number of people decided to stay – is attributed by those concerned to the extra feeling of community solidarity and identity which the existence of the

Teatro Povero provided. (That the theatre had contributed to a rise in the village birth rate was a standard joke for some time, but it also appeared to be a truth based on statistics.)

Arturo's speech from 1980 paints a picture of vigorous year-round debate provoked by the need to work out ideas for the next script – ideas which in those days involved interpreting and understanding the experiences which the village collectively had been through. The writer of this study, to his regret, cannot speak from experience about the atmosphere that far back in time; but encouragement of a systematic programme of consciousness-raising through group discussion would have come in any case from a different source – that is, from the events regularly organised by the Italian Communist Party to promote general political awareness in its members and voters. Even though the Teatro Povero had some less left-wing people at its centre (including the priest Don Vasco Neri, still remembered with huge affection by people of all political persuasions), the climate created in this predominantly left-wing culture would have harmonised perfectly with what the Teatro Povero thought it was doing for the community. The Monticchiellesi who have stayed in the village now love their environment and do not regret their choice; but there is a strong feeling that for some, at a crucial moment, the atmosphere produced by the theatre provided an extra reason for staying. They felt that it was giving them a common purpose, and that the content of the plays was helping them to assess what had been happening in their lives. Rightly or wrongly, this also gave them a feeling of some control over what might happen next.

The first productions in Monticchiello were paid for out of such meagre resources as could be found, and used very basic equipment. From the very beginning, an extra source of income was a 'popular restaurant' opened in the church crypt for the duration of performances; this still flourishes, is owned by the Teatro Povero, and is a well-used venue for the villagers themselves during their festival period and for audiences who have to fit in a meal with a fairly complicated evening journey. The formation of the cooperative in 1980 made the theatre eligible for state arts subsidy, channelled through the Region of Tuscany: it no doubt helped that all the local administrations up to that regional level are solidly left-wing, and would have official sympathy with the aim of presenting the peasant view of recent history. Public grants enabled the company to equip itself with a good stock of stage lighting to rig up in the central village square (Piazza San Martino) which is the open-air theatre; and to acquire a structure of raked seating for an audience of 200, which is dismantled and stored for most of the year.

During the 1980s and early 1990s, all this gave the Teatro Povero a considerable sense of financial security. In 1986 the offer of sponsorship by a food company could be rejected, and was even treated with some satirical derision in the *autodramma* performed that year. Since then Italian public finances have been under pressure, and cultural expenditure has been heavily curtailed. From the mid 1990s, the productions have been more reliant on gate money in order to break even: the run of each *autodramma* has been increased from two weeks to three, and sponsorship has had to be accepted – not only from the post office, for a while, but from the Monte dei Paschi bank in Siena which has a centuries-long tradition of supporting local cultural life. Meanwhile, the spin-off from the project in economic as well as social terms has been considerable. Despite its relative difficulty of access, the village is visited by a trickle of tourists throughout the season, and has to cope with a major influx during the performance period. A certain number of people from Italian cities have bought property there, attracted specifically by the particular atmosphere created by the presence of the theatre: house prices in the village are thus now very high, even by Tuscan standards. Younger residents still have to make difficult choices about career and employment, as they do everywhere in Italy; but for its size the village can regard itself as much more affluent than it would ever have dreamed it could be, thirty years ago.

So what has been dramatised in Monticchiello, over more than thirty years, which has been so empowering?

Individual plays have varied quite considerably in content, style and technique. They have also varied in quality – it is unrealistic to expect a limited number of people, beset with the ups and downs of their personal circumstances, to produce the best of which they are capable every July over such a long period. (*Alizzardo* of 1995, evoked

at the beginning of this essay, was certainly successful but not out-
standing.) In some years (for example, 1992) a piece of astonishingly
moving and effective dramaturgy may appear in the same play as other
sections which are failures. Risky experiments may reveal that they
really were risks, and cause some controversy (1989, 1991 and the
aforementioned 1992). Occasionally a whole show has been miscon-
ceived, to the extent of making one fear that inspiration has finally
been exhausted. This happened, in my experience, in the *autodrammi*
of 1987 and 2000, yet in each case a sense of focus was re-established
the following year by drawing in some new way on the company's
established proven strengths.

The type of dramaturgy and performance which has been most
characteristic, and which seems truly to find no parallel in any other
Italian theatre whether amateur or professional, has been the exploration of the lives and attitudes of sharecropping peasants. By definition, even in the earliest years, this meant seizing a world which
had already disappeared and recreating it with hindsight on stage –
its family structures, its hierarchies, its attitudes, its social and economic predicament. (Also its language: actors both young and old have
learnt to preserve and deploy the local dialect from before 1960, which
nobody now speaks in its pure form, although everyone can still recognise it as the substratum of the vernacular they do use.) Defiantly,
press releases and prefaces have always spoken of dramatising 'peasant civilisation' (*civiltà contadina*), aware that they are finally giving
a posthumous voice[16] to a system of behaviour and values which had
its own validity, and even some complexity, in the face of the automatic contempt with which it was visited by Italian urban society –
that is, by those who, etymologically as well as in other ways, claimed
to have created 'civilisation' in the first place. The dramatised voice
was indeed posthumous, from the start, even though in the early 1970s
the world of *mezzadria* was not very distant in the memories of those
who scripted and performed it. The Monticchiellesi have always been
aware of the irony in the fact that they could at last express their
world and their history only after it was already over. The exercise
has made them particularly conscious of how they have been moving willy-nilly along with the rest of Italy into the modern world, and

made them wonder how much of the affluence they have been embracing has really been accepted from choice, and how much just through having no alternative.

To begin with there was uncertainty both about the way in which the peasant family should be presented and about the purpose of presenting it at all. During the 1970s some of the company felt that it was being sentimentalised and reduced to a series of patronising comic vignettes. To a reader of the scripts, after the event, their discomfort seems only partly justified. When exploring themes such as the predicament of women in a highly patriarchal society – *Quelle e queste donne* (*Women Then and Now*), 1977 – dialogue and situations brought out at least some of the harshness and rigidity which was internal to peasant society as well as being imposed on it. The fundamental economic subjection to the landlord, and the injustices of the sharecropping contract, were dramatised to devastating effect, especially in *Contadini o no* (*Peasants or Not*) of 1974 and *La dura terra* (*The Hard Earth*) of 1980.[17] Even after the major change in scriptwriting personnel, quirky characters (especially those played by Alpo Mangiavacchi) went on providing elements of humour in the peasant scenes, along with the general tendency towards pithy undermining sarcasm which Italians see as characteristic of all Tuscan conversation. But Mario Guidotti was suspected of presenting too rosy a view, and of wanting to create a sentimental picture of earthy rural harmony, unrecognisable to those who had actually been there. Worse still, he seemed to be promulgating the view that contemporary Monticchiello represented some kind of rural utopia, outside the ills of modern society. Since 1981 – despite a running unease about some of Andrea Cresti's more experimental imaginings, felt by some to be too abstruse – the village has been happy with its collective ability to evoke on stage, with a plausible mixture of exasperation, bitterness and unavoidable nostalgia, the formative experience which the older Monticchiellesi will carry with them until they die, and which the younger ones have learnt to recognise as an explanation of what the community has since become.

For a surprisingly long time, however, texts of the Teatro Povero returned at intervals to pick at one particular open sore in the memory of Tuscan *ex-mezzadri*: the confused way in which *mezzadria* came to an end, and the mythical 'lost opportunity' associated with the early 1960s. (According to a hindsight view which is debatable but very widely held, there was a failure of nerve among both political leaders and the peasants themselves, at the moment when more of them might have bought their *poderi* from the departing landlords.) The dramatisation of peasanthood as such was often inseparable from this one political obsession, to which I have devoted a previous study.[18] However, in the process a stage picture of the peasant family evolved which has attracted and enchanted regular audiences.

A classic way in which the *famiglia contadina* was evoked, but then also used for a wider purpose, appears in the *autodramma* of 1983, entitled *Zollet*. This play dealt overall with contrasting attitudes to money and spending, held by the modern and peasant worlds. After a prologue set in the present day, scenes alternated between careful evocations of family life in the 1950s, and satirical futuristic predictions of the more lunatic directions in which a modern economy could drive us. A single protagonist linked it all together, entering as an adult the world which he had inhabited as a child, and trying to avoid becoming trapped in the future. The peasant scenes dealt with the impossibility in those days of spending any money you did not have in your hand (so a daughter's wedding had reluctantly to be postponed); and then with the crisis which came around 1960, when peasants were faced suddenly with the chance to buy their land and become independent, but many of them could not face the thought of the resultant debt. In the first of the futuristic scenes, a law had been imposed whereby people were selected by lot to throw out a room's worth of furniture and buy another set, in order to keep the consumer economy going. (In a memorable sequence the population were lulled away from their rebellion into a soothing waltz, to soundtrack music with the theme 'Buy . . . Consume . . . Throw away . . .') In the second of the scenes, Monticchiello had been turned into a supermarket, which no one could enter without a trolley. The only commodity on sale, in various sizes of packaging, was the local earth – which the peasants had missed the chance of buying in 1960. The *zolle*, clods of earth which had been the peasant's object of desire and at the same time the rack of labour on which he was stretched, were transmuted into the purposeless consumer product 'Zollet', stacked on the shelves.

The audience in 1983 were left to make up their own minds about the relative merits of the old system and the new; and this open-ended contrast between the peasant world and the modern one was a standard feature of Teatro Povero dramaturgy for some time. From around 1994, however, as new generations grew up, it ceased to be taken for granted that the whole of the village's thinking could be based on receding memories of a vanished world. More recent *autodrammi* have undertaken to question the function and utility of such memories, and indeed of memory as such. In the 1994 script, *Sfratti* (*Evictions*), the peasant drama became a play within a play, and was openly challenged on stage by representatives of the modern unemployed. The company had to justify to itself its own obsession with the campaigns of the peasant leagues in the 1950s; it did so on this occasion by offering the spirit of solidarity which prevailed at that earlier time as a principle which could still be used in confronting modern economic problems. Since then, the question has refused to go away, and 'memory' has been a theme, implicit or explicit, in many *autodrammi*. At the same time, an obstinate attachment to the countryside and the rhythm of the seasons, reinforced by such memory, has been offered as a necessary 'natural' part of human inheritance, and Monticchiello has effectively been saying to the urban world that we abandon the resources and the insights of the rural world at our peril. Confrontations with intrusive representatives of official modern culture – bureaucrats, managers, salesmen and also academics – have been a repeated theme over the years. They are handled sometimes with foreboding, but more often with satirical sarcasm, combined with a rueful perception of the ambiguous position in which the new affluent Monticchiello actually stands in relation to such alleged 'invasions'.

From 1999 to 2001 the plays attempted to build a kind of trilogy in which the predicament and the prospects of small rural communities, nationwide, was investigated from different angles. In *ManONèAbusoDIpodere?*,[19] of 2001, the village pretended that it had invited three marketing consultants to offer a solution to its isolation and alleged economic unviability. The experts proposed that Monti-cchiello should draw its future income from mounting a complicated lottery game, for which the prize would be the chance to spend time in a 'virtual' peasant environment in a local converted farmhouse (*podere*). Unfortunately, the *podere* which would be needed was owned by six obstinate old peasants, who were insisting on staying there and living as they did forty years ago. In the second half of the play, we saw those six people, and witnessed their determination to stay put even in the face of pleas by their despairing children, who were motivated by a mixture of genuine concern for their crumbling parents and greed for the money which would be brought in by the sale.

The scripting and the casting pulled the audience firmly on to the side of the elderly 'monads' – they were played by actors who have enough track record, reputation and overwhelming stage presence to attract sympathy from both the local and the less knowledgeable spectators. Towards the end they produced a choral narrative about their generation's attachment to possession of their own plot of land – a potted history of yearning, acquisition, desolation and rebirth. There were few dry eyes left in the house (or, to be pedantic, in the *piazza*). The message was that the generation of *ex-mezzadri* might soon be coming to an end, but that in Monticchiello at least they had used the theatre to come to terms with their lives, past and present, and were not going to abandon their identity or their self-knowledge. The other Tuscans who formed the majority of their audience had clearly seen their own history articulated by this one small village over the years, and had experienced indeed a level of empowerment. The danger of sterile nostalgia always threatens, perhaps; but communities, like individuals, must ultimately be allowed to use their own past for whatever purpose they choose. It is, after all, the only one they have. To dramatise it, ruefully and ironically as well as nostalgically, is more productive than to forget it.

The empowerment has been individual, as well as collective. To highlight a list of names (and to leave out others) risks both unfairness and an invasion of privacy, but a selective impression has to be conveyed. In the 1970 *autodramma* a young man appeared in his own identity as a person who could see no future in Monticchiello and was aiming to move to Florence. In 2002 he was still in the village, a successful businessman and property holder, regularly involved in productions as actor, organiser or prompter. In an interview given to a British student,[20] he said that it was the collective activity of the Teatro Povero which reattached him to Monticchiello, and which corrected his temperamental tendencies to isolation and even to selfishness. The same British student recorded a conversation with an *ex-mezzadro* who has been one of the company's leading actors since the very beginning, has been a consultant for years on all aspects of peasant language and dialect, and has been moved to write some one-act plays of his own. This relatively uneducated man has had his life both transformed and defined by the theatre, and has used it to build his own relationship with a past life the loss of which he regrets. Other former peasants regard themselves as less backward-looking, but still see their long experience of 'performing themselves' as a crucial part of their lives: the best known of them all, Rino Grappi, gave a moving public declaration at a conference in 1992 about his absorbed affection for every production in which he has appeared, good or bad. 'It's like a parent who has ten children; so, if one is uglier than the others, you still have to love him, because he's still your child.'[21]

The personalities of so many of the villagers – artisans, clerks, tradesmen, manual labourers, housewives, but also the village doctor and a retired professor of Chinese – have been marked and altered both in public and in private by what they have done for the theatre and what the theatre has done for them. And those who are reluctant to take leading scripted roles nevertheless signal their participation by appearing in the crowd scenes, the *scene di popolo*: every *autodramma* contains at least one moment when as many as fifty people, aged literally from seven to seventy, may be on stage as choral representatives of the community.

A special word has to be said in conclusion about women's contribution to the Teatro Povero. In 1969 peasant women were barely emerging (if they were emerging) from a culture in which they were expected to keep quiet and let the men do the talking. (Lots of age-old proverbs told them explicitly that this was what they should do; some have been quoted in scripts from time to time.) When women were immediately needed to perform in the plays, it was at first quite hard to find any who could break out of that habit of silence. The earliest actresses tended to be from the village rather than the farms – women from families of small property owners, shopkeepers and artisans. Many of the peasant women were too old to change, and their participation (sometimes very important) was limited partly to backstage work, but also to feeding their memories and opinions into the discussions which helped to structure the early scripts. Well into the 1990s, there were old women who regularly turned up to rehearsals in order to check that any representation of the past, even indirect representations of real village characters, conformed with their memories.

At the same time, the educational activities and propaganda (already mentioned) of the Italian Communist Party made great efforts to address and to involve women members, with a good proportion of women speakers and organisers being sent round to set an example. This created a climate of greater equality as regards participation in politics and in society. In 1977, during the first energetic flourishes of Italian feminism, the *autodramma* was devoted entirely to the roles and predicaments of women, past and present. By the end of the twentieth century, a good number of women old and young, locally born and more recently arrived, had passed through the casts of *autodrammi*, and some of them have stayed to perform every year. There are now women whose stage talents are as forceful, individual and practised as those of the men. The world has moved on around them in any case, and their presence now provokes little comment; but at a time when it was necessary, the Teatro Povero helped to empower them, too.

NOTES

1. 'Ma Cristo! Succede sempre cosí. Ci si accorge che le cose 'un vanno come dovrebbero andare, quand'è bell'e troppo tardi! [. . .] Sapete . . . quando venivo da queste parti, qualche volta mi fermavo giú in mezzo al campo, e pensavo a come sarebbe stato giusto se ogni contadino fosse doventato padrone. Ora mi rendo conto che ci hanno fatto prendere una cosa per un'altra. Ecco

perché ci voleva piú convinzione. Ci hanno fatto giocà su un banchettino dove c'erano, no tre, ma trecento carte, e tutte truccate. Una beffa dopo l'altra.'

(The language contains elements of the local dialect of the Val d'Orcia.)

2. I have attempted to give a more detailed account of the system of *mezzadria* in a previous study: R. Andrews, *A Theatre of Community Memory: Tuscan Sharecropping and the Teatro Povero di Monticchiello* (Exeter and Leeds: Society for Italian Studies, 1998), ch. 1, pp. 1–7. An even fuller description is found in Frank M. Snowden, *The Fascist Revolution in Tuscany, 1919–1922* (Cambridge: Cambridge University Press, 1989), pp. 7–69.

3. The size of a 'normal' family of *mezzadri* is still subject to debate, but it is clear that whereas as many as twenty was common in the nineteenth century, the average had dropped considerably by the Second World War, perhaps to as few as seven people including children. See Snowden, *The Fasust Revolution*, p. 20 and accompanying footnotes.

4. A fuller narrative of the political process which led to the collapse of *mezzadria* appears in Andrews, *A Theatre of Community Memory*, pp. 7–22. It is a story still rarely told, even by Italian historians.

5. For population statistics, see Vasco Neri, *Monticchiello, storia di una comunità* (Siena: Cantagalli, 1986), pp. 121–2. The author was the village priest, a competent scholar, and closely involved in the earliest theatre projects.

6. I must acknowledge here, as on other occasions, the help of extremely useful exchanges with Margaret Sheehy, a practitioner and scholar of community plays.

7. A number of Italian towns perpetuate local dramatic traditions by mounting community performances of dramas (usually in verse) with a historical or legendary content. An example very close to Monticchiello would be the so-called 'Bruscelli' in Montepulciano: the author of the 1967 play in Monticchiello had also written Bruscelli. Although some texts are of relatively recent composition, the dramatic structures and verbal styles always

clearly mirror those of pre-humanist plays from the early six-teenth century.

8. The most comprehensive study of the Palio in English is A. Dundes and A. Falassi, *La Terra in Piazza. An Interpretation of the Palio of Siena* (Berkeley and Los Angeles: University of California Press, 1975).

9. For more details of this play, *Noi di Monticchiello*, with some translated extracts, see Andrews, *A Theatre of Community Memory*, pp. 25–9.

10. See *ibid.*, pp. 30–9, with fuller Italian extracts on pp. 106–11.

11. In 1975 *Quel 6 aprile del '44* was revived from 1969, to mark the thirtieth anniversary of the Liberation of Italy.

12. The programmes were broadcast on RAI3 in 1995 and 1999. The first, *Storia di una banda e di un paese*, dealt with conflicts in the early twentieth century between the village priest and the anti-clerical schoolmaster; the second dealt with events of the Second World War. Both made use of the lucid on-camera reminiscences of Signora Lidia Virgini, born in 1908. Lidia has been one of my own most precious and informative resources; sadly, she died in June 2002.

13. These proposals appear in the script of *La dura terra* (1980), and are reproduced in Andrews, *A Theatre of Community Memory*, on p. 102. The current constitution of the cooperative appears on the Teatro Povero website, at http://www.teatropovero.it, under the heading 'Compagnia'.

14. 'Il fatto è che il teatro è tutto a Monticchiello. Il teatro è lo spetta-colo, ma è anche il problema, la questione, la condizione sociale. Il teatro è tutto, è anche fatto practico. Il teatro si occupa delle nostre strade che vengono trascurate, della condizione della nos-tra gente, dei problemi della comunità e anche dei singoli. Il teatro non c'è soltanto d'estate quando recitiamo qui in questa piazza, non c'è soltanto per le feste di Natale quando recitiamo in tav-erna. Il teatro c'è sempre, in tutte le stagioni dell'anno, quando ci riuniamo, quando parliamo, quando ci scambiamo battute che non sono quelle d'un copione.'

15. The whole play, in response to this provocation, dealt with the threat posed to small communities (those below Monticchiello's 'quota' of 300) in the modern economy. A futuristic situation was dramatised in which such villages would be closed down, and their inhabitants deported to larger centres.

16. The importance of a 'voice', in various senses, has been explored more fully in R. Andrews, 'Finding a Voice: a Theme in the Community Drama of Monticchiello', in *New Theatre Quarterly* 25 (February 1991), pp. 77–96.

17. A complete Italian/dialect text of *La dura terra* is reproduced as an Appendix to Andrews, *A Theatre of Community Memory*, on pp. 78–105.

18. See Andrews, *A Theatre of Community Memory, passim.*

19. This title is the most complex pun which Andrea Cresti has so far come up with, from a mind always fecund with mischievous verbal mystification. 'Ma non è abuso di potere?' would mean 'But isn't it an abuse of power?'. *Potere* (power) is deliberately conflated with *podere*, the word for a farmhouse or its surrounding plot of land, under *mezzadria*. Then certain letters are capitalised to spell 'MONADI' ('monads'), the word having the sense, more viable in Italian than in English, of people adopting their own unique lifestyle without reference to a norm.

20. Chris Aaron, who did a study project in Monticchiello in 1993, on a research grant from Warwick University.

21. Rino died on 19 April 2002, while this present essay was still being completed; his death was announced nationally on RAI teletext on 23 April. His departure is a grievous blow to the Teatro Povero (as it is to the present writer): for an assessment of his importance to the company, see Andrews, *A Theatre of Community Memory*, pp. 42–3. For a transcribed version of his conference contribution, see M. Fresta (ed.), *Il Teatro delle Radici: Teatro Povero di Monticchiello. Atti del Convegno, 16/17 maggio 1992* (Montepulciano: Editrice Le Balze, 1996), p. 153.

4 'What happened to you today that reminded you that you are a black man?' The process of exploring black masculinities in performance, Great Britain

MICHAEL MACMILLAN

Blacks – in particular, black men – swap their experiences of police encounters like war stories, and there are few who don't have more than one story to tell.[1]

Henry Louis Gates, Jr

While there has been much written about the experience of African-American men, a similar body of literature does not exist for issues of black masculinity in a British context. In Britain there has been a pathologised approach which sees black masculinity as constructed within a deviant youth subculture as a substitute for powerlessness. As bell hooks argues: 'The portrait of black masculinity that emerges in this work perpetually constructs men as "failures", who are psychologically "fucked up", dangerous, violent sex maniacs whose insanity is informed by their inability to fulfill their phallocentric masculine destiny in a racist context.'[2]

Power is central to any discussion of black masculinity, but different from the wider gendered power relations in society. Black masculinity can be best understood as an articulated response to structural inequality, acting out and subverting hegemonic definitions of power and control, rather than an alternative to them. Living in a culture where racist colonisation has designated black men as more body than mind, I am witness to, and participant in, the black bodily experience as collective memory. The severing of the mind from the body and the soul suggests a fragmentation of identity in the construction of black masculinities. But it is the utilisation of creative tactics in the domain of performance and orality that enables these fragmented identities to coexist. If Richard Schechner delineates performance as 'behaviour heightened' or 'twice behaved behaviour', then black masculinity is a site of performed cultural discourse around 'index and symbol, multiple truths and lies . . . [and an] arena of struggle'. Moreover, masking as an ancient African ritualistic practice was adapted by slaves as a survival strategy during colonialism and later fabricated as roles, façades, shields, fronts and games to facilitate an ontology of being in the face of that ongoing hegemony.[3]

> We wear the mask that grins and lies,
> It hides our cheeks and shades our eyes,
> This debt we pay to human guile;
> With torn and bleeding hearts we smile,
> And mouth with myriad subtleties.
>
> Why should the world be otherwise,
> In counting all our tears and sighs?
> Nay, let them only see us, while
> We wear the mask.[4]

To peel away the mask, we have to transcend the oppressive representation of black masculinity as homogenous by first exploring its construction as performative behaviour and rehearsed ritual, customs and rites of passage. The workshop process, in the context of performance, enables us to unpack difference in the heterogeneous construction of black masculinities by empowering the subject. It is also a strategy of resistance, subversion and affirmation, framed by the dialectics of race, gender, sexuality, class and desire. Through a critique of various projects working primarily with black men, it is hoped therefore that some light can be shed on the discourse of black masculinities.

A performance-orientated workshop setting has been the site of this exploration, and my approach as practitioner in this process has not been as a teacher but as a facilitator. The aim in this context has been to create the conditions that will foster a safe space based on trust, where participants can feel free to express themselves. A fundamental condition is that the workshop facilitator is not a voyeuristic observer, but a participant prepared to share himself or herself as subject as much as other members of the group share themselves. Another aspect of this levelling is the demystification of language, its uses and meanings, where writing and performance can be a means of expression in a personal context.

Orchard Lodge Resource Centre in Anerley, London, is a multidisciplinary client-based service with residential places offering secure, open and daycare placements. Among the services and facilities it provides is a formal education structure for boys and young men from the age of eleven to sixteen years old. I was invited to work with this client group and produce a collection of writings. The aim was to give creative expression to the experiences, emotions, fears, frustrations, dreams and aspirations of boys and young men who had been previously disadvantaged in vital elements of care, and/or who had committed criminal offences. This was not a psychoanalytic investigation into the 'criminal mind' to reveal answers to questions which society wished to ask. Rather it was giving a space to voices made silent in a hegemonic white patriarchal culture, where talking about, much less exploring, one's feelings is usually suppressed and or oppressed. 'Language is not a virgin, but a bastard', as Deborah Levy once said, and coded in the language of male oppression is power, violence and fear.[5] At Orchard Lodge, through writing and performance, we attempted to construct a 'feelings vocabulary', of which many young men are too often afraid.

The outcome of this process was a published anthology of poetry and prose. It gave pride to contributors and empowered others to try their hand at poetry and publish a collection, even to take up GCSE English. I could identify with the young men I worked with, given my own experience as a relative outsider in the British education system. Among the ugly and dirty realities that this collection of pieces highlighted was how race is immersed in the stream of popular and public consciousness, and how the trauma of racism is embedded from an early age. Years before the public debate about the educational underachievement of boys in general, there were cries from the black communities about the plight of black boys from parents exasperated by the disproportionate number of exclusions and expulsions of black children.[6]

Born and bred in the UK, of parents from St Vincent in the Caribbean, I had to negotiate daily the invisibility of my cultural experience and the visibility of stereotypes of colour and gender in the British education system. My parents, like many immigrants from the Caribbean and South East Asia, had been educated in a colonial system left by the British. As immigrants trying to survive in a hostile society, they were the greatest exponents of the Protestant work ethic and the teachings of the Bible. Some of this generation were activists in labour struggles, or set up voluntary self-help organisations; they were also concerned to defend the rights of their children in the British education system. But to many the teacher was omnipotent, and it was heresy to think that their children might be stereotyped with low expectations by those who taught them. (Tony Sewell has written extensively, if not uncontroversially, on the complexity of racism in British schools; space constraints do not allow me to do his arguments full justice, but I should acknowledge that he does provide a context in looking at the performance work with black men discussed in this essay.)[7] Psychologically, many young black people still find it a struggle to transcend the denigration of their self-esteem and the sense of alienation and disenfranchisement that the British education system created.

In Ralph Ellison's novel *Invisible Man*, the anonymous, naive protagonist, alienated from the reality of his existence, descends physically into an underground cavern and wires his space with 1,369 light bulbs with power diverted from the electricity board.[8] In his cosmic 'black hole', time and space are suspended as he begins to celebrate the advantages of his invisibility. Ellison's allegorical narrative formed the basis of *Invisible*, a one-man performance piece, in which an unknown black man as 'persona' (see below) lives in a timeless pit of sand. He is comforted by the jazz music of Louis Armstrong as he attempts to deconstruct the ontology of his invisibility through flashbacks and dreams. Houston A. Baker, Jr explores this rite of passage as symbolised tropically by a Black Hole, a scientific entity where time,

space and light have been conflated to zero.[9] In the black ontology
of being, this subjectivity has a rationality, given the history of black
disempowerment. But within the dominant culture this identity crisis would be seen as irrational, and the subject sectioned as mentally
ill, or on the verge of a nervous breakdown.

As a writer on theatre and performance, I share Claire
MacDonald's view that:

> writing what I call 'texts for the theatre' has in my experience
> been a much more eloquent form to discuss cultural identities
> and difference than the play text. This is because 'the play' is
> perceived to be dependent on character, while the 'text' can
> explore persona or personae in all their strangeness and
> complexity. Fanon's insight into the colonised psyche, having
> to intimately know the heart and the mind of the master
> better than the master knows those things himself, finds its
> bitter truth in the text for performance . . . Persona literally
> means the masks through which we speak. For those of us
> who negotiate the everyday by using many voices, many
> guises and strategies because we have to, the performance text
> in the hybrid form can transgress the traditions and
> conventions of the play and give voice to our experience of the
> contemporary world – with all its mixed messages.[10]

The oppositional and countercultural political framework underpinning interdisciplinary and post-disciplinary practice therefore invites
a paradigm shift, or at least an overhaul. Julie MacDougall's perception – 'As a displaced person moving between cultures, I am viewing
identity as a work-in-process, a disappearing act, a performance' – has
a poignant resonance.[11] Underpinning this process is the adaptation
by the media of Foucault's notion that power consists of being able to
act, and to act on the action of others; in other words, a social intervention which turns individuals and groups within a specific society
from being the objects into being the subjects of their own history.[12]
In Forum Theatre, part of Augusto Boal's Theatre of the Oppressed,
spectators are invited to challenge the role of the acting protagonist
and themselves to change the course of the story, thereby becoming

'spect*actors*'. 'We tried to show in practice how the theatre can be placed at the service of the oppressed,' Boal writes, 'so that they can express themselves and so that, by using this new language, they can discover new concepts.'[13]

In my work as a practitioner using theatre and performance, this approach has been empowering in a workshop context, where Forum Theatre deconstructs collective oppression as a means of finding group solutions. And in the context of unpacking representations of black masculinities, Forum Theatre has a relevance in identifying the execution of oppression in terms of institutionalised racism in the British education system, the labour market, the police, housing, Social Services, and so on, and in formulating strategies of resistance. But Forum Theatre offers only a two-dimensional expression of more complex psychological dynamics where, for instance, oppression has been internalised.

> . . . we had a very interesting experience in the U.S., comparing social values in the segregationist South with those in New York, where 'integration' appeared to be more advanced. We showed a dozen or so dolls to hundreds of black children. We asked them to point out the prettiest and the ugliest. In the South, where the segregated blacks had better kept their aesthetic values (along with other values), the children said that the prettiest was the black doll and the ugliest the white one. In the North, where 'integration' imposes the values of the white society, the results were just the opposite: the white doll was the prettiest and the black the ugliest. The black kids had acquired the white values.[14]

Boal developed 'cop in the head' as a derivative of his Forum Theatre approach when he went to work in France and found that while participants felt no obvious oppression, Europe had a higher suicide rate than Latin America. To counter this repressive and seductive process of 'osmosis', as Boal describes it, 'cop in the head' as a workshop approach challenges the oppression that takes place inside the head of the protagonist.

Power, control and authority as prevailing definitions of masculinity were historically denied to the black man; consequently there emerged the contradictory formation of a subordinated masculinity. The black male youth today is stereotyped as the 'mugger' or 'rioter', constituting a violent threat to white society, according to Kobena Mercer 'the objectified form of inarticulate fears at the back of the minds of "ordinary British people" made visible in the headlines of the popular tabloids'.[15] Historically, black male identities have been culturally constructed through the complex dynamics of power in Western patriarchy, which cannot be simply stripped away to discover some essentialist 'natural' black male identity that is 'good, pure and wholesome'. 'There is a further contradiction,' Mercer continues, 'another turn of the screw of oppression, which occurs when black men subjectively internalise and incorporate aspects of the dominant definition of masculinity in order to contest the definitions of dependency and powerlessness, which racism and racial oppression enforce.'[16]

Michael Hamilton is a friend and fellow practitioner I have known and worked with for years. We have done extensive work with boys and young men in a range of different contexts: sexual health, community education and in schools. An exercise which I developed with Michael was based on a simple question: 'What happened to you today that reminded you that you are a black man?' We were asked to lead a day-long workshop with a group of young black men at Crofton Park Secondary School in South London and we asked this question, expecting answers such as 'passing a white woman clutching her handbag' or 'a gaze of suspicion when we entered a shop'. Instead, most of the participants said that when they woke up, they looked down and realised that they were black men. The meaning of this, their response to a symbolic image, was that they believed the myth that having a big penis defined them as black men. Needless to say, we had an uphill struggle to convince them otherwise, to perceive definitions of themselves other than biologically reductionist ones. Among their peer group, hyper-masculinity as currency was circulated, perpetuating the colonial mythology around black sexuality. Black sexuality is fetishised in the representation of black popular culture, be it music, fashion or the vernacular. Urban youth culture is both a performative transience and a transcendent expression of style, where a consumer-led 'street cred' is what you wear, the way you look, the way you speak and what you think.

Many of the assumptions about black sexuality emanate from a view which sees the black family as deviant, dysfunctional, disorganised and pathological, and therefore failing to socialise its offspring into 'correct' societal norms. As Frantz Fanon argues, in *Black Skin, White Masks*, myths about the violent, aggressive and 'animalistic' nature of black sexuality were fabricated and fictioned by the all-powerful white master to allay his fears and anxieties as well as to provide a means of justifying the brutalisation of the colonised and assuaging any vestiges of guilt.[17] These fictions of the sexually active savage have entered into the social construction of black masculinity today. With the black man inscribed as the Other, black sexuality is constructed as an object of desire, while ambivalently feared at the same psychological level. Kobena Mercer, in *Fear of a Black Penis*, points out that:

> psychoanalytic concepts now float freely in debates on cultural politics, but there is still a stubborn resistance to the recognition of unconscious phastasy as a structuring principle of our social, emotional, and political life . . . It is in the domain of race, whose violent and sexy phastasia haunts America daily, that our need for an understanding of the psychic reality of phastasy, and its effect in the body politic, is greatest.[18]

From a post-modernist perspective, prison represents the absolute separation that society wishes to impose between acceptable and unacceptable forms of subjectivity. Black men are othered as unacceptable subjects and therefore, in the USA and Britain, constitute a disproportionate percentage of the prison population in relation to their overall representation in the wider population. Prison is also highly theatrical as a site of contestation between good and evil. Consequently there have been some innovative theatre projects carried out in prisons. Working with black male inmates, performance ensembles such as The Hittite Empire have done groundbreaking creative work in

American state penitentiaries, and practitioners such as Martin Glynn have used rites of passage as a concept to empower incarcerated fathers in British prisons.[19]

Other than under the more humane regimes of uncommonly enlightened governors, which may include innovative education departments, prison is still predominantly a place of punishment rather than rehabilitation. I was aware of this reality when I began a four-week intensive workshop course in Theatre Skills at HM Prison The Mount in Hemel Hempstead. Race relations in the British prison system are still largely a paper policy, and I was conscious of my invisibility in an institution where 60 per cent of the inmates were black and/or non-European. Prison culture operates as judge, jury and executioner, and prison officers (the 'screws', as they are so touchingly termed) are at the top of the chain of dehumanisation. I may have been police-checked, but I was under surveillance like everybody else. I was reminded of this daily, when I had to remember to walk in with my passport, as the gatekeepers would never recall me from the day before. I did not dress to a particular formal code or carry keys, and this 'deinstitutionalised' my position, allowing me to be more informal with inmates; the price paid, however, was to be accidentally (or sometimes deliberately?) mistaken for one of them. Conscious of how my actions were perceived and by whom, I wore a mask of conformity.

Freedom can be exhilarating, liberating, intoxicating and empowering, but it can also be frightening, involving the loss of safe, non-threatening conventional structures. Many participants in the workshop situation can feel terrified of letting go of trusted conventions and modes of perception: in other words, they can question their own ontology when involved in a situation where one has to open up and be honest with oneself creatively as a means of engendering a sense of trust. And trust is fundamental here, where one is unsure of what will happen next, of what one will be asked to do, of other participants (including those leading the workshop) . . . 'Will I look like a fool if I do this exercise?', 'What do they think of me?', 'Will I be exposed?', 'Why don't they ask the next guy?', 'What will I get out of it?', 'Will it change me?', 'Will I need counselling after this experience?'

The workshop process consisted of sharing personal stories, performance writing, improvisation and ritual, all with the subtle intention of achieving 'cop in the head' outcomes. Using games and exercises which loosened inhibitions and enabled sharing, nobody seemed to mind making a fool of himself in front of others. We utilised an exercise I first saw used in a workshop led by Keith Antar Mason of The Hittites. Each person was lifted aloft by the group and carried around the room like a champion, with his name being chanted. In a patriarchal society, where male competition is advocated and coded as a badge of masculinity, celebrating each other as simply men is often suppressed, apart from in the sexual and sports arenas. One would expect the ego to step forward, but instead embarrassment brought on false modesty; there were claims of being too heavy to be lifted, or fears of being dropped. But once the nervous threshold was passed, every person who went through this exercise felt exhilarated and closer to other participants in the group. Complementing this series of trust and status-based games and exercises were those focusing on breathing, relaxation, visualisation and body stretching to empower and liberate the mind, body and soul towards performance. After this warm-up we would then go on to devising performance pieces from oral testimonies based on the theme of freedom, although this was only symbolic as the work was taking place in a prison.

I found that being incarcerated was itself inhuman: 80 per cent of one's energy could be devoted just to surviving. The boundaries of personal physical and spiritual space enclose a force-field of self-preservation: I watch you, watching me, watching you in a paranoid climate of mistrust. Returning the male gaze is either read as a threat or sexualised. And the mask of emotional coldness operates as a means of protection and warning in this encounter. In the West there are prescriptive cultural codes of conduct for male bodies touching each other which have their roots in cultural norms around violence and sexuality. (For instance, the Western cultural tradition of shaking hands says to the recipient, 'I present you with an open hand without a weapon and without any intention of violence.') The operations of power and control make prison a microcosm of society, and in a closed male environment the intrinsic relationship between power and sex is sometimes manifest.

The transient nature of prison life prevents close relationships from being made: life is continually shifting, unstable, ephemeral, unsafe and frightening. Its culture is dominated by a regime which is itself a prisoner and hostage to its own rules and regulations. The notion that inmates are of a particular social type is a myth: they are simply people who have ended up for one reason or another in confined spaces. By the fourth week we were beginning to trust each other and open up. It was then that we started to dream and allow our desires to manifest themselves as we constructed our freedoms as spiritual as opposed to material.

We had been using a Multifaith Room as our workshop space, although nothing in prison can be relied upon and we could have lost the space at any moment. So said, so done: the month of the Muslim Ramadan arrived and the room was out of use to us. A music studio was the only space available. But the inconvenience eventually proved an asset, as we were able to use the technology there and collaborate with other inmates learning music in bringing together our performance presentation. An accident of fate had enabled us to fuse the art forms of performance, music and writing through a number of jamming sessions and some 'bad' recordings.

After four weeks together I was able to use the word 'feminine' with the group in describing how they had connected with themselves emotionally, without them feeling paranoid. It was unfortunate that the prison regime was not enlightened enough (and/or was too afraid) to allow us to perform in front of other inmates. Nevertheless, we used the waiting involved in a prison sentence as a motif in the performance setting of a train station, where improvised drama and written poetic monologues punctuated the tedium in real time. Each performer took on personae as masks, which allowed them to be someone else, a vital strategy for survival in prison.

Projects of this nature break the monotony of prison life, and inmates look forward to taking part each week, almost to the point of dependency. One criticism of this project would be that there was no follow-up: I have often asked myself since whether the workshop had any lasting affect on the participants' lives. Depending on their sentence and movements within the system, I might have returned in a year to find the same people living the same routine. But just as with the young men at Orchard Lodge, the inmates I worked with at The Mount were I hope able, through sharing, to shed a little light on their lives.[20]

At The Mount I led a two-day workshop with black inmates, and among this cohort was someone with the surname Bogle. I don't know why I was curious, but on the second day I asked this inmate whether he was a descendant of the Jamaican national hero, Paul Bogle, a Baptist preacher who led a slave revolt in the nineteenth century. It turned out that Paul Bogle *was* his ancestor, but he was indifferent to that history, and to the irony of his legacy. Instead, the subject in front of me was more interested in his peer status as matriarchy worshipper, while being a patriarchal misogynist. This had nothing to do with race, as the dominant male discourse dictates that the remedy for emotional constipation is silent violence. 'Black men are densely mythogenic, the object of layered fictions produced by others . . . And like other mythogenic people, Black men are, as if in self-defense, prolific generators of self-descriptive legends.'[21]

As storytellers we are mythmakers, and the narrator can mask his or her identity to be someone else. Subjectivity in the black diaspora has an ontological relationship to the concept of masking, mediated culturally within a ritual context and historically through colonialism. America cannot be understood without an understanding of the race politics that have shaped that society, and blackface minstrelsy was its first theatrical prototype, where burnt-cork-faced white entertainers appropriated and ridiculed black life. The die had been cast in the representation of the black subject, as black actors even in Hollywood had to imitate whites caricaturing blacks.[22] In spite of this colonial fantasy, freed slaves in the Americas held on to the performativity of the mask as masquerade. Using African trickster figures such as the spider, Anancy, to inform a subversive philosophy, slaves incorporated a performance strategy as mask. They would smile and grin at the agents of colonial power, but suck their teeth when white backs were turned. This beguiling deference to authority as a means of survival has echoes in old proverbs such as, 'Play fool to catch wise.' In *Invisible Man* Ellison's deranged veteran advises the protagonist 'Play the game, don't believe in it.' Black men experience their social predicament as a game. 'The game is ironic. It is also oblique, since many Black men, players all, don't even know the object of the contest, have no clues of the rules, the stakes, or even that they are both in the game and the quarry.'[23] In this game the trickster cannot resist the temptation to mask his identities, to manipulate the masks, through myths created around them, where multiple personalities improvise fantastic identities.

As already noted, there are legitimate historical precedents for the mask as illusion.

> The profile of today's gangsta rapper, scaled down last season to the ultimate, low metabolism vibe of Dr. Dre and Snoop Doggy Dogg, evokes an affectless masculinity, conceived under siege, and resonating with a long history of presenting a neutral face as a mask of inscrutability to the white gaze.[24]

From a reductionist perspective, the impervious mask often adopted by black people in relation to whites can be seen as facilitating internal balance. But a consequence of this post-modernist adoption of multiple subject positions is that the question of who is really speaking becomes highly problematic. In the summer of 1994, during a one-day workshop, twelve black men of African descent, and as different as can be, attempted to peel away this impervious mask for a moment. The workshop was led by Keith Antar Mason of The Hittites, and in that space we began to break the silence of our private and public truths. During the 1990s performance work which foregrounded black masculinities as subject matter was humanised by the work of the The Hittite Empire; work such as the *The Underseige Stories* and *The Punic Wars*, both performed at the Institute of Contemporary Arts (ICA).[25] If women cultural producers coined the phrase 'the personal is political and the political personal', then they were also prophets on this occasion: it was Catherine Ugwu and Lois Keidan, Live Art programmers at the ICA, who first invited The Hittites, and, after their groundbreaking performance, it was the performance poet, live artist and producer SuAndi who invited them to collaborate with the Black Arts Alliance (BAA) on a number of subsequent projects. SuAndi has been at the helm of the BAA for more than ten years, and the group has made many significant interventions within Live Arts for black cultural practitioners. The Hittites returned and joined with BAA to produce *Man in the Belly of a Slave Ship*.[26] In the bowels of an actual ship, as dark and as eerie as any slave vessel, they told their stories.

However, in the media the representation of black people is generally fixed within a tropic repertoire of images and mythic narratives (which is why O. J. Simpson had so much attention, and how Made in Da Shade, the Netherlands-based black performance ensemble, made the connection between him and Othello in *OJ Othello*, performed at the Riverside Studios, London, in 1999). Fear of black men, coded as anger, lurks beneath the surface of a review of The Hittites' work by Alexis Greene:

> Hatred of those in power was also the thrust of The Hittite Empire . . . One central image of *49 Blues Songs for a Jealous Vampire* became more lame than serious, as Mason, sitting in a chair at the edge of the stage, continually ripped pages out of several books, and harangued white Americans to 'catch up with me' . . . 'How the fuck do you think you're going to ever make me shut up?' he thundered. While Mason raged at the audience, five other men, dressed only in red briefs, incanted phrases of despair and enacted the humiliating rituals of black men's existence in America: slavery; unwarranted police investigations; the white woman's/white America's fantasies about the black man's potency. 'What is the size of Clarence Thomas's penis?' The image of the nearly naked men underscored their historical experience as powerless objects of both desire and barter – but that was an intellectual connection, made with the realisation that their performance offered no reality for me to get inside their anger.[27]

Inscribed in the colonial fantasy is a fear of the Other rebelling against their oppression. Historically, meetings of black people were always viewed as seditious. While religious gatherings were accepted, slave revolts of the nineteenth century and mass revolts and civil actions had been inspired by religious leaders. Perhaps because violence is often associated with men, male gatherings are feared more than gatherings of women. If you substitute race for women's demands for exclusive spaces, gatherings of black people of African descent suddenly become viewed as 'separatist' and 'racist'. Even in a 'live and let live' liberal humanist discourse, fear of the Other still exists.

I attended the One Million Men March on 15 October 1995 in Washington, DC. Being a Muslim, a card-carrying member of the Nation of Islam, or an ardent follower of Louis Farrakhan was irrelevant as motive for travelling to this event. What motivated me was rather the idea of a safe space for men in the African diaspora to share, touch skin and break the silence. Returning to England, I wanted to create a performance piece which would give voice to British black male experiences, as opposed to the hyper-masculine representation constructed via the hegemonic imperialism of African Americans. As the project matured, the idea of unpacking the baggage of not sharing, not crying, not feeling, not loving began to take shape.

Ntozake Shange's *for colored girls who have considered suicide when the rainbow is enuf* had a seminal influence not only in terms of content, but also in terms of form.[28] It was an explosive story exploring black women's identities, as well as being a formal experiment in fusing performance, music, dance and poetry: a choreopoem. Coupled with the liberating critiques of black women writers such as Alice Walker, Toni Morrison, Zora Neale Thurston, Paula Marshall, Sonia Sanchez, June Jordan, bell hooks and others, the self was being foregrounded as subject in cultural production. In this feminisation of the narrative, othered voices that spoke of differing desires in the areas of race, gender and sexuality began to be heard.

These voices also opened the discourse around black masculinities, about which Kobena Mercer and Isaac Julien have written extensively. *Brother to Brother: New Writings by Black Gay Men*, edited by Essex Hemphill and conceived by Joseph Beam, provided a vocabulary for me to explore the feminine side of masculinity. The term 'Brother to Brother' was further popularised in Marlon Riggs's film *Tongues*

74

Untied, which was concerned with the lack of dialogue between black men who formed erotic relationships with one another.[29]

In 1996 *Brother to Brother*[30] became a workshop process and eventually a performance piece, devised collaboratively with three black male performers (Benji Reid, Ekundayo and Michael Mannash-Daniels). It attempted to situate a black male narrative within a British context, linked to, but separate from, the mainstream popular representation via the 'Black Atlantic'.[31] Stories of love, self-doubt, foolishness and terror were encased in a performance of narrative with slide projection and music. The performers had worked with director Denise Wong, whose devised performance pieces for Black Mime Theatre empowered the performer as a collaborative artist, as opposed to training the 'actor' to become a directed automaton.[32] This was why I cast these practitioners to take part in *Brother to Brother*, which was essentially a Live Art project, with the emphasis on performance fusing art forms in an interdisciplinary context. It began with chatting, reasoning and rapping over three days, where we explored complex answers to the question: 'What happened to you today that reminded you that you are a black man?' One of them was, 'No, white woman, I don't want your handbag.'

RED: Now in the nineties,
         it's like I got eighty per cent written on my back.
         I'm looking at a woman,
         she looks at me,
         she looks at her bag,
         she grabs her bag
         and turns to the side.
         All I wanted to do, was tell her that her bag was
             open.
         Or sometimes I'm standing at a bus stop
         and I'm thinking instead of being a rude boy,
         like I normally do,
         let me go and wait in the queue.
         But she's still watching me.

CHORUS: Oh my god, this man's gonna do something to me!
Oh my god, this man's gonna do something to me!
Oh my god, this man's gonna do something to me!

(Flashback to the plantation mansion where Red is trying to resist the sexual advances of the slave master's wife.)

RED: I brought the milk Miss Elemay.
Why do you want it in the bedroom Miss Elemay?
Why are you taking off your clothes Miss Elemay?
What do you mean Miss Elemay?
Miss Elemay!
No Miss Elemay!
What if master comes Miss Elemay?
What if I come? *(Pause)*
And the bag slowly slips on the other side.
You can feel her edging forward into the next woman.
I don't wanna feel like I'm pressurising the woman,
but something wants me to just lurch for the bag.

CHORUS: And I just wanna freak her out!
And I just wanna freak her out!
And I just wanna freak her out!

RED: But you can't do that can you,
cause the minute you do that,
a Babylon is on your back.
So I stand back
and I bump into the next woman,
who's hiding her bag as well.[33]

Part of this deframing and reclaiming process was the questioning of the patriarchy of our fathers and the dominant male discourse of our peers in the acquisition of power, the maintaining of authority and the ownership of the material world and nature. An element of this process was coming to terms with our own emotional illiteracy. Our families, for better or worse, still shaped our identities, in terms of relationships, loving ourselves and loving someone else.

> Dad don't read the newspaper
> I'm talking to you
> Dad turn off the TV
> Dad turn off the radio
> this is not cricket dad
> it's me.
> Remember that time
> when I came second in a competition
> I came home with a trophy
> about the same size as your own
> I put it down with the certificate
> on the TV
> you made a cup of tea
> and decided to put it on my certificate
> remember that dad
> remember that big brown stain
> right over my name
> next day my face was in the newspaper
> you got to the centre page
> all the family was waiting for you
> we'd all seen it
> but you skipped over it like there was nothing there
> Remember
> like you were frightened to see it
> it's the same paper
> go to the middle page
> look at it
> if you can
> that's me
> that's your son
> I'm your legacy.[34]

We remembered the deferred dreams of our parents, their puritanical discipline, and the way they were alienated from their own emotions as a means of survival in racist Britain. Going in search of our fathers as a theme resonated with being fathers ourselves and the fear of failure in patriarchal terms to be 'men', faithful partners, reliable enough to hold our families together.

> My daddy taught me
> I must be perfect
> I had to know everything
> that feelings got in the way
> I'm afraid that I might be
> repeating it all over again
> like father like son.[35]

Echoing Paul Gilroy's *There Ain't No Black in the Union Jack*, a full-size red, gold and green Union Jack was made as a transgressive motif and prop: it was a burial wrap for an unknown black man (a symbolic memorial to death by murder or suicide), it was a rope to hang from a tree, it was the placenta in a birth ritual.[36] As British citizens, we celebrated the flag and sang 'Rule Britannia' ('Rule Britannia/Britannia rule the waves/Britons never never never shall be slaves') and played the national anthem ('God save our gracious Queen/God save my black skin').[37] Flashbacks to slave plantation society punctuated the present, where the present echoed screams from the past and fears of the future.

Historically, there is a metaphorical and material connection in the black diaspora to trains and railways. Many West Indian immigrants were invited from the Caribbean to come and work on British Rail, and railways to the North signified freedom for runaway slaves in Sojourner Truth's Underground Railway.[38] And the train serves as metaphysical rite of passage in the black church as the final journey of life, transcending the pain of this world and transporting us into the next. A Tube train in a tunnel became a recurring motif as part of a layered sound score. In popular culture the sexual discourse of black popular music enables and invites the listener to find a means of making sense of their feelings. It is the 'key site in everyday life where men and women reflect on their gendered and sexual identities and make adjustments to the images they have of themselves'.[39] Consequently we used manipulated samples of Stevie Wonder, Marvin Gaye and Diana Ross, Curtis Mayfield, and Jungle, intercut with the hymn 'Jerusalem' and with an interview with the then Home Secretary, Michael Howard, who publicly defended the statement made by the Metropolitan Police Commissioner, Sir Paul Condon, that 80 per cent of muggings in London were committed by black people.

Our approach, as in effect producer, director and writer of the devised text, was multimedia in a Live Arts context, and we received a grant of £5,000 from the Arts Council of England to facilitate research and development. Black masculinity would for many white-run conventional theatre companies, with their patronising views of Black Arts, be a closed subject, while for black theatre companies (the few that there are in the UK), it could be a charged issue. Black Arts practitioners are generally just as excluded from the means of production and distribution as others of our communities, which turns us into innovative *auteurs*. 'Who feels it, knows it' can become an answer to an indifferent marketing officer in a well-resourced venue who thinks he or she knows how to attract black audiences. The project was produced on a shoestring, but at least we as collaborators aimed to be – and were – in control of the process, the product, its distribution and marketing. We were also able to use the public relations momentum of Black History Month in October, when money seems to come from nowhere to support black cultural production.

We premiered at The Green Room, Manchester, and went on a month's national tour, with a package of workshops for, with and about black masculinities. Intensive outreach and networking in the 'community' to recruit black men to free workshops received positive telephone enquiries, but few who were interested turned chat into action. We seemed to be encountering from potential participants the same enigmatic 'mask of inscrutability' of black masculinity that we were attempting to explore in *Brother to Brother*. Apathy was an internalisation of the powerlessness of their condition. Many could not understand why black men would want to come together, unless we were gay or for social reasons. Insecurity breeds fear: fear of sharing, fear of loving oneself, fear of anyone knowing that one was afraid.

In retrospect I felt that the original workshop process of *Brother to Brother* did not explore in depth the construction of black male sexuality. The reasons are complex, and not central to this essay. As previously noted, black sexuality has been fetishised, mythologised and pathologised; and sexuality, pleasure and desires are contested sites within the black communities. Imagine then three black men on stage attempting to unpack through performance the construction of their oppressions. The intertextuality and performativity of the black male body is a charged zone, with a hegemonic repertoire of images. In theatre the work of Amiri Baraka and the Black Arts Movement showed black men exploiting the contradictions of the dominant ideological regimes of 'truth', in such plays as *The Dutchman*.[40]

But these structures of representation, which marked the black liberation movement of the 1960s, were politically limiting, because the cultural reconstruction of the black subject was masculinist, and at the expense of black women, gays and lesbians. Eldridge Cleaver, for instance, promoted a heterosexist version of black militancy, masking a hidden homophobic agenda, which came out in his attacks on James Baldwin. In Britain revolutionary nationalism emphasised politics as 'frontline confrontation' in a macho-orientated notion of black struggle where the term 'black youth' really meant black male youth. Some male activists and intellectuals have romantically taken this to embody the 'heroic' essence of black resistance.[41] Until the arrival of Ntozake Shange's *for colored girls who have considered suicide when the rainbow was enuf* in the 1970s, black women were not foregrounded as characters, much less as writers and directors, in an emerging black theatre movement in Britain. Unless it had a feminist/womanist, gay or lesbian agenda, the cultural politics of sexuality, desire and pleasure were not explored in black theatre. Within black music, sexuality, pleasure and desire are expressed through ever-fresh critiques of black relations. But in the trenches of the black struggle, historically inscribed as very much macho-orientated, gender and sexuality only got on the agenda because of interventions made and leadership taken by black women. As Cheryl Clarke demonstrates in her essay 'The Failure to Transform', the issue of homophobia in black communities cannot be ignored any longer. Here, homosexuality is tabooed as a 'white man's disease', yet 'lesbians and gay men have always been an integral part of black society – active in politics, the church and cultural activities like music, literature, and art', even if self-appointed 'community leaders' would publicly deny and disavow their existence.[42]

While we were attempting to reconstruct the black male subject in *Brother to Brother*, by resisting the safe mask of inscrutability as another form of 'emotional illiteracy', we were perpetuating another form of oppression-as-repression. In a heterosexual vernacular context, for black men to talk of sexuality means not only risking been seen as gay, but as betraying the struggle. So in the workshop process, self-righteous black nationalism became paranoia verging on the homophobic whenever we attempted to discuss sexuality.

I was never happy with this situation even when we took the show on tour and were rightly criticised for this mis(sed)-representation. The piece had been devised collaboratively, and I was faced with the dilemma of choosing one set of ethics over another. But if *Brother to Brother* was going to have an enduring relevance to the intertextual discourse of black masculinity in Britain, it would have to be reworked. Given this ethical imperative, I copyrighted the piece as the author and rewrote the character of 'Blue' as a black gay persona when Michael Buffong directed the play for Talawa Theatre in a second production. 'Blue's' sexuality is treated as incidental to his characterisation rather than as central. This was one small intervention in the project of encouraging black men to engage in dialogue with each other regardless of sexuality.

Towards the end of a year-long Artists Agency residency in Newcastle in 1992, I worked with people infected by HIV/AIDS. It was challenging on a personal and on a creative level. A few black women students became involved, but only one gay black man, whose glory was to be a drag queen in Newcastle's gay clubs.

While in New York on an artist's fellowship, I had met the playwright George C. Wolf, who showed me a video of Pomo Afro Homos (Post-Modern African-American Homosexuals). I was taken with their in-your-face feistiness. They were three black gay men from the North American West Coast, and through dramatic tableaux, song, dance and some serious snapping and voguing their performance piece *Fierce Love* took a challenging look at the struggles that black gay men face in defining their communities and sexuality in finding their way home. They were not limited to a black gay agenda, but attempted to open up a discussion about the state of black masculinity as challenged by the experience of faggotry. Black men loving black men is a revolutionary act, and does not just involve gay-identified black men, but black men, period. Yet black theatre companies in the USA chose to deny Pomo Afro Homos's existence in banning them from attending the 1991 National Black Theatre Festival in Winston-Salem, North Carolina. Brian Freedman of Pomo Afro Homos argued for the need for black theatre to embrace performance as a genre, and for the need for black men to re-educate ourselves about the diversity and difference of our practices in our cultural, political and personal agenda.[43] I invited Pomo Afro Homos to come to England and present their performance piece *Dark Fruit* as part of the North East HIV/AIDS Arts Festival, a multi-event programme that I coordinated with Photographer in Residence Nick Lowe as a culmination to our joint residencies. Pomo Afro Homos were a hit and surprised the largely white gay community in the North East. Not satisfied, the Pomo Afro Homos guys wanted to take on black audiences in black-run venues. The work of black performance/Live Art artists has usually been stereotyped as too avant-garde, experimental and inaccessible. Add sexuality to the mixture, and we knew that it would be an uphill struggle to find a venue with a mixed black audience.

Maybe we were naive, as the stonewall of silence and unanswered calls in London served only to perpetuate the myth that black people are more homophobic than whites. Pomo Afro Homos did get a black audience of sorts eventually, although they were bussed in as friends of friends of the Drill Hall Arts Centre, which had a predominantly white gay and lesbian constituency. The writer Biyi Bandele believes that:

> there has been a backlash on political correctness, where the black and white intelligentsia have played into the hands of right-wing cultural commentators, and which has meant that

the most offensive things can then be written and excuses given that they are simply being politically incorrect and therefore get away with it . . . you can be racist, homophobic, misogynist . . . atavistic instincts which had been suppressed coming to the surface.[44]

Inevitably the theme of fathers recurs in my performance work with men, irrespective of age, race, class, education or sexuality, and it did with *In My Father's House*, a collaborative performance piece produced by the BAA. A vision of a hundred men of colour drumming collectively on a stage was conceived by the poet SuAndi, the strength of whose vision enabled the project to be sold and funded by the Arts Council. As producer/director, SuAndi brought a femininity to the process which served to enhance our exploration of the emotional territory of our masculinities. Ronald Fraser-Munro, Mem Morrison, Kevin Johnson, Max Alder, Dinesh Allerijah and I were brought together as lead artists to plan a workshop programme which would culminate in a performance production. Some of our cohort were Asian and Turkish, so, in this context, the term 'black' took on a political definition as opposed to a culturally specific one. As sons, we researched relationships with our fathers. It was envisaged that each of us would work with a subgroup of participants to devise material that would be integrated into a larger piece. As live/performance artists, we wanted a mixed-media fusion of art forms which would include dramatic tableaux, poetic monologues, performance, movement, music and mixed audio-visual media.

As always, recruiting men to work of this nature was frustrating and did not really begin until the two weeks of intensive workshops before the first performance. Attendance was sometimes hard to maintain, and the process went beyond the professional in being sensitive to the lives of the mainly young group of black men I was working with at The Zion Centre. We used games, exercises, workshop techniques and ontological approaches to ritual, which I had developed in my practice over the years of doing performance work with men. I used a basic hot-seating exercise, where individual performers construct a persona based on answers to questions about their character from other members of the group. Using improvisation, recorded interviews and soundbites, we devised a series of sketches which I then scripted into a text. Material from the lead artists' groups was then brought together in our regular production meetings at BAA's office, to make an overall storyboard and script. It was not our aim to produce the definitive representation of the theme around fathers and fatherhood, but instead to create a series of powerful yet layered performances, with oral and visual motifs based on stories we had gathered.

SON: Dad you wore the trousers in the house,
you were the boss and all.
But outside you wore a suit,
all posh with a handkerchief in your breast pocket.
When you saw people in the street,
you were like,
Yes Sir,
Yes Mam.
It's like they were a King or Queen.
I knew about racism,
but you were different,
like another person I didn't know.
It made me furious,
I was embarrassed,
ashamed,
you didn't have to talk like that to them.

Sins of the father,
are the sins of the past.
I look at you now,
and my eyes turn inward with anger.
I was your son,
but I was left to fend for myself.
Independence is great,
but when I needed someone to talk to,
someone to turn to,

Where were you?
Nowhere.
I asked for help,
but you chucked it back in my face.
What was I supposed to do?
The sins of the father.
Am I gonna repeat them with my own children?
Do I want to do that?
You could have treated me like your son.
I felt lonely, angry, depressed –
resorting to violence,
wanting to kill myself.
The sins of the father
are the sins of the past.[45]

Meanwhile, a large group of twenty drummers, who would provide a musical backdrop, link sections and evoke moods, rehearsed
in parallel to the workshop performance process. Community performance projects of this nature are never funded adequately and produce
work on a shoestring. Yet *In My Father's House* achieved what many
well-funded, professionally trained performance practitioners could
not achieve. It was a raw 'work in progress' that could have done
with more of a narrative structure sewing all the disparate elements
together. But many of the participants were drawn from a cross-section
of ethnic background, age, education, profession and family responsibility, who had little or no performance experience. Had the process
been longer than two weeks, it would have been extremely difficult
to maintain commitment. The ensemble was forty to fifty strong, and
it was impossible to synchronise all of us in the same place and at
the same time. Consequently, while this added stress (and panic) to
the process, it was not until the day of our first performance at the
Contact Theatre that the whole company was present. To use a cliché,
'the show must go on', and the performance was cathartic for the audience and performers. There was real courage from this loose group of
men of colour who got up on stage and broke the silence of emotional
constipation through sharing their vulnerabilities.

SON: Should I shout it?
Should I speak it?
Should I whisper it?
Should I sing it?
How do I say this to you?
How do you expect me to say it?
What do you want me to say?
How do I bring myself to say it?
Could I live with myself if I didn't say it?
I'm more of a man than you,
because I found it in my heart to forgive you,
and wish you all the best for the future,
because,
I love you Dad.[46]

Brother2Brother became the title of the final project examined in this discussion, but it had different aims and objectives from previous, related work. It was initiated by the Young People's Health Project as part of Lewisham, Southwark and Lambeth Health Action Zone's Bridging the Gap Project.[47] In 2002 Michael Hamilton and I began a series of meetings with black male youth workers from South East London who would go on to recruit participants from their youth centres. The aim was to create a programme of workshops exploring issues of working with young black men. The idea behind this strategy was that, while there are many projects targeted at the alienation of young men under the auspices of government policies towards social inclusion which produce positive empowering benefits for their participants, how are these projects followed up once the funding has dried up and the workers have moved on? And what are the key ingredients that make such a process successful? One of the aims of this project was to formulate models of good practice in informal education which could be adopted by youth and community practitioners. The process was just as important as the end product, which would be performance presentations for both a closed (black men only) and an open, mixed, audience.

A researcher was allocated to the project who would document the process with the aim of producing a final report. But having a white male researcher observing young black men explore personal issues in a workshop was highly problematic, even though we sought permission from participants. We did not want to perpetuate the paternalism of race politics, where black subjectivity can be legitimised and validated only through a white observer as voyeur. We opened up the issue for discussion and it was decided to bring in a black male researcher, to collaborate with our first researcher and attend sessions which were for black men only. When seeking mechanisms to document adequately a process which could not be measured as a formal structure, the two researchers were able to brainstorm on complex issues.

In the institutionalisation of the arts education sector, effective art practices have been appropriated and repackaged as models of good practice which tick the boxes in a hierarchy of oppression: racism, sexism, homophobia, class discrimination, ageism, and so on. And as an arts practitioner of African-Caribbean descent, one is stereotyped with many others who share a black body as being able to comment, explore and make work only about race. Where the skills, experience and knowledge of black arts practitioners can be most effective is deemed to be in working with the deprived, alienated and disenfranchised, especially if they are black as well. This paternalistic and patronising approach is also evident in policies which consider the only worthwhile work with men to be work with young male offenders and those excluded from the education system. While recruitment for working with men is difficult, in *Brother2Brother* we chose not to target those in apparent need of the process, but rather those who expressed a desire to participate and contribute to it.

The process began with a residential workshop at Woodrow High House, with nine young black men aged from fifteen to twenty-five years old and four black male workers. Sharing this short, intensive time together meant that we achieved what would normally take weeks. A set of workshop ground rules was agreed, such as active listening, respect and confidentiality, which helped in establishing trust among participants and facilitators. We could explore a range of issues and themes in depth: society's stereotyping of black men; the construction of individual identities; the myths and realities of our sexuality; love and relationships; fathers and fathering. Through discussion, exercises, games and writing, material emerged that formed the basis of the performance presentation. One particularly powerful exercise was where participants were asked to create a character through hot-seating and use it as a mask to talk to their imaginary fathers in an empty chair. This revealed much that was personal even with the mask as protection.

SON: Can you come and watch me play football tonight?
DAD: You know I work late on Mondays.
SON: Can we go ice skating after school on Tuesday then?
DAD: I promised my work mates I'd go out with them for a drink.
SON: There's an open evening at school on Wednesday.
DAD: Working nights again. Why don't you ask your mum?
SON: Mum always comes.
DAD: What about Thursday, I'm free that evening.
SON: Football practice. Don't suppose we can go cinema on Friday?
DAD: Going away on Friday.
SON: Can we go out over the weekend then? You're not working.
DAD: Not coming back till Sunday.
SON: But you promised.
DAD: I'm sorry, son.
SON: What about next week?
DAD: Let me get back to you on that.[48]

Without domestic distractions, youth workers and participants 'talked the talk' enthusiastically about continuing the process at the end of the residential workshop. But in returning to the diversions of daily life, we had to 'walk the walk' in trying to maintain commitment to regular evening workshops. To continue active participation it was crucial that workers made some personal investment in the process that went beyond the professional. Otherwise, as older men they would perpetuate the same issues of unreliability that so many sons experienced with their fathers. The focus shifted to looking at our connections as older men in relation to our fathers and how we shared those experiences with younger men. Cooked food also provided a sharing communal event in subsequent workshops with participants. To enhance the production of the performance presentation together, we went on a final intensive residential workshop, where we rehearsed and saw the piece take shape.

> If one begins with the threat of concrete nihilism, then one must talk about some kind of politics of conversion . . . Nihilism is not overcome by arguments or analyses; it is tamed by love and care. Any disease of soul must be conquered by a turning of one's soul . . . This turning is done by one's affirmation of one's worth – an affirmation fuelled by the concern of others. This is why a love ethic must be at the center of a politics of conversion.[49]

As artists, practitioners and cultural workers, we are engaged in this politics of conversion as a struggle to develop and practice pedagogies of resistance. Brecht argued that art is not truly revolutionary unless it is revolutionary in *form*. Among the creative arts projects I have cited here which explore black masculinities, we see a subversion and fusion of art forms. Moreover, these hybridised practices reflect more than the polyphonic nature of black culture. Their aesthetic representations signify a re-invention and re-imagining of the self in a cultural political context, where identities are continually fragmented and hybridised. Given the body-politic discourse around black masculinity, performance offers an empowering space where the construction of those identities can be taken apart and reconstructed. The challenge for practitioners is to take on this challenge, where the personal becomes political and the political personal.

NOTES

1. Henry Louis Gates, Jr, 'Thirteen Ways of Looking at a Black Man', in *New Yorker*, 23 October 1995, p. 58.

2. Cited in Kwesi Owusu (ed.), *Black British Culture and Society: A Text Reader* (London: Routledge, 1999), p. 375.

3. Richard Schechner, *The Future of Ritual: Writings on Culture and Performance* (London: Routledge, 1993).

4. Paul Lawrence Dunbar, 'We Wear the Mask', in *Lyrics of Lowly Life* (New York: Dodd Mead, 1896). Dunbar was an African-American poet who was the first black person to support himself financially as a professional writer.

5. Deborah Levy, quoted during the Institute of Contemporary Arts (ICA) Conference 'Working with Fanon: Contemporary Politics and Cultural Reflection', London, 13–14 May 1995.

6. Orchard Lodge Residency, 1997–8. *If I Could Fly: An Anthology of Poetry and Prose from Orchard Lodge Residency Centre* was published by Southwark Social Services in 1998.

7. See Tony Sewell, *Black Masculinities and Schooling: How Black Boys Survive Modern Schooling* (Stoke-on-Trent: Trentham Books, 1997).

8. Ralph Ellison, *Invisible Man* (Harmondsworth: Penguin, 1965).

9. See Houston A. Baker, Jr, *Blues, Ideology and Afro-American Literature: A Vernacular Theory* (Chicago: University of Chicago Press, 1984).

10. Claire MacDonald, from an interview at De Montfort University, Leicester, 1995.

11. Julie MacDougall, discussing the plays of Lebanese writer Abla Farhoud: 'Growing . . . Growing . . . Growing . . . Growing . . . Growing . . . Growing . . . Growing . . . Growing . . . Analysis of a Work-in-Progress', cited in bell hooks, 'Performance Practice as a Site of Opposition', in Catherine Ugwu (ed.), *Let's Get It On: The Politics of Black Performance* (London: ICA/Bay Press, 1995), p. 213.

12. Michel Foucault, *The History of Sexuality*, vol. I (London: Allen Lane, 1978).

13. Augusto Boal, *Theatre of the Oppressed*, trans. Charles A. and Maria-Odilia Leal McBride (London: Pluto Press, 1979). Forum Theatre is a kind of theatre developed by the Brazilian Boal. He has worked to create a number of participatory forms of theatre

which have been taken up by community theatre practitioners throughout the world. In Forum Theatre performers act out a scenario dealing with problematic issues identified by the participating group. The scene is then played back and audience members, called 'spectactors' by Boal, are asked to come up on stage and act out alternative approaches to resolving difficulties in order to explore avenues for change. See also Boal, *Rainbow of Desire* (London: Routledge, 1992) and *Legislative Theatre* (London: Routledge, 1998).

14. Augusto Boal, 'The Cop in the Head', in *Tirlare Drama Review*, vol. 34, no. 3 (Fall, 1990), p. 37.

15. Kobena Mercer, 'Racism and the Politics of Black Masculinity', in R. Chapman and J. Rutherford (eds.), *Male Order: Unwrapping Masculinity* (London: Lawrence and Wishart, 1988), p. 153. See also Mercer's *Welcome to the Jungle: New Positions in Black Cultural Studies* (London: Routledge, 1994).

16. Mercer, 'Racism and the Politics of Black Masculinity', p. 153.

17. Frantz Fanon, *Black Skin, White Masks* (New York: Grove Press, 1967).

18. Kobena Mercer, 'Fear of a Black Penis', in *Artforum*, vol. 32 (April 1994), p. 122.

19. Martin Glynn is a black writer and performance poet who has extended his drama-as-rites-of-passage work with fathers in British prisons to state penitentiaries in the USA.

20. Theatre Skills workshop, HM Prison The Mount, February 1995.

21. Clyde Taylor, 'The Game', in Thelma Golden (ed.), *Black Male: Representations of Masculinity in Contemporary American Art* (New York: Whitney Museum of American Art, 1994), p. 169.

22. Paul Carter Harrison, *The Drama of Nommo* (New York: Grove Press, 1972). See also Donald Bogle, *Toms, Coons, Mulattoes, Mammies and Bucks: An Interpretive History of Blacks in American Films* (New York: Bantam Books, 1974), and Tejumola Olaniyan, *Scars of Conquest/Masks of Resistance: The Invention of Cultural Identities in African, African-American and Caribbean Drama* (Oxford: Oxford University Press, 1995).

23. Taylor, 'The Game', p. 169.

24. Andrew Ross, 'The Gangsta and the Diva', in Golden, *Black Male: Representations of Masculinity in Contemporary American Art*, p. 161.

25. *The Hittite Empire: The Underseige Stories* (London: ICA, 1994), and *The Punic Wars* (London: ICA, 1995).

26. *The Hittite Empire: Man in the Belly of a Slave Ship: Walk the Plank, Floating Theatre Ship at Salford Quays, 1315* (The Hittites: Keith Antar Mason, Gerard Williams and Kirk Washington, Jr; UK artists, Douglas Russell, Joseph Jones and Delroy Williams. Manchester: Black Arts Alliance, 1997).

27. Alexis Greene, *Theater Week*, 17 August 1992, cited in Keith Antar Mason, 'Revisionist Examination', in Ugwu, *Let's Get It On*.

28. Ntozake Shange, *for colored girls who have considered suicide when the rainbow is enuf* (London: Methuen, 1978).

29. Essex Hemphill (ed.), *Brother to Brother: New Writings by Black Gay Men* (Alyson Publications, 1991), and Marlon Riggs, *Tongues Untied* (1991).

30. Michael MacMillan, *Brother to Brother*, in *Black & Asian Plays Anthology* (London: Aurora Metro Press, 2000), p. 139.

31. Paul Gilroy, *The Black Atlantic: Modernity and Double Consciousness* (London: Verso, 1993).

32. Formed in 1984, Black Mime Theatre (under the artistic direction of Denise Wong) produced groundbreaking, non-text-based pieces, such as *Super-Heroes*, *Drowning* and *Earliest Date of Release*, which attempted to subvert and transgress the traditional representation of mime arts.

33. MacMillan, *Brother to Brother*, pp. 139–40.

34. *Ibid.*, pp. 168–9.

35. *Ibid.*, pp. 156–7.

36. Paul Gilroy, *There Ain't No Black in the Union Jack: The Cultural Politics of Race and Nation* (London: Hutchinson, 1987).

37. MacMillan, *Brother to Brother*.

38. Sojourner Truth fought for the desegregation of public transportation in Washington, DC during the Civil War. She refused to face

the indignities of segregation on streetcars, and was an abolition-
ist, women's rights activist and preacher.

39. Kobena Mercer and Isaac Julien, 'True Confessions', in Golden,
    *Black Male: Representations of Masculinity in Contemporary
    American Art*, p. 199.

40. See Amiri Baraka, *Dutchman and The Slave: Two Plays* (New
    York: William Morrow, 1964).

41. Mercer and Julien, 'True Confession', in Golden, *Black Male:
    Representations of Masculinity in Contemporary American Art*,
    p. 198.

42. Cheryl Clarke, 'The Failure to Transform: Homophobia in the
    Black Community', in Barbara Smith (ed.), *Home Girls: a Black
    Feminist Anthology* (New York: Kitchen Table/Women of Colour
    Press, 1983), cited in Mercer and Julien, 'True Confession', in
    Golden, *Black Male: Representations of Masculinity in Contem-
    porary American Art*, p. 199.

43. Brian Freeman from Pomo Afro Homos, in an interview with
    Michael MacMillan (1993). *Dark Fruit* and *Fierce Love* were per-
    formed at the Drill Hall Arts Centre in London in 1992 and 1993.

44. Biyi Bandele, interview with Michael MacMillan, London, 1995.
    See also Michael MacMillan, 'Passports to Possibilities', in New
    Playwrights Trust, ed., *Black Writing: A Guide for Black Writers*
    (London: London Arts Board, 1998).

45. *In My Father's House*, Black Arts Alliance, Contact Theatre,
    Manchester, 2001.

46. *Ibid.*

47. Formed in 1996, the Young People's Health Project, led by
    Michael Hamilton, has used a range of activities to make young
    people aware of sexual health issues such as puberty, periods,
    intercourse, pregnancy, contraception, and so on.

48. Michael MacMillan, *Brother2Brother* Project, London, 2002.

49. Cornel West, 'Nihilism in Black America', in Gina Dent (ed.),
    Black Popular Culture (Seattle: Bay Press, 1992), p. 43.

5 Wielding the cultural weapon after apartheid: Bongani Linda's Victory Sonqoba Theatre Company, South Africa

STEPHANIE MARLIN-CURIEL

The years leading up to the first South African democratic elections in 1994 were marked by a sharp increase in violent clashes between the black nationalist Inkhata Freedom Party (IFP) and the non-racial African National Congress (ANC) led by Nelson Mandela.[1] In its determination to win the elections, the apartheid government led by the National Party both funded and fuelled the IFP's campaign against the ANC. The government trained and armed Inkhata hit squads that became incorporated into the KwaZulu police force to keep 'law and order' in their regions. Despite the 1991 National Peace Accord between the ANC and IFP, the violence continued. The IFP formed 'Self-Protection Units' (SPUs) while the ANC formed 'Self-Defence Units' (SDUs) recruited from radicalised youth in order to protect their respective communities.

When ANC military cadre Bongani Linda was asked in 1991 to train the ANC Student Defence Force's Self-Defence Unit outside Johannesburg, he courageously decided to try to negotiate with the IFP rather than fight them. 'Why should the oppressed kill each other?' he asked himself. To him it was clear that the violence between ANC township residents and IFP migrant workers living in hostels on the township's edges was 'orchestrated by the white man'. Since Linda was both Zulu and ANC, brokering peace with the IFP would be a task of not just political, but also personal reconciliation. He proposed that the two sides hold a battle on the soccer field with a ball, instead of in the streets with guns. Both sides resisted the idea, but in the end they agreed to the match. He then managed to convince the ANC and IFP teams to join forces to challenge the local police unit on the soccer field. After a rousing victory the next step was to switch the emphasis from sport to culture. Securing funds from the French Embassy, Linda organised a cultural festival in the Alexandra community hall and invited hostel groups to share the stage with township groups. From the IFP's slogan, 'Victory is ours', and the ANC's slogan, '*Simunye Sonqoba*' ('Together we will be victorious'), the Victory Sonqoba Theatre Company (VSTC) was born.

This chapter examines the influences of Linda's personal and political history on the development of VSTC as a model of Theatre for Development (TfD) that offers sustainability through professionalisation and effectiveness through peer education. My discussion refers both to past plays performed by VSTC and current productions I witnessed at first hand. During three weeks in August 2001, I met the casts of all three branches of Victory Sonqoba, in Soweto, Alexandra and KwaZulu-Natal (KZN), where I spent ten days with Linda and his company members at his complex in rural Osizweni. During my visit the Soweto cast of Victory Sonqoba Theatre Company was performing *Shaka Zulu: The Gaping Wound*, a piece advocating a resolution to the violence in KZN. The Alexandra cast was performing *Kuku Roof* (Afrikaans for *Cake Robbery*), addressing the horror of rape and the failure of South African institutions to root out and punish rape offenders; and the KZN cast was performing *Vuka Uma Ulele* (*Wake up and Smell the Coffee*), analysing the social factors that contribute to the rampant spread of HIV/AIDS in rural areas. *Shaka Zulu* and *Kuku Roof* were performed primarily in English, while *Vuka Uma Ulele* was performed primarily in Zulu. My descriptions of the plays and workshops are based on what was said in English or explained to me in English by cast or audience members, or by Linda himself. These plays are constantly evolving according to context and in response to workshops. Where possible, I have tried to indicate what some of these alterations have been as Linda has conveyed them to me, but my descriptions are primarily based on the performances and workshops I witnessed during my visit.

Theatre for Development: education via mobilisation

VSTC performs what Linda calls 'Theatre for Education' and 'Theatre for Conflict Transformation', both of which can be considered under the rubric of Theatre for Development (TfD). By the time Linda heard of TfD while studying at the University of the Witwatersrand, he had already been using several standard TfD techniques such as interviewing, storytelling and developing plays through workshops. Although TfD had been widely practised in many parts of Africa, it was not used as extensively in South Africa until after apartheid as the anti-apartheid struggle demanded the full attention of cultural activists.[2] What did exist in South Africa was a strong anti-apartheid theatre tradition. This included the protest and resistance theatre movements[3] that exhibited strong physical theatre and 'Poor Theatre' techniques, as well as a combination of township theatre and Brechtian techniques that contributed revue, song and dance to the genre. TfD in South Africa is practised by artists and activists to a greater degree than by educators and development workers, and has been strongly influenced by the resistance theatre of the anti-apartheid struggle. Zakes Mda contends that this makes South African TfD 'very strong on the mobilisational aspects and rather weak on the creation of a critical awareness among the target audiences'.[4]

I would argue that critical awareness is only as important as it leads to behavioural change. Mobilisation, in addition to sustainability and community building, is necessary to behavioural change since it provides a social context in which to develop and transmit critical awareness to target audiences. I would further argue that in South Africa, where youth activism triumphed over apartheid, mobilising youth might be a fruitful strategy for improving the country's future. With Linda's personal history as a veteran of the struggle, as well as his rigorous physical training techniques, he saw his cast as soldiers in the fight against crime and AIDS, as their predecessors had been in the fight against apartheid. The apartheid resistance fought an ideological and intellectual struggle, before taking up arms. Linda's critical awareness stems directly from his rigorous political training by the ANC and is reflected in his plays.

As a former MK soldier, Linda freely admits to his heritage as a mobiliser. He often wears military fatigues in rehearsal, recalling his years combating apartheid as part of the ANC's military wing, Umkhonto we Sizwe (literally 'Spear of the Nation' in Xhosa, and abbreviated to MK).[5] In the 1980s, Linda recounts, he was 'a stone-thrower by day, and a theatre director by night'.[6] His first play, *Born to Suffer*, was a protest theatre play, aimed at the consciences of oppressors. After having been detained twice for breaking the law against holding gatherings of more than three people, he wrote the play *Black Blood*, a resistance theatre play aimed at recruiting youth into the MK, and then joined himself. When he returned from exile in 1989, Linda's loyalty towards the ANC and anger towards the government drove him to commit politically motivated armed robbery. Once acquitted and released from prison, Linda committed himself to putting his energies towards more constructive endeavours. He attended university, where he majored in film and television production and design, but then reacted against the world of academe and became a community organiser committed to theatre as a reaction to violence. Linda calls himself a 'cultural combatant' because he 'believes theatre is a weapon to change people's minds, as well as a political instrument that encourages people to oppose injustice'.[7] He recruits his 'cultural combatants' from youth-at-risk populations in order to conscientise and restore communities that have been broken by violent crime, political violence and AIDS.

'Each One Teach One' and the peer education approach
Linda's production of *Black Blood* in the 1980s included two survivors of the 1976 Soweto riots. 'I've always had that strategy,' Linda says. 'I choose people who have a story to tell.' Thus acting talent is not his primary consideration when selecting a cast. He gives preference to people who have personal experience of whatever issues he is trying to confront in his play, such as HIV, rape and other crimes. Linda calls this methodology 'Each One Teach One'.[8] 'Each One Teach One' is a peer education model in which peers belonging to the same group as the target audience perform plays and conduct workshops to promote

education and behaviour modification on both individual and societal levels.

Studies have shown peer education to be highly effective because peers have insider status and knowledge and because the approach is participatory.[9] Critics of peer education have pointed out, however, that volunteer peer educators working for NGOs often work themselves up the ladder of NGO culture and become estranged from their communities.[10] In other words, many peer educators are primarily motivated by the opportunity to acquire skills that will help them to better their own lives rather than by the opportunity to change other people's lives. Linda's theatre company offers a rigorous training in acting, singing and dancing that has already led to several successful television acting careers in major series such as *Yizo Yizo*.[11] However, many VSTC members also learn to appreciate the less glamorous life of community theatre and the impact it can make on young people. In the words of one aspiring thespian:

> After completing my matric I found Bongani Linda. He has played an important role in theatre, especially in Jo'burg. I've read about him in the newspapers. I've seen his actors on TV so I thought maybe one day my dreams will come true. In the future, I want to have my own group, so I've learned a lot from him. He has helped my life through discipline. He is a perfectionist. He does not compromise. If something is wrong, it's wrong. I learn discipline and to be a role model for the youth . . . [which] is important especially for teaching about HIV and AIDS . . . not roaming around with the girls in the community and being a party animal. [I need to be] a disciplined young man so young heroes will say this is our role model. That is very important to me.

If VSTC breeds commitment *to* the community, perhaps it is because the company remains embedded *within* the community, both geographically and conceptually. Unlike an NGO, the headquarters of which would likely be located in an office building in an urban centre, VSTC rehearses in community halls and churches, and performs in the languages and cultural idioms of its audiences, addressing the particular problems they face. VSTC goes beyond youth-teaching-youth to facilitate peer education between ex-criminals and potential criminals, between HIV-positive youth and their sexually active peers, and between reconciled ANC and IFP supporters and their unreconciled colleagues. His actors teach the lessons that saved them from continuing to destroy themselves and others, thus setting a powerful example of behavioural change.

Community activist as professional artist

Most TfD practitioners are 'outsiders' who work with a given 'community' on a one-off basis. Linda, however, is an *insider* in many of the communities he works with. He has been at least a part-time resident of Soweto, Alexandra, KZN and the prison system, and now creates sustainable programmes within those communities by regularly employing members of his target audiences as actors in his company.

At the moment Linda employs fifty-two young people in three branches of VSTC operating in the urban townships of Soweto and Alexandra, and in the rural areas of KZN. Sowing the seeds for independence and self-sufficiency, Linda trains his casts to rehearse and arrange performances on their own, usually assigning an assistant director. Although his companies do reach a saturation point, several members have 'graduated' to high-profile acting jobs, thus making room for new recruits.

He pays his actors only per rehearsal or performance. Although he aims to treat them as professionals, he is dependent on grants and cannot promise a steady salary or 'daily bread'. The Nelson Mandela Children's Fund and the National Lottery Board are his only South African funders. The remaining money comes from overseas funders such as the Ford Foundation, the Swedish, the Dutch and the Swiss. With each pay cheque cast members receive a lecture about not becoming dependent on money. Commitment should be their primary motivation.

Like many South African community theatre practitioners, however, Linda refuses to be considered an amateur and to have his work labelled 'community' theatre rather than 'art' theatre.[12] Combining the influences of Gibson Kente, the father of the commercially successful township musical, and Black Consciousness playwright Matsemela Manaka,[13] Linda's goal is to prove that issue-based theatre can be entertaining and performed at a professional level. Like Kente's, Linda's rehearsal regime emphasises physical fitness, vocal exercises and dance routines.

The difficulty that township-based theatre practitioners face is that only the largely white urban audiences can afford to pay for tickets. Whites are still unwilling to travel to see professional theatre in the townships: the perception is that anything worth seeing will come to the Market Theatre. Since 1977, when the ban on multiracial casts and audiences was lifted, the route to success for black theatre practitioners has been through urban theatre venues such as the Baxter Theatre[14] in Cape Town and the Market Theatre in Johannesburg. The lifting of the ban was pioneered by the Space Theatre in Cape Town[15] and by the Market Theatre.[16] Although the Market opened with masterpieces of European theatre, it quickly gained a reputation for turning protest plays from the townships into international commercial successes. Politically committed theatre practitioners, however, criticised the Market for being run by well-intentioned whites with capital rather than blacks who lived the struggle day to day. It was not only the directors of the Market but also the audiences that compromised politically motivated work. Presenting at the Market to predominantly white elite audiences meant that the political content of the plays was not reaching the target audiences.[17] Little has changed in terms of Market audiences. Linda comments:

> The reason we move to the city is because we are running after the white audiences. It is easy for them to see 'reality' in a protected environment. The Market Theatre was a safe haven where white audiences could watch because they want to feel guilty and politically correct, to be seen to go to the Market Theatre, and to be in love with a dreadlocked guy.

The venue is now run by John Kani, one of the original actors from the quintessential protest theatre piece, *Sizwe Bansi is Dead*, and one of the most famous black actors in South Africa (and beyond).

While black audiences at the Market have increased, the audiences still remain middle class.[18]

Adding commercial success to community-based popularity does not mean that Linda intends to ignore his target audiences. The plays have always combined entertainment with education, what Linda calls 'edutainment'. This strategy raises questions as to whether it is possible for commercial audiences who do not belong to the target audiences to become target audiences and to be educated as well as entertained.

VSTC has been successful in performing to non-target audiences in the school environment. In 1993 Linda recruited youth from both the hostels and the townships to perform *Divide and Rule* about the role of the riot police in perpetuating violence between the ANC and the IFP in Alexandra township. They took the play to a girls' school in Balfour Park, a white suburb just outside Alexandra, to enlighten students about the conservative forces behind what the media was calling 'black on black violence'.[19] Students and teachers were extremely affected to learn what was happening right next door to their own neighbourhoods. They devised the Get to Know Your Neighbour Project, which was intended to bring students from the white suburb of Balfour to spend a weekend at VSTC cast members' homes in neighbouring Alexandra township and learn what it was like to wake up in a one-room house. They would then collaborate on a play that would explore their perceptions of each other. According to Linda, 'white people's perceptions of black people are defined by their interactions with their domestic servants, while black people learn about white people by stealing from their homes'.[20] Alexandra parents were extremely receptive to the project, but Balfour Park parents were too afraid for their children's health and safety to let them spend the weekend in Alexandra, so the project was never carried out.

Trying to educate commercial theatre audiences who have paid for a night of entertainment would be a far greater challenge than presenting educational theatre to student audiences. Since South Africa remains geographically divided largely along lines of race and class, the location of a performance plays a significant role in how that performance is received. Most TfD and other educational theatre is produced in the townships and in rural areas where poverty and lack of access to education, healthcare and jobs produce socially corrupt and risk-taking behaviour. Elite audiences who go to see such theatre 'because they want to feel guilty and politically correct', as Linda put it, ultimately do so as a form of entertainment. As the majority of these audiences have not engaged or no longer engage in crime or risky sexual behaviour, they are not the target audiences for these productions. Even if these audiences might be persuaded to help to improve the conditions of township and rural residents, audiences would be unlikely to carry this impulse home from the theatre. Whatever is viewed from the plush seats at the 'safe haven' of the Market does not intrude on the comfort of middle-class life. The Market is still considered a safe haven compared to the townships, despite its reputation for 'alternative', politically charged theatre, although its location in the city centre of Johannesburg is considered risky by some suburban residents.

White audiences' reluctance to see theatre in the townships was made clear during John Hunt's 1999 production, *Stand in the Sun*. This play displays the ironies of the 'new' South Africa through a confrontation between an Alexandra resident and a Sandton resident whose car breaks down on the highway that divides the two areas (Sandton is a largely white, affluent and thriving commercial district of Johannesburg). The play was staged simultaneously at venues in Alexandra and Sandton with the intention of bussing audience members from Alexandra to the Sandton venue, and vice versa. The Alexandra performances were soon discontinued for lack of audience. Why did these potential audiences refuse to go to Alexandra in a luxury bus specially provided to take them there and back? One audience member's comment would indicate that this was more a matter of psychological than of physical safety: 'It was easy to imagine that what was being presented to us – an uneasy meeting, but a meeting nevertheless – represented what was happening in the real world. Once back outside, however, I saw the stark reality of just how divided these two worlds are. That sense of possibility about the 'hands across the highway' just evaporated.'[21] Amid the squalor of Alexandra, white audiences felt that the material differences between their lives and those of their neighbours widened the cultural gap to an unbridgeable degree, making the performance feel morally 'unsafe'. The run did continue in Sandton, however, where the performance felt less of an indictment than a humorous treatment of the bumps and stumbles of a new democracy.

'Unsafe' theatre is not only a product of white people's fear and guilt after the collapse of apartheid. Theatre potentially becomes 'unsafe' when it leaves the auditorium for the street. I use the term 'street' here in its broadest sense, as denoting any manner of public space, or even private space, not specifically designated for performance, such that performing in that space constitutes a potential act of intervention into everyday reality or transgression of social or legal boundaries.[22] In South Africa theatre practice has historically constituted political action, often by the simple fact that it took place at all, thereby breaking laws against congregation and racial integration. While the Market Theatre technically broke laws when it first opened by allowing multiracial casts and audiences, it became a protected space, strategically overlooked by the apartheid government because of its links to liberal capital and its international visibility.[23] Meanwhile, people such as Linda, who were making theatre in the townships under the State of Emergency, were detained.

VSTC has a history of performing risk-taking, 'unsafe' theatre in 'unsafe' places. The risk is increased by the fact that VSTC actors are performing situations they have lived for those who are still living them. For example, VSTC's first Theatre for Conflict Transformation play, *Never Again*, staged the story of the conflict between the ANC and IFP as played out between brothers born of a Xhosa mother and Zulu father. It was performed by a cast of ANC and IFP supporters for both ANC and IFP audiences. ANC audiences were extremely receptive, but the IFP audiences were more suspicious. When Linda drove his company into KZN for a performance, bullets were shot into their vehicle, killing three of the actors. The group nearly dissolved, but members came back together with renewed strength.

Another less successful experiment was *Thetha Ngikhulume* (*Speak So That I May Speak*), a play dealing with the unresolved pain and anger of the past provoked by the Truth and Reconciliation Commission. Linda wanted to create a play for his friends and neighbours in Alexandra that would give voice to their untold and unresolved stories. In the second scene of the second performance, the actors, audience and even the director crumbled into tears. 'It became so real,' Linda has said. 'The actors were so touched. We couldn't differentiate between playing and reality. I wanted to provoke and to challenge the TRC, but I ended up opening up the wounds and making people cry and be more hateful.' Linda promptly cancelled the play.[24]

Performing *Never Again* became physically unsafe, while performing *Thetha Ngikhulume* became psychologically unsafe. This is not to say that such risks cannot be successfully curtailed. The core of Linda's current work, for example, includes bringing youth at risk of offending into prisons to see anti-crime performances by prisoners. Not only do the plays help to deter potential criminals, they also help to reintegrate ex-convicts into the community once they are released. These plays have thus far taken place without serious incident.

Shaka Zulu: The Gaping Wound

Shaka Zulu: The Gaping Wound is the play that Linda currently intends to perform in English for urban, commercial audiences, and in Zulu for target audiences in rural KZN. *Shaka Zulu* is one of VSTC's Theatre for Conflict Transformation plays focusing on ANC–IFP rivalries. The play is conceived in two parts, with the second part in the process of being written. In the first part Shaka is killed by his brothers in a struggle for the throne. As he dies, he curses the kingdom, pronouncing that the area will forever be plagued by violence and ruled by whites. The second part will be based on a 2000 newspaper story that caught Linda's eye. A *sangoma* (traditional healer) goes to King Zwelethini and reports that Shaka has come to her in a dream. He declared that there will always be violence unless the royal family performs a cleansing ritual by slaughtering a cow and apologising on behalf of Shaka's assassins. The king ignores her because she is a commoner and thus KZN continues to be wracked by violence. Linda plans to write the second part after interviewing the *sangoma* and the royal family, and then to stage the play in KZN in an effort to call attention to Zulu-against-Zulu (ANC v. IFP) hatred in the area. 'Everything in KZN happens in the extreme,' Linda says, 'faction fighting, natural disasters, accidents and AIDS. If we need to secure a peaceful KZN, let's deal with our past, rectify it so we can understand our future.'

The legend of King Shaka Zulu, founder of the Zulu kingdom, has been popularised so that he is now an icon of post-apartheid South African national culture. Add to this an evening of bravado singing and dancing and the show is destined for success. Linda's *Shaka Zulu* is not concerned, however, with celebrating the legendary battles of the past (as did Mbongeni Ngema's recent production, *The Zulu*); the first and second parts of Linda's play taken together reflect the relevance of the myth to the violence that continues in KZN today.[25]

The use of *Shaka Zulu* as a theatrical device not only secures the play's commercial appeal, but also functions as part of Linda's conflict resolution method. In the play Linda expands upon the strategies he used in *Never Again*. Both plays begin by invoking the ancestral period before delving into the contemporary moment, as if to encourage audiences to return to an imagined state of unity. Using culturally specific imagery plotted on a historical trajectory (division v. unity, past v. present) dramatically augments conflict while simultaneously providing a motivation for resolving it.

This device helps set the scene for 'Each One Teach One', which in this case functions, according to Linda, as 'conflict resolution by example'. The cast is composed of ex-IFP artists from the Alexandra, Nancefield, Jeppe and Jabulani hostels as well as ANC artists from Alexandra, Soweto and Durban townships. The make-up of the cast is revealed during the post-performance discussion as 'a living example of tolerance'.

During my visit VSTC performed Part I of *Shaka Zulu* as a fundraiser without a post-performance discussion, so it was not possible to see these conflict resolution methods in action. The fundraiser was presented at a church in Soweto to young, non-target audiences, and only a nominal fee was charged. This particular performance was not intended for conflict resolution purposes, but to build future audiences for professional theatre in the townships. *Shaka Zulu* Part I has since played in both national and international venues with the intention of 'informing' white audiences about Zulu history from a Zulu perspective.[26] The production not only reclaims Zulu history, but challenges the white domestication of 'the Zulu' as cultural commodity, as evidenced by the 1974 hit show *Ipi Tombi*, which packaged the image of the dancing female Zulu to satisfy the appetite of colonial desire. Even in the 'new' South Africa, the image of the 'traditionally' clad Zulu has become a cultural icon of the rainbow nation. The challenge on both national and international soil, then, will be to combat exoticisation with enlightenment. To the extent that the colonial gaze is an integral aspect of colonial structures, the reception of *Shaka Zulu* on the international stage depends on the mode and mechanism of its presentation. Ironically, however, what is most enlightening about *Shaka Zulu* for white audiences is that it is not addressed to them.

Kuku Roof (Cake Robbery)

Like *Shaka Zulu*, *Kuku Roof* was originally intended for commercial, as well as target, audiences. The show contains an uplifting song and dance number in which students promote the virtues of education (recalling Mbongeni Ngema's Broadway-hit production *Sarafina*), as well as several other solo and ensemble musical numbers intermixing Broadway and township styles. Despite these hallmarks of an entertainment genre, it is difficult to conceive that a play that explores rape as anything other than a plot device or character history would ever be taken on as a moneymaking venture.

Kuku Roof was originally commissioned by the Gender Commission to be performed in schools. In the townships women who do well in school become victims of the 'Pull Her Down' (PHD) syndrome and face an increased risk of being raped and shamed into silence. Linda highlights not only the devastation of rape, and the sickness of rapists, but, equally important, critical awareness of the corruption of the prison and educational systems in present-day South Africa that silently support rape as a reinforcement of male power. The play depicts a system in which rapists are able to bribe their way back on to the streets, and guards solicit sex from victims as payment for keeping their rapists in jail. The young schoolgirl is raped not only physically, but psychologically, many times over. Even her teacher, who was her role model, attempts to rape her. When the teacher is arrested, he also buys his way out of prison. While *Kuku Roof* did not finally go along the commercial route, its performances have raised questions as to how to create 'safe' theatre from 'unsafe' content in non-commercial venues.

In the workshop process Linda discovered that one of his actors had been gang-raped with her sister, who later committed suicide. The surviving sister agreed to let her story be performed and to play herself in the performance. Because the audience was not made up exclusively of rape victims, the actor could feel safe that the audience of students had no reason to suspect she was acting out her own story. The rape victims who were in the audience could similarly feel safe that they had not been identified as victims, only as potential targets. Here, safety becomes a matter of whether the proximity of the content to the audience's (and in this case the performer's) experience is kept private. Because neither performers nor audience had to reveal their real-life experiences during the performance, *Kuku Roof* successfully created safe space for post-performance discussion. Until the post-performance discussion, no one's identities had been revealed. When the actor revealed that she had in fact been a rape victim, she voluntarily cast off the veil of ambiguity. Students who had been living with trauma resulting from rape felt empowered to speak for the first time.

While some of the performances may have created a psychological safe space for female students, they also created the potential for physical unsafety for male students and teachers. Teacher–student rape in schools is a serious problem and VSTC targets schools with a high rate of corruption among teachers. Linda reports that:

> there was great tension between students and teachers, because some teachers were dating students. The first obstacle was the response of some of the teachers in schools. The corrupt teachers tried in vain to disrupt our performance in Alexandra Township and Thembisa . . . The play nearly caused violent confrontation between the male teachers and the male students.[27]

In the schools the performers focused on creating a safe space for victims, but not for perpetrators.

Perpetrators, however, were addressed in the prison performances. I attended a performance of *Kuku Roof* at Leeuwkop Medium C prison, where the exclusively male prisoner audience included convicted rapists. It is not a maximum security prison; rather it is a place for those who are trying to change their lives. Life-skills workshops are regularly held at the prison to rehabilitate prisoners and build their self-confidence. As with the school performances, VSTC met with resistance from the institution's officials rather than from the target audiences. According to Linda, prison officials have tried to shut down the performances, but have not succeeded because of the prisoners' commitment to the project. Neither a school nor a prison, then, makes the performances 'safe' for everyone. It is the safety of these institutions that is being attacked in the play, and therefore the officials of these institutions feel 'unsafe'.

The play not only accuses teachers and prison guards, but also intends to show rapists that 'they are sick' and that 'rape is not a woman's problem, but a man's problem', according to Linda. The play uses graphic imagery, such as the gang-rape of a mother in front of her children, and vulgar language, such as when the teacher sings, 'Girls go crazy when they see my car. I just put them in my bedroom and I fuck them all one by one.' But for the unreformed convicts in the audience, these images may have been more entertaining than shocking.

Officially the prison authorities refused me permission to interview the prisoners and take photographs, but one prisoner in the audience kindly agreed to circulate a survey on prisoners' reactions to the play and sent me the results. Many prisoners commented in the survey that they actually found the gang-rape scene the most moving because they imagined the victims as their own family in the same situation. One observed, however, that he did not understand why the rapists chose to rape the older woman as opposed to the young girls. Many prisoners wrote that since the prison and school systems were so corrupt, their only choice was to 'change society' and 'take justice into their own hands'. For some, this could mean taking responsibility for their actions; for others, it could lead to the commission of acts of violent retribution. One prisoner felt that displaying the ease with which offenders could buy their freedom encouraged rapists further, emphasising that they would be able to rape again and again without consequence.

If, for some, the play reinforced rape in South Africa as a non-punishable crime, others who have raped may have felt shamed by the play, as one inmate indicated to me: 'Taking from what I have witnessed and the comment of my fellow inmates, I can say the play had a positive impact on some, and to those who raped and are currently serving rape sentences, they seemed to be embarrassed and feel remorse for what they did.' Perhaps those prisoners who whistled at the actresses' short schoolgirl outfits did so because they had no reason to be remorseful; or perhaps it was to *cover* their remorse. For some prisoners, the outfits erased any feeling of sympathy. A prisoner sitting near me said, 'The play only showed one side. It blamed the men. It didn't talk about the women's part, how they make themselves attractive.' While blaming women for rape is clearly not appropriate, the play, which was devoid of male role models, may have been perceived as too anti-male.

During post-performance discussion Linda injects a strong dose of humour to get the prisoners laughing and paying attention as he delivers his message that 'rape is sick'. A social worker sits in the audience and participates in the discussion, reinforcing the idea that rape is a reflection of low self-esteem. They both emphasise the importance of thinking of oneself in a familial relationship – son, husband, brother, father – to a woman to deter them from raping. Linda asks, 'How would you feel if your daughter was raped and the rapists were coming to share the cell with you?' These ideas and the importance of the life-skills workshops are reiterated by the audience in answer to the question of how rapists can reform themselves while in prison. Because neither audience members nor performers have disclosed whether they have, in fact, committed rape, the discussion continues in these general terms.

With sensitive issues such as rape, performers and audience members may be reluctant to disclose their histories. Some cast members admitted to me that they had been in prison, but no one admitted that they had served time for rape. Since the audience is only partly made up of rape offenders, those offenders in the audience do not necessarily identify themselves as such when they choose to speak. Cast members do not participate in the post-performance discussion and therefore also do not reveal themselves as either rape convicts or victims.

If everyone's identities remain concealed, how can 'Each One Teach One' be effective? If audience members do not know that cast members have overcome the same negative behaviours they currently engage in, how are they to benefit from their example? Linda says that VSTC has since dealt with this problem by requesting prison audiences made up solely of rape offenders so that audiences can speak about their experiences. In this scenario 'Each One Teach One' benefits the performers as well as the audience. Linda suggests that 'some of the boys that are in the play were convicted of rape and they were afraid to disclose, but now that our focus is more on the rapist than the rape survivor, they are beginning to open up'.[28]

Even when such self-disclosures do not take place, 'Each One Teach One' operates within the playmaking process. The stories are drawn from those of the cast members, specifically those who have lived with the issue the play addresses. The play then becomes a screen whereby cast and audience can see themselves represented without necessarily having to be seen by those on the other side. Even if 'Each One Teach One' does not take place directly during the play or the post-performance discussion, there is a final stage in which VSTC cast members work with prison inmates to help them to create their own plays. The performance and post-performance discussion become part of the process of creating a safe environment for peer education to take place.

Vuka Uma Ulele (Wake up and Smell the Coffee)

The KZN branch of VSTC also faces challenges to peer education, owing to the sensitivities of disclosing HIV status. In KZN a cast including HIV-positive youth performs *Vuka Uma Ulele (Wake up and Smell the Coffee)* to audiences of slightly younger HIV-positive and potentially HIV-positive youth. In KZN school-going youth, particularly young women, have the highest rate of HIV infection in the province, requiring urgent action in AIDS prevention. The KZN cast members were trained as AIDS counsellors by the Madadeni and Newcastle Provincial Hospital and began by conducting door-to-door community outreach in order to disseminate information and research local perceptions of AIDS. In the rural areas there is little access to media and the population depends on outside experts for information. The company members report that the people to whom they speak often believe that HIV/AIDS originates from the townships, and that rural people can only be infected from involvement with a prostitute. One cast member reported that Christians in the region learn in the churches that if AIDS comes from sexual contact, it cannot be a deadly disease because 'God made man and woman to have intercourse.' *Vuka Uma Ulele* was created from both the realities and the perceptions of HIV/AIDS and it is being performed before audiences of high school students, adult farmers and prisoners.

As in the other plays, the issues are dramatised in the context of family relationships. The play opens with the wedding of a rural man to his second wife, who comes from the city. Tension between two wives creates a rift between the man and his brother, who sides with the first wife. Their father, representing the voice of 'tradition', says that each must sacrifice a goat to the ancestors for bringing violence into the family. The elder brother refuses, deciding instead to go to Johannesburg to find a job. While the traditional wife suspects nothing, the 'modern' wife displays her urban savvy when she prophetically announces to the audience that fighting over a husband is stupid, because all husbands leave their wives to get jobs in the city, only to contract AIDS and come back and infect them. Indeed, this is what happens.

The father invites a 'traditional healer' to help his son, while the second wife invites a 'Christian fortune-teller', with whom she has secretly been having an affair. The healer decides that the family's curse can only be lifted through bloodletting. He proceeds to cut every member of the family, infected and healthy, with the same razorblade, infecting them all. The healer also prescribes that the sick husband must sleep with a virgin. (This is a common 'cure' promoted by traditional healers in KZN.) It is decided that he must have intercourse with his brother's daughter. She contracts HIV and is harassed by the other students at school for what happened to her. Before the husband dies, he says that his brother must now take his HIV-infected wives as his own, as is customary in the rural areas. In the final scene the chief declares that no one with AIDS will be buried in his land and the family carries the dead body away.

The plot, therefore, centres on four main issues that contribute to the spread of HIV/AIDS in the rural areas: polygamy, labour migrancy, the influence and misinformation of traditional healers, and the hypocrisy and denial of churches that preach abstinence rather than condom use. Since the play was developed through interviews with farmers and the elderly in rural KZN, the play emphasises these issues when it is performed to this audience. The play has latterly been performed in prisons, where its focus has radically changed to draw attention to the transmission of HIV through homosexual rape by male prison gangs, as well as through the sharing of tattoo needles and razorblades.

When I saw the KZN branch of VSTC perform the play in schools, they performed the original plot. VSTC has since changed the play in response to the post-performance discussions with school-going audiences. While the issues in the original plot do impact on youth, the post-performance discussions revealed that students wanted to focus on issues of particular relevance to them. For school-going youth, the most important scene, for example, was a minor one in terms of the plot, in which the virgin daughter's schoolfriends try to convince her to fall in love with a taxi driver. In post-performance discussions both male and female students responded to that scene by talking about peer pressure and sex.[29]

In one of the post-performance discussions, for example, some of the boys brought up the fact that girls are promiscuous and this is why they contract HIV/AIDS. They claimed that the girls wanted material possessions, and if one man cannot provide for a girl, she moves on to another one. The girls admitted that many of them come from poor families and are tempted by money. They counterargued, however, that it is the men who pay attention only to the girls with the fanciest mobile phones and shortest skirts, thus throwing the responsibility back on them for producing their desire for material possessions in the first place. The girls added that they feel pressured to have sex, knowing that, if they refuse, a man will just find another girl who will. In fact, this sexual peer pressure exists not only between men and women. Studies show that men are pressured by men to have multiple sex partners as evidence of manliness, while young women who are virgins are treated as children by other women and excluded from conversations dealing with sex.[30]

Linda informs me that, in response to these concerns, he has since added scenes that address peer pressure for both sexes and the gendered inequalities underlying poverty, materialism, virginity as a cure for AIDS, condoms and abstinence.[31] The format of the performance has also been changed. When I saw the play, the entire student body of a school would flood the hall. Those who could not fit in peered in through the windows. Now Linda insists on performing to only one class at a time so that he can stage a more interactive performance. The company now positions actors within the audience to encourage audience involvement, and the scenes accommodate dialogue between the actors and the audience during the course of the play, with the direction of each scene determined by audience response.

The performances I saw, however, were uninterrupted and were followed by a post-performance discussion. Although the cast members are trained as AIDS counsellors, Linda says that when they conducted the post-performance discussions, audience questions tended to focus on acting rather than on HIV/AIDS. At one time, one of the actors who was HIV-positive ran the workshop. Sometimes he would disclose his HIV status and sometimes he would not, depending on whether he felt safe with the group. The sensitivities of disclosing HIV status here affected not only the performer, but also the director. Since this cast member is HIV-positive in real life, Linda was unsure about continuing to have him run the workshops. As director, Linda did not want the actor to think his HIV status was being exploited. 'Each One Teach One', therefore, is also adapted according to the sensitivity of the issue and the boldness of the performers.

Linda felt, however, that – if possible – it was important to have someone run the workshops who would identify himself or herself as HIV-positive and be able to keep the discussion focused on the issue. He therefore hired an 'expert' from the National Association for People Living with HIV/AIDS (NAPWA) to run the workshops. As a young, independent woman, she was an important role model in the context of gender relations in KZN. She was new to the project when I was there and drew on her training as an AIDS educator, lecturing the audience on facts and statistics and handing out worksheets to the teachers that tested the knowledge she communicated in the workshop.

Once the scientific lecture was over, Linda joined in to give practical advice to the young women in plain language, such as: 'It's your right to say "No", otherwise it's rape. You are not the only partner that person has had.' To young men he talked about honesty, and about repairing the image of the Zulu male, saying, 'Masculinity should be about respecting women.' Linda the teacher-storyteller speaks to the attitudes of young people using the most direct and simple language. 'For three minutes of moaning and groaning,' he says, 'you will suffer for the rest of your life.' He tells the young men to 'go to the toilet and jerk off if you are aroused'. The students bring up their questions about condoms, such as whether they are worth using since they often break, or whether they actually carry the virus (a widely held perception). One student explained that he had even conducted an 'experiment' proving that condoms carried the virus. He had put a condom in boiling water and put it out in the sun. 'The next day it was rotting with maggots in it. That proves there is HIV in the condom,' the student said. Although condoms are discussed, the emphasis is on abstinence: 'Sex is not worth your life.' Between Linda and the NAPWA representative, the post-performance discussion addressed both the lack of knowledge about AIDS and the need for behaviour change, while the play provided a social context that analysed the social, political and economic factors that contribute to the spread of AIDS.

While condom use is brought up in post-performance discussion, AIDS testing is not. Condom use is not only considered risky because of breakage and because of the myth that it actually carries the virus; it also carries several meanings relating to a general lack of trust between men and women in South Africa.[32] Talking to cast members revealed that issues of privacy, access, fear and the social stigma of AIDS prevent people from going to get tested. Those cast members who admit to having been promiscuous in the past report that they now engage only in monogamous relationships or abstain from sex completely. VSTC seems most successful in the alteration of gendered behaviour, in how masculinity and femininity are performed. This is in keeping with current trends in peer education in South Africa that emphasise teaching 'life skills' to 'the whole person' rather than attempting to deliver non-specific, uncontextualised health prevention messages.[33]

Despite the fact that HIV-positive actors did not identify themselves and interact with audiences during the post-performance discussion, 'Each One Teach One' does take place behind the scenes. As with the *Kuku Roof* performances in Leeuwkop prison, performances of *Vuka Uma Ulele* are followed up by training sessions so that students can learn to create their own plays. After the post-performance discussion, VSTC distributes questionnaires to the school groups to test their knowledge about AIDS. One cast member then returns to the school to distribute informational pamphlets on HIV/AIDS, and helps the students to form an 'AIDS team'. The VSTC delegate trains 'the team' in theatre techniques and playmaking with the goal of having them develop an educational play based on their experiences at school. The themes include drug use, promiscuity, homosexuality, condoms and abstinence. Every year on 1 December, World AIDS Day, pupils from all the schools come together to watch the plays. VSTC thus helps to involve students in the creation of a culture of AIDS awareness and prevention.

Although developed independently, the VSTC approach is comparable to the Drama Approach to AIDS Education (DramAidE) programme. DramAidE is a peer education programme that draws heavily on Augusto Boal's participatory theatre techniques.[34] The programme has been in operation in the KZN area since 1991 and has been reported to be effective in performing and implementing drama-based AIDS education in the secondary schools. I have never seen DramAidE in action, but by all accounts the process is similar. The actors present a play and hold a post-performance discussion, teach life skills by engaging students in participatory Boalian Forum Theatre exercises, train teachers and eventually help students to create their own plays.[35]

Just as many VSTC company members used to belong to target audiences, DramAidE workers are made up of people who themselves had been targets of NGO peer education programmes. Unlike VSTC company members, however, DramAidE educators had already been acculturated to social volunteerism before their recruitment to the organisation. Most DramAidE volunteers have already served as community leaders or have otherwise worked within community organisations.[36] As VSTC company members are recent recruits who struggle with the specific issues being targeted and whose social base is still in the community, they more closely fit the description of 'peer' in peer education. While some of Linda's cast had been working in loosely organised, community-based AIDS awareness initiatives before joining VSTC, many were simply seeking an opportunity to perform and became 'turned on' to AIDS activism. Others were just out of school, wandering the streets without direction, and as Deborah James observes of many who become involved in peer education, 'looking for a better life'.[37] In communities where poverty and powerlessness are often a motivation for anti-social behaviour, material reward may be an important incentive for changing behaviour. If the core of peer education is to set an example of behavioural change, and if involvement in community work has bettered the lives of VSTC members materially as well as morally, they may successfully rival the gangsters as role models for youth who are seeking self-sufficiency before self-improvement.

Conclusion

In this chapter I have suggested that Bongani Linda's Victory Sonqoba Theatre Company extends the efforts of most TfD and peer education endeavours. While most of these are designed by outsiders, Linda is an insider who both lives and works among his target communities. 'Each One Teach One' ensures that his actors are insiders as well. This methodology goes further than most peer education programmes that concentrate their recruitment efforts on youth who have leadership experience in the target community, but who may not necessarily have personal experience of the issues at the core of the awareness campaign. For Linda, prior leadership, or acting, experience is not necessary. Rather what primarily qualifies 'cultural combatants' is to have first-hand experience of the issue being addressed. While most peer education programmes use NGO-developed sociological literature as informational resources, VSTC plays are developed in workshops from the real-life experiences belonging to or gathered by the cast.

The 'Each One Teach One' method may encounter a potential obstacle when a play attempts to deal with sensitive issues such as rape or AIDS. Those who have personal experience of these issues do not necessarily feel comfortable talking about their experience or guiding others through it. When possible, Linda finds people who do feel comfortable disclosing their status, even if he has to look for a higher level of expertise. When it is impossible to find such a person, the play and post-performance discussion serve to build safe space for the more personal interaction that takes place when 'cultural combatants' work closely with members of the target population in developing their own plays.

That 'cultural combatants' live within the communities they serve is an additional advantage from a peer education point of view. Their peers may witness the transformation in their lives before they even see a play. Many of these young people turned from being criminals to being contributors to society, and from being irresponsible and carefree to being respectful and cautious in their sexual lives.[38] Perhaps even more initially enticing to young people lacking direction and in need of earning a living is that VSTC company members have found a worthwhile occupation with income and promising career opportunities.

By employing and training members of the target community, Linda sustains not only the future of his company members, but also that of his company. As part of his plan for sustainability, Linda creates entertaining, professional-level, educational theatre intended for commercial, as well as target, audiences. While some of Linda's theatre may achieve commercial success among white audiences in the urban venues, bringing white people into the townships regularly is still a distant goal. Thus, for the time being, white people will continue to view educational theatre as having to do with problems affecting 'others', and they will attend as a leisure activity in the relative 'safety' of an urban theatre venue. Until the country achieves a redistribution of wealth and a more radical restructuring of the arts institutions, it may be too soon for Linda's ultimate goal of producing sustainable, professional theatre for township audiences.

Other than its potential for commercial viability, other indicators of VSTC's sustainability include its national reputation as a valuable communication tool, earning the company invitations from numerous institutions and organisations, and the impact that participating in peer education through theatre has on VSTC company members themselves. It remains a problem that very few studies have been conducted to evaluate the success of peer education programmes.[39] Since VSTC members belong to the target population, the impact of VSTC on their lives is a strong indication of the impact that VSTC is likely to be making on its audiences. Theories of peer education suggest that those who are valued by individuals or communities can serve as role models and bring about behavioural change by influencing group norms.[40] By both living and working in the communities, Linda and his company members become respected citizens who provide positive role models for youth. Linda's heritage as veteran of the struggle against apartheid is deserving of admiration in itself. What makes him such a powerful role model, however, is that he has not stopped fighting, but instead of combating injustice with violence, he now combats it with culture.

NOTES

1. In 1975 Mangosuthu Buthelezi consolidated the Inkhata Freedom Party as a Zulu representative body of the ANC resistance movement. Buthelezi had originally used his alignment with the ANC

political movement as a means of rivalling the power of the royal family in Zululand. In the late 1970s, however, the ANC, influenced by the Black Consciousness Movement, objected to any blacks participating in any government-sponsored institutions or policies (such as the Bantustan policy, which Buthelezi had used to develop his own power in the region). The rift between the ANC and IFP grew when the ANC movement campaigned for economic sanctions imposed by the international community, while the IFP supported a free market economy. When the ANC decided to engage in armed struggle, the IFP favoured a political battle fought from within Bantustan policy. The struggle for power between the United Democratic Front (the front organisation for the ANC while it was banned by the government) and the IFP in KwaZulu-Natal (KZN) erupted into violence. For more information, see Georgina Hamilton and Gerhard Maré, 'The Inkhata Freedom Party', in Andrew Reynolds (ed.), *Election '94: The campaigns, results and future prospects* (David Phillip Publishers, 1994), pp. 73–87, and the *TRC Final Report*, vol. III, no. iii, on the Truth and Reconciliation Commission Website CD-ROM (Copyright Steve Crawford & the Truth and Reconciliation Commission, Cape Town, 1998).

2. Health education theatre, such as that facilitated by Barney Simon in the 1970s, used similar methods to those of TfD, although it was not called by that name. See Loren Kruger and Patricia Watson Shariff, ''Shoo-This Book Makes Me to Think!': Education, Entertainment, and Life-Skills Comics In South Africa', in *Poetics Today*, vol. 22, no. 2 (2001), pp. 475–513, 493.

3. Protest theatre in South Africa referred to those plays that appealed to the conscience of the white oppressor. Athol Fugard's plays are a prime example. Resistance theatre, typified by Black Consciousness playwrights Maishe Maponya and Matsemela Manaka, was aimed instead at mobilising the oppressed to become active in the resistance movement against apartheid.

4. Zakes Mda, 'Current Trends in Theatre for Development', in Derek Attridge and Rosemary Jolly (eds.), *Writing South Africa:*

Literature, Apartheid and Democracy, 1970–1995 (Cambridge: Cambridge University Press, 1998), p. 259.

5. The MK was a highly disciplined, volunteer guerrilla army formed in 1961 after the ANC was banned in 1960, making it more difficult to conduct a non-violent struggle. The MK was established to fight the South African Defence Force (SADF) and the South African Police (SAP), which were increasingly raiding townships, dragging people out of their houses in the middle of the night, and attacking and killing young activists. After the tear gas and bullet attacks on students in the 1976 Soweto student uprisings, thousands more youths went into exile to join the MK. Inside South Africa they performed sabotage operations, planting bombs at several key SADF facilities, command centres and fuel reserves. Surrounding countries also fighting South African and US-backed rebel groups in Angola and Mozambique offered to host training camps for the MK.

6. Unless otherwise indicated, this and all subsequent comments from Bongani Linda, company members and other participants in this account were made to me during the three weeks of my visit in August 2001.

7. Bongani Linda, email correspondence with the author, 7 July 2002.

8. 'Each One Teach One' is a common name used for various peer education programmes, but Linda claims that his method and its name are self-invented.

9. See Nicholas D. Richie, PhD, and Adelaide Getty, RN, BHS, CHES, 'Did an AIDS Peer Education Program Change First-Year College Students' Behaviors?' http://www.interactivetheatre.org/resc/peered.html, n.d., and 'Peer Education and HIV/AIDS: Concepts, uses, and challenges', UNAIDS, Geneva, Switzerland, 1999, http://www.unaids.org/publications/documents/care/general/peer.pdf.

10. Deborah James, '"To Take the Information Down to the People": Life Skills and HIV/AIDS Peer Educators in the Durban Area', in *African Studies* 61 (January 2002), p. 183.

11. *Yizo Yizo* (Zulu for *That Is How It Is*) is a popular educational television series designed to inform the public about the conditions of learning in township schools and to educate young people about sex, crime and violence. Its graphic content has raised controversy over whether or not it helps to deter or reinforces criminal behaviour.

12. For a discussion of the community theatre activists' objections to the distinction between art and social criticism, see Loren Kruger, *The Drama of South Africa* (London: Routledge, 1999), p. 200.

13. Manaka's musical play, *Koma* (1987), aimed at increasing the literacy rate among black youth and performed in the rural areas, was perhaps one of the first TfD efforts in South Africa.

14. The Baxter Theatre opened in 1977. It maintained a policy of 'open to everyone' even at the height of the apartheid regime.

15. The Space Theatre opened in 1972, despite police interference, with Athol Fugard's *Sizwe Bansi is Dead*, but closed in 1981.

16. The Market Theatre opened in 1976 with *Marat/Sade* and *The Seagull* and is still in existence.

17. Martin Orkin, *Drama and the South African State* (Johannesburg: University of the Witwatersrand Press, 1991), pp. 212–13.

18. Even in the field of TfD, Linda is weary of being managed by whites. Linda recounts that the Community Theatre for Development Trust was ultimately a white-led organisation even though it was primarily aimed at theatre work being done in black communities. The Community Theatre for Development Trust was established in 1992 to provide additional training in community theatre work to that provided at the Market Theatre Laboratory (the Lab) and universities. Established in 1989 to provide training to black students and community theatre groups, the Lab is still the usual opening for community theatre groups seeking urban audiences. Linda showcased his play, *Kuku Roof*, at the Lab with the hope of eventually taking it to the Market Theatre, but he was insulted when the Lab assigned an undergraduate student to work with the group. When Linda refused to work with anyone of less than professional level, he was cut off from the Market Theatre's resources, including venues, and National Arts Council funding.

Linda has since had to take his work to the cities of Durban and Pretoria and rely on more funding from overseas. It is ironic that this government agency has discontinued funding VSTC. Linda reports that he has some overseas funders who only fund work that is in opposition to the government, when much of his work reflects initiatives within certain departments of government: *Kuku Roof*, for example, was commissioned by the Gender Commission. The Department of Land Affairs commissioned VSTC to make a play about a project concerning rights and access to land for women. VSTC helped the Department of Justice challenge the Ministry of Justice's sympathy to perpetrators of rape, and the South African Revenue Services to lobby for tax exemption for community-based organisations and non-governmental organisations dealing with education and HIV/AIDS. Linda comments, however, that '[w]e've always maintained our freedom of expression and choice to do what we know and what is real in every project. Our work has challenged, criticised, praised and inspired the government departments to work hard in fulfilling their promise to the people.' Linda, email correspondence with the author, 25 July 2002.

19. Bongani Linda, interview with the author, Johannesburg, 27 January 2000.

20. *Ibid.*

21. http://www.worldbank.org/html/fpd/urban/urb_age/disastermgt/hands.htm.

22. For further discussion of the broad applications of 'street' performance, see Jan Cohen Cruz, *Radical Street Performance: An International Anthology* (London: Routledge, 1998).

23. Loren Kruger, *The Drama of South Africa: Plays, Pageants and Publics Since 1910* (London: Routledge, 1999), pp. 154–5.

24. I have written in detail about this play elsewhere. See Stephanie Marlin-Curiel, 'The Long Road to Healing: From the TRC to TfD', in *Theatre Research International*, vol. 27, no. 3 (October 2002), pp. 275–88.

25. In the months preceding the second democratic elections in 1999, old IFP–ANC rivalries resurfaced as conflict between the

IFP, the ANC and the United Democratic Movement (UDM), an opposition party to the ANC formed in 1997 by alienated ex-National Party leader Roelf Meyer and ousted ANC leaders Bantu Holosima (Transkei military leader made deputy minister of the ANC in 1994) and Sifiso Nkabinde (secretary general of the ANC and KZN Midlands regional leader who was not only accused of spying for the apartheid government, but is widely believed to have been responsible for sixteen political murders of which he was acquitted). Nkabinde's assassination shortly afterwards set off a wave of killings that continued through the year 2000. Although political violence in KZN since 2000 has lessened greatly, the area has still been plagued by violent clashes between taxi companies.

26. Linda, telephone conversation with the author, 15 October 2002.
27. VSTC Narrative Report, unpublished, n.d.
28. Linda, email correspondence with the author, 7 July 2002.
29. Neither the play nor the post-performance discussion touched on homosexual transmission. Heterosexual sex is by far the more common mode of transmission in South Africa, and homosexuality is a taboo subject in Zulu culture. Linda did say, however, that he was planning a future play on the subject.
30. Liberty Eaton, Alan J. Flisher and Leif E. Aaro, 'Unsafe Sexual Behaviour in South African Youth', in *Social Science and Medicine*, 3599 (2002), pp. 13–14.
31. Linda, email correspondence with the author, 7 July 2002.
32. Examples of the social stigma associated with condom use are: i) it is commonly believed that condoms can disappear in women, causing injury or death; ii) many also think that using condoms is offensive since it makes the partner feel as though he or she is dirty (Eaton *et al.*, 'Unsafe Sexual Behaviour', p. 13); iii) people associate condoms with casual sex partners rather than permanent ones (Quarraisha Abdool Karim and Janet Frolich, 'Women Try to Protect Themselves from HIV/AIDS in KwaZulu-Natal, South Africa', in Meredeth Turshen [ed.], *African Women's Health* [Lawrenceville, NJ: Africa World Press, 2000], p. 76); iv) not only do condoms diminish pleasure, but since condoms

also prevent pregnancy, they are not popular because fathering children is one way in which men prove their love and virility; and v) hormonal contraceptives are perceived as more effective than condoms. Some mothers in rural areas who feel that they cannot control their daughters' sexual behaviour take them to receive hormonal injections that prevent pregnancy but not STDs; this encourages young women to have sex more freely but discourages use of condoms (Eaton *et al.*, 'Unsafe Sexual Behaviour', p. 14).

33. See James, '"To Take the Information"', p. 173.
34. See Michael Carklin, 'Rainbows and Spiderwebs: New Challenges for Theatre in a Transformed System of Education in South Africa', in Marcia Blumberg and Dennis Walder (eds.), *South African Theatre As/And Intervention* (Amsterdam: Rodopi, 1999), p. 164.
35. *Ibid.*, pp. 164–5.
36. James, '"To Take the Information"', p. 171.
37. *Ibid.*, pp. 185–6.
38. Those who were sexually promiscuous by their own account have now become more sexually responsible. This has not, however, been verified by third party sources.
39. See James, '"To Take the Information"', p. 180.
40. UNAIDS, 'Peer Education and HIV/AIDS', p. 6.

6 Dance and transformation: the Adugna Community Dance Theatre, Ethiopia

JANE PLASTOW

In addition to the life-death cycle basic to nature, there is also an unnatural *living death*: life which is denied its fullness.

Men will be truly critical if they live the plenitude of the praxis, that is, if their action encompasses a critical reflection which increasingly organises their thinking and thus leads them to move from a purely naïve knowledge to a higher level.

Paulo Freire, *Pedagogy of the Oppressed*[1]

Junaid: *My bones, joints, skin, mentally and physically – all move in contemporary dance. I can create and say anything. Sometimes I feel like God, creating through contemporary dance.*

Minyahil: *I have a photo from before I joined Adugna and a recent photo. There is no Minyahil before. Now I am very strong and healthy. Before Minyahil spoke very bad language and was aggressive. Now I like to read and do all politely. It is a big, big change. As if I were not there before.*

Meskerem: *They didn't only teach dance, they gave us life. How to live and change others. This is life and what Ethiopia needs.*[2]

It is lunchtime in *Kebele* 43,[3] an average slum ward in Addis Ababa, and the stony tracks are busy with children coming back from the first sitting at school;[4] with petty traders squatting over their meagre piles of vegetables or secondhand clothes; with goats, chickens and donkeys. The car cannot get near to the *kebele* administrative buildings, so I pick my way over lumps of rock, past the erosion gullies and around puddles to the paint-flaking building and the senior citizens' dance class.

There is nowhere else in this city where old people have such a class, but here, every week, twenty-two elderly people, men and women in roughly equal numbers, gather in good time for their session with members of the Adugna Community Dance Theatre. There is no Lycra here. The women are in long dresses, the men in ancient jackets, patched trousers and an eclectic variety of headgear.

Meseret leads off with some gentle stretching exercises, while Andualem and Mekbul move among the group, helping and explaining the instructions. There is an air of high seriousness, frowns of effort, and a quiet concentration which is a world away from the racket and grime outside. This is a dance class.

The class move into a circle with some difficulty. It does not seem to be a concept which comes easily, but everyone is trying to follow the gentle teacher (a third their age), as they attempt to move in unison to music from the small 'ghettoblaster'.

After the warm-up and the exercises comes traditional Ethiopian dance music. The energy level rises, stiff bodies move in the shoulder-shaking shimmy so characteristic of Amhara dance. Smiles break out as men and women lean shoulder to shoulder and the pace quickens, with individuals moving to centre stage for short extrovert solos. The class lasts for an hour. It has been filmed for a video on the Ethiopian Gemini Trust to which Adugna belongs, and some of the participants are interviewed. Belay Anbawe speaks of the health benefits: 'I've been coming to these classes right from the start. If I miss a class I find that my body seizes up.' But it is Shifera Belihu's response which moves me. 'Dancing', he says, 'helps me to get rid of the old person in me.'

The class is free, part of an outreach programme involving some 300 people on a regular basis, which extends to kindergarten and schoolchildren, unemployed youth groups, disabled dancers and these elderly men and women. The impact it makes on the economy must be negligible. No one has evaluated what it means to those who take part, and providing for the cultural wellbeing of elderly slum dwellers doesn't figure in any development or funding plan I have ever seen. But this is a class to which everyone comes on time, in a place where time is not usually any sort of a priority. It provides a focus, companionship, enjoyment, culture and fitness for people whose lives are usually confined to one or two crumbling rooms, with no scope for creativity. How do you put a price tag on such an event? How do you value *fun*? How do you ask funders who want measurable development outcomes to support a group that wants to offer a dance class to a group of economically useless, illiterate, old slum dwellers?

The genesis of a dance project

Dance is still an unusual form in the area of development projects. The origin of this article was my desire to explore how dance works in a development context and what might be unique as well as generic to cultural development projects privileging dance. However, a project can only work in a particular situation, so this essay will also look at how Adugna came into being, in Ethiopia, and will seek to understand its growth through the voices of those most closely involved in the project.

> Shiferaw: *I never forget the first day we began. I was looking for education, for exercise books. Even when I was introduced to Mags and Royston I had no idea. I was still looking for books. They gave me a T-shirt and shorts, but even after six months I was just following. I had no idea what I was doing.*

Shiferaw is not the only person involved with Adugna who has been through periods of confusion. Precisely because dance and development are so unusual a pairing, there was little prior wisdom for the project to draw on. Adugna's conception was almost serendipitous, and its growth has been mirrored by constant struggles between Western dance practitioners, development professionals, young participants and an Ethiopian culture which traditionally looks down on artists, young people and street dwellers, as all involved have sought to understand and work with languages and mindsets originating in profoundly different places.

The project came into being through a meeting between Carmela Green-Abate, an Anglo-American doctor married to an Ethiopian who conceived and now chairs a major Ethiopian non-governmental organisation (NGO), the Ethiopian Gemini Trust, and British filmmaker Andrew Coggins, who came to Ethiopia to make a film about street children.

Gemini began in 1983, when Green-Abate was working as a pae-diatrician and was appalled at the number of infant deaths of twins born to desperately poor women in Ethiopia.[5] With the help of a sin-gle initial benefactress she set up an emergency feeding programme for some of these women. Over the years Gemini (named after the heav-enly twins) has grown into a major programme involving over a thou-sand families, and around 7,500 people. Since twins and their mothers do not exist in isolation, the project has sought to be holistic, looking at the whole family. Emergency feeding still goes on for malnourished infants and their mothers, but healthcare is available to the whole fam-ily. All children in the families have their education costs covered. There is a kindergarten to enable mothers to work. Work-creation schemes employ nearly 200 parents of Gemini twins. Some funds are available for upgrading housing and for crisis aid. The project also runs a major citywide, community-based reproductive health programme, and takes a leading role in a coalition of development agencies which seek to work together to improve the lives of the huge number of street dwellers in Addis Ababa. Gemini has received support over the years from a great variety of funders – including such major names as Oxfam, Christian Aid, Comic Relief, UNFPA and UNESCO – and has its own British support group. It has been visited by every luminary travelling to Ethiopia, including the Archbishop of Canterbury and the Secretary General of the United Nations.

By the early 1990s many of the children of Gemini families were growing up. Some had become school dropouts, failing the com-petitive end-of-year exams, while others needed educational support to enable them to keep going in the system. So the Gemini Youth Club was founded, both to give extra classes in subjects such as English and maths and to provide a safe recreational space (a respite from the dangerous life on the streets), a centre where young people could receive support and have fun. It is a pretty basic place: a part of a compound shared with the kindergarten and the health clinic, with some rough ground, a small library, a couple of metal transport containers converted into work spaces, and a wooden office.

When Andrew Coggins arrived in Addis Ababa in 1995, he had already worked in Ethiopia on a couple of occasions, most recently in 1994 when he had been filming for the BBC, looking at the impact of Bob Geldof's Live Aid initiative a decade after the famine that gave rise to a huge public outpouring of support for Ethiopia's millions of starving people. Coggins says he cannot remember just who it was, but as he was driving across the main city square an Ethiopian passenger suggested that he should make a film about Ethiopia's street children. Coggins had been appalled, like many who come to Ethiopia for the first time, by the numbers and plight of young children living and working on the street, polishing shoes, selling fruit, chewing gum and cigarettes, begging, sniffing glue and getting involved in petty theft and violence. He took the idea away with him, and after discussions decided that there had to be street children behind as well as in front of the cameras. He also decided that he wanted to use dance in his film, because dance seemed to be such a central means of cultural expression at all ceremonial occasions in the country. He made enquiries as to who might be a suitable person to lead on dance elements in the film, and the name Royston Muldoom kept coming up.

Coggins and Green-Abate met as he was seeking pre-production money for his proposed film; she suggested that it would also be a good idea if some of the young people could be employed in the filming. Meanwhile, they were having difficulty in enticing Muldoom to Ethiopia. Muldoom had himself been a street dweller as a young man. He has worked in community dance not only in some of the rougher areas of working-class Scotland, but also in a number of other countries (including South Africa), and at the time was involved in a major project in Croatia.

Eventually Coggins said, 'Just come for the weekend.' It is a long way to go for a weekend, but Muldoom went. He was immediately struck by the vulnerability of the street children, some of whom were at that time being picked up by the police and dumped outside the city boundaries as a means of clearing the streets. Muldoom said he would work with them, but it had to be for a performance to raise consciousness about the children's plight. *Adugna*,[6] a piece using the music from *Carmina Burana*, was rehearsed in eighteen days, using more than a hundred street children, some brought in by Gemini, others attached to various support programmes operating in the city. Muldoom wanted to do something to make a difference fast. He had used his choreography for *Carmina Burana* in a number of other countries. It is a piece about the search of the oppressed for freedom through love, but hardly one member of what would become the Adugna dance company understood it at the time.

> Getachew: *I didn't like the costume and I didn't understand*
> Carmina Burana.
>
> Assrat: *Before* Carmina Burana *it was not clear and it was boring, and I was shy and afraid of all those involved. And even with that show, I didn't like it, but after that I got a little more happy.*

The production was mounted in 1996 for five free performances at the prestigious City Hall Theatre, and even if the dancers did not understand what they were doing, the evidence that they could entertain, that street children could *do* and *be* something, made a profound impact on a number of important audience members. Venus Aswaran of UNICEF, who has subsequently become a member of the Gemini Board in Ethiopia, commented:

> Before I saw this show I always thought, OK, yeah, we need to help street children – give them some used clothes and help them – some charity. But this has changed my whole attitude. Because I see something deeper within the beings of street children. They're just like us. They can learn and they can move on. And actually, you know, they can entertain us. That was a very good performance tonight.

As a result, the British Ambassador asked if the dancers could perform a piece in the central Meskel Square as a major part of the British Embassy's 1996 centenary celebrations. Muldoom came back to Addis Ababa to work with his hundred dancers, this time putting on a piece choreographed about their own lives, with which the performers were much happier. More street children were employed to marshal the crowd of some 250,000, and it turned out to be another major artistic and public relations triumph.

I am not sure if anyone knows just when the notion of the film evaporated, but in its place were developing two ideas: to train a group of young street dwellers in film skills so that they could articulate their lives from the inside, and to offer dance training in order to raise public awareness about the vulnerability of street children and develop community dance opportunities. Green-Abate, Coggins and Muldoom were all convinced of the need and scope for providing arts training to enable street children to develop their own performative voices. So a video training programme (GEM TV) was set up with twelve participants, and Adugna was established with eighteen young people selected in a process that looked at aptitude, attitude and what Muldoom admits was partly just his own gut feeling. The dance training lasted, not for the eighteen months envisaged at the beginning, but for five years, coming to a close at the end of 2001.

Dance and development: a conflict of visions?
The project caught my imagination. It was something new and offered new skills. Traditional development wasn't getting anywhere. The average standard of living has gone down over the years and malnutrition among children is rising.

Caroline Green-Abate

This question about what constitutes valuable development, and what has been the value of more traditional, usually economics-driven, development programmes, comes close to the heart of why an Adugna-style initiative has caused such controversy, yet been so passionately supported by those at the heart of the project. The Gemini

Trust has been offering ameliorative support to the poorest of the poor in Addis Ababa for twenty years. It has undoubtedly saved hundreds of lives and offered a bearable standard of living to many more. But Green-Abate sees the need for help like that offered by the Gemini Trust only increasing, and the children growing up with Gemini support still failing to find employment in large numbers. 'If we really want to see change,' she said, 'we need to invest in our young people; give them the tools by which they can find their own voice and become leaders within their communities.'

Rosemary Arnott, a board member of the Trust and head of the British Council in Ethiopia, independently corroborated Green-Abate's view, arguing that initiatives such as Adugna and GEM TV offered the possibility not just of amelioration of appalling living conditions, but of transformation, firstly for the trainees, and potentially, through outreach work, for enormous numbers of people.

On the other hand, a number of supporters could not believe it to be right that the Trust was pouring such relatively large amounts of money, time and resources into what they saw as a programme for a very few young people, who would then be disproportionately privileged. Some key Ethiopian staff had similar reservations, coupled with a persistent cultural sense that the arts are not a proper profession, and a concern that too much exposure to European ideas might make the young people involved disrespectful and unable to negotiate their own society.

Adugna has had an easier time obtaining funding than GEM TV, but one of the major funders, the UK agency Comic Relief – despite its own high-profile arts connections – has quailed at the cost of a professional-level training, and at the small number of direct immediate beneficiaries of the project. It did maintain support for the project until the end of the training period, but its unease often came through loud and clear.

This issue of professional-level training, and its cost, is – along with the focus of the project being dance – what has caused most unease. It has been impossible to obtain full figures for the costs involved, partly because so much has been given as voluntary assistance, but also because much falls within an integrated set of Gemini activities. However, between July 1999 and June 2000, recorded Gemini expenditure on Adugna came to just over £52,000, so one might reasonably extrapolate that the whole programme has cost at least £200,000–£250,000. Despite development agencies now being responsible for sponsoring huge proportions of all professionally produced performance work in countries such as Uganda, Tanzania and Burkina Faso (under the umbrella of arts for development), most of this work is cheaply commissioned from existing companies, which are often in a weak bargaining position, and usually produce very didactic theatre to order. The methodology of arts within a development context is almost wholly unexamined by NGOs, which predominantly use the arts simply as an entertaining means of transmitting their messages. Some organisations have sponsored training work for development arts practitioners, but this has usually been short-term and about passing on basic skills in such forms as Forum Theatre.

The vision behind the training of Adugna has been arts- (rather than development agency-) led, and has consequently had some very unusual priorities for an arts and development project. The training programme, large parts of its implementation, and all of its supervision have been rigorously devised by Muldoom and his collaborator Mags Byrne. Their idea was to give the members of Adugna the best possible training in contemporary Western and traditional Ethiopian dance, with the following intentions:

- the students would become exemplary practitioners of dance, and thus demonstrate the potential of all street children;
- there would be no question of providing second-rate training for a Third World country (a common scenario), one that effectively traps the recipient nations in a circle of dependency and a continuing sense of inferiority. These would be dancers on the same terms as dancers anywhere in the world;
- the group would be given the potential to become economically independent;
- the dancers would be encouraged to develop their own dance 'voices', to develop their human potential, and to articulate their sense of being;

- the dancers would be encouraged to use their skills on behalf of street dwellers and communities of the poor to advocate change.
- members of the dance group would become community arts trainers who would begin a process of extending the benefits and joys of dance in ever-widening circles throughout Ethiopia.

I asked Muldoom to explain how dance could be a powerful tool in a development context:

In dance we take away words. Often we use words to say what we don't mean, as a protection from revealing who we are. When they are taken away, you leave a person very vulnerable, bare and transparent. The audience also lose a crutch. They have to absorb the experience directly; communicate at a non-verbal level. The body is a powerful indicator as to who we are, what we feel and what we experience. It always responds to our state of mind. We move in response to how we see ourselves.

As a psychologist works through mind and observes changes in the body, we can work the other way. Changes in movement make people change the way they think and behave. The taking part and the process is the most crucial. The passing on of self-esteem and skill to others is most important. Teaching and workshopping is as important as performance and direct messages. When you work with others with low self-esteem they only take the space they think they are worth. They can't stretch or raise their heads. Through controlled pleasurable experience they can extend and take space. They are unlikely to go back. Dance affects their idea of self and place in their world. Passing that on is paramount.

Dance means extending yourself to others – giving examples of good practice in life. Lifting and supporting are equally valuable. Mutual support is necessary. It becomes harder to be violent to other bodies, hard to maintain prejudice when you are involved in the intimate, physical, emotional process of problem solving with another human being.

If delivered right it is joyful. Most human beings aspire to dance. It is an obvious place to start to contact people as nearly all, and especially young people, dance or want to dance.[7]

Muldoom's vision is essentially *human-to-human* led. This contrasts with many aid programmes which, however much they may espouse participation and Freirean philosophies of mutual learning, remain materially and economically motivated, and dominated by funders' agenda. This is not to deny that such initiatives as emergency feeding programmes, provision of clean water and medical care are not often absolutely essential, but what projects like Adugna – especially within the wider context of Gemini as a whole – ask is how much long-term use *is* aid, or even skills training, if it does not seek to liberate and empower human potential, and to build supportive contact between human beings? Do we wish to ameliorate human misery or to liberate human lives?

Becoming Adugna

The training programme extended from eighteen months initially to three, and ultimately to five, years, because everyone had underestimated the tremendous journey that would be necessary for a group of poor school dropouts from the city's slums to become confident, creative, dance leaders.

> Nuria: *I used to sell coffee. I followed the lorries, I collected spilt coffee from the ground, washed and sold it in Mercato. Before, I was the boss for violence, I controlled other children and hit those who didn't listen to me. When I joined Adugna I was the youngest. I was thirteen.*

Other members of the group had previously sold reject oranges and secondhand clothes, shined shoes, made paper bags, minded cars on the street and generally done anything in the way of petty trade and street hustling to earn a few *birr*[8] for their families. They lived in an atmosphere of overcrowding and dire poverty. Although Meseret, for example, is from a Gemini family and is clearly one of the most intellectually astute of the trainees, she had had to leave school in grade eight because there were nine children in her family and they needed her to start earning money.

Nearly all the trainees said that before they joined the programme they were constantly sick and hungry. They also spoke of violence as a constant factor in street life, and of the temptation to resort to glue-sniffing and drugs to escape its misery. In this context it is not surprising that the young people signed up for Adugna training without knowing anything of what would actually be involved. The chance to be given food and clothing, and the possibility of acquiring a skill – in no matter what – was a once-in-a-lifetime chance that no one could afford lightly to turn down.

The training base was on the Youth Club compound; the dance studio a three-sided breeze-block room, some ten metres long, with a corrugated iron roof (which has had to be lifted as the students' jumps got higher) and a concrete floor. Basic showers were put up next to the classroom, and students were provided with food, clothing and transport money. The training programme, running five days a week, concentrated on Western contemporary and Ethiopian traditional dance, but there has also been regular teaching in English, maths, computer and administrative skills, social skills, yoga and health awareness. In the last year emphasis was also placed on production management, costume design and costume making. Not only were a number of the students dubious about the sense and worth of what they were doing in the early stages, but several were also under pressure from their families who were missing the small but crucial income their children had previously been bringing home.

> Getachew: *When I was on the streets, I used to give some money to my family. But after I joined Adugna, they hated me and stopped giving me food or greetings. After one year the families were invited to see a show. My mother liked it and persuaded the others to accept me and give me food.*

In contrast Guenet's family was supportive from the start:

Guenet: *My family was very poor and wanted me to learn*
more, and they really liked me coming to Adugna
and supported me every time. I saved my taxi money
and gave them some small coins, then Gemini gave
us some money. They are very proud of me.

Gemini was forced to realise the acute stress that the loss of income
was causing families. Consequently an allowance system was set up
offering families the equivalent of six pounds a month in lieu of their
children's lost earnings, and for many this immediately resolved significant tensions. The exception was among the families of Muslim
students, who, despite attempts by a number of Gemini staff to gain
support for the students involved, have resolutely rejected dance as
a respectable way to earn a living, whether their children be male or
female.

Mekbul: *I am not supported by my family because I am*
Muslim. Especially in Ethiopia it is the religion. I
am alone. I have made this alone.
Nuria: *I am a Muslim. In the beginning my family didn't*
know [about Adugna] and didn't mind. But then
they found out, especially my father, sometimes
they beat me. It is still going on and until now they
don't appreciate it.

Many students also reported that their friends at first thought them
crazy to work so hard on the dance programme, and urged them to
leave.

Given all these stresses, the fact that trainers were not con-
tinuously present in the early days, and that many students did not
understand the nature of their training or the relevance of their first
performance piece, it is a considerable achievement that all eighteen
young people have lasted the course.

The turning-point for many seems to have been the second production they created with Muldoom. Entitled *Street Dreams*, it was
a direct reflection of life on the streets and has remained a central

part of the repertoire until today. *Street Dreams* begins with a group
of street children gathering, playing cards and starting to argue. A
policeman enters and starts to lay into them with his truncheon –
a common experience for many street children. The children break
and run. The following high-energy dance, backed by Adugna members playing local drums, centres on shoeshine boxes and petty-trade
goods, as the children dance their life on the streets.

> Shiferaw: *The second performance,* Street Dreams, *the story
> was all our lives. Royston told us the story and it
> took all my pain.*
>
> Guenet: Street Dreams *was my life and all the message and
> content was clear for me, and this was the first
> thing I understood.*

I asked Muldoom why he chose to begin his work in Ethiopia
with *Carmina Burana*, which emanates from a musical tradition and
philosophy that is Eurocentric rather than Ethiopian. Partly the production was dictated by the perceived need to put on a large-scale piece
quickly. Muldoom argues that its message is universal, but of course
he at that time knew very little about Ethiopian culture, and since he
had previously succeeded with the production in a range of nations
it seemed a valid choice. The success of the production undoubtedly
gained Adugna a following among both street children – all major performances have free showings for street children – and the Ethiopian
and expatriate elite, which in itself raises interesting questions about
ownership and understanding of material.

Meanwhile, a number of training concerns were developing.
Muldoom could not be in Ethiopia permanently. He did not wish
to live there, had other training commitments and needed to earn
more money than Gemini could afford to pay him. Mags Byrne has
often alternated with Muldoom and has been in Ethiopia more con-
sistently than any other trainer. There have also been a series of spe-
cialist trainers. Sylvan Prunenec, a French choreographer and dancer,
inspired an upsurge of interest in choreography among students.
Sheila Raj, who danced for the Royal Ballet and Merce Cunningham

companies, worked on yoga, breath control and improvisation skills. Richard Hilton ran a course, particularly popular with male students, on hip-hop and break-dance techniques, while Germaine Acogny, a leading Senegalese dancer, began the important process of widening Adugna's contacts with African dance practice. However, students had to be given assignments while trainers were away, and a number of tensions tended to arise in these periods with some Ethiopian Gemini management staff who felt that students were losing respect for their authority as they fell under the Western influence of imported trainers. There were also problems in chains of communication, with all sides believing – often with some justification – that they were not kept fully informed by others who did not understand their needs and priorities as dance trainers, trainees or Gemini managers.

Finally, in terms of delivering dance training, there were continual problems in finding the right Ethiopian traditional dance trainers. Ethiopia has more than sixty ethnic groups, but the capital is dominated by the Amhara, and although the city's four major theatres all have their own traditional dance troupes, the groups are simply taught to reproduce a version of particular ethnic dances. Negash Abdi of the National Theatre was able to give students some background information about the history of dances, but little thought has been given among Ethiopian dance professionals to how traditional dance can be developed and drawn upon beyond mere commercialisation. No one involved in Gemini had good access to the rather incestuous world of Ethiopian performance, and therefore locating the best local teachers was a problem. This area has continued to prove difficult. The group now acknowledges that it needs to find first-hand teachers in the regions who can teach both movement and the significance of particular dances, but an initial research trip to northern Ethiopia in 2001 failed to identify appropriate figures, through lack of good contacts. One perhaps unfortunate result has been that although some members of Adugna express a preference for traditional dance, many more choose contemporary dance as their favourite form.

Getachew: *Traditional dance makes me think of my culture and my people.*

Guenet: *I like traditional and contemporary dance together because you can express yourself through both and join them together to give messages.*

Minyahil: *Contemporary dance is everything: life, sadness, happiness, politics. Much more than I can tell in words.*

Of course, expressive possibilities can be present in traditional dance, but only when one has teachers who have a real engagement with the cultures concerned plus ideas about developing and adapting dance forms. Only in the last eighteen months was a new teacher (Abby Mekonnen) located, who has been able to work in partnership with Western trainers, has taught Adugna many new Ethiopian dances, and – crucially – has had the skill and flexibility to fuse traditional and contemporary forms.

Theatre training

Adugna is formally called the 'Adugna Community Dance *Theatre*', and since 1998 there has been a recognition that not only would theatre training add to aspects of the group's expressive skills, but in running issue-led workshops and projects the use of drama might allow closer scrutiny of complex issues than is possible in dance alone. I therefore began some drama training, based around Boalian concepts of Forum Theatre, in 1998, and since that time leading community theatre practitioner Gerri Moriarty (who discusses her work in Northern Ireland earlier in this volume) has made five training visits to the group.

These skills have been particularly utilised in relation to projects such as the Police Training Programme and the Nazret work on issues such as HIV and drugs use among street children (these projects are discussed below). A minority of students have a particular interest in theatre, and not only enjoy acting but also wish to develop scripting and directing skills. I certainly found that their dance training had already given the Adugna students poise, confidence and improvisatory skills when I first began working with them; they have been quick to develop the ability to improvise scenes around a range of social issues, and to be able to take on the role of the Boalian 'joker', in drawing responses out of the client groups they have worked with.[9]

In terms of making 'dance theatre', there has been insufficient time, particularly with dance and theatre trainers both present, to develop the kind of syncretic dance-drama performances which have made strong impacts on audiences – especially when they utilise traditional dance forms with which mass audiences can identify – in other parts of Africa. Since Ethiopia has very few trained community theatre workers, there is likely to be considerable demand among NGOs and similar agencies for such issue-based theatre workshops and productions. At present Adugna uses a mixture of dance performances with forum-type improvisations in its issue-based projects. But this raises questions for me about whether there is a danger that a rather utilitarian approach to theatre might compromise the wider aims elucidated by Muldoom in relation to dance. There is also the possibility that a group less skilled in theatre than in dance may be pushed into making a series of basic issue-led drama pieces for future client groups who see theatre as less abstract than dance. Finally, the perceived need for drama training raises the issue of just how far dance can be utilised within the currently recognised parameters of development programmes, which are usually run by people who have no training in the possibilities or methodologies inherent in any kind of arts and development programmes, and who are therefore likely to feel more comfortable with the commonly used form of theatre, particularly when it can be more obviously employed to discuss, inform and educate regarding the very concrete issues, such as HIV/AIDS, clean water programmes or drugs use, that agencies may be specifically concerned with at any one time.

Personal journeys

The most difficult part of the process of Adugna training to document has been the journey of personal transformation undergone by the trainees. Junaid perhaps encapsulates the sense of the nature of the journey that I feel many members of Adugna have undergone.

Junaid: *'Junaid #1' has gone. I have gone through a lot of*
Junaids. I can help others change now. Around ninety
per cent of the community is in very bad condition
and I can help now. I can explain without being
aggressive.

Just as in Minyahil's description of his journey at the beginning of
this article, so Junaid explains his sense of transformation. These
young men articulate a sense of having sloughed off a series of previous embodiments associated with ill-health, violence, poverty and
misery, to emerge, as Junaid said, feeling 'like God' through their art.
It has taken a lot of talking, a lot of nurturing and, most profoundly,
a lot of dancing. To reiterate Muldoom's argument: 'The taking part
and the process is the most crucial. The passing on of self-esteem and
skill to others is most important.'

Ethiopian culture, conservative and, after hundreds of years of
rigid hierarchical dominance by both church and state establishments,
deeply suspicious of innovation and creativity, is often particularly
repressive towards women. Women are expected to do all the domestic
work, are often married off in their early teens, and are traditionally
taught to defer to the male sex in all things. The six girls who came
to Adugna were very withdrawn. They claimed minimal space and
almost no voice in the early stages of training. Guenet and Meseret
explained to me how the process of change worked for them.

Guenet: *[Female submission] began back in the family. We*
cannot eat together with the boys and play with the
boys. And when we came here we had to work with
the boys. And after a lot of pressure from our
teachers and performing with boys, and lifting
boys, which amazed audiences, I realised we are all
humans.

Meseret: *Although the lessons were equally for boys and*
girls, usually the girls were retreating behind. And
later I realised that because of bad training in
Ethiopia I was in a bad way. I have to throw that
away. I started to listen and to see on video

> European women, and I thought, 'They are women,
> why not us?' And I started to compete with the
> boys and now I have no problem.

It is undoubtedly true that the training influences, including that of Sue Pendlebury who visited specifically to work with the girls and build their self-esteem, have been predominantly European, and that some Ethiopian Gemini staff have worried about Eurocentric influence, but even the boys have eventually come to value their female dance partners. Yidnekachew is now a husband and father.

> Yidnekachew: *In the beginning I was a boy who didn't want girls near and neglected them. But after many lessons . . . I changed, I started to think that they have the right to work as equals. Now we all work equally. I really love my current life with my wife and daughter. It gave me more responsibility and that is what I want.*

As evaluator, theatre trainer and part of the forward-planning team, I made trips to Ethiopia in 1998, 1999 and 2001, as well as spending some time with the group when they performed in England in 1998. The sense of emerging beings has become apparent to a degree unparalleled in my experience of any other arts training projects, in both the UK and Africa, with which I have been involved.

Partly this has been to do with the low level of the starting-point. Muldoom speaks of the impossibility for people with low self-esteem to claim space, and the students I first met, particularly the girls, huddled in small corners in the back of the studio, begging to be ignored. I also remember an exercise I conducted with the group in 1998 in which I asked them to show each other their wildest dreams for the future. What I was shown were images of people with enough to eat, people with shoes, or people with petty-trade goods to sell. Such seemingly small happinesses were the greatest they could imagine.

Three years on, I see the results of the most intensive arts training course I have had experience of, a course about which I was initially dubious because of the lack of experience among the trainers of arts and development thinking and because of the Eurocentric emphasis in training and support. These concerns have persisted, but the evidence of the glowingly healthy, physically assured students cannot be ignored. Their dance skills go from strength to strength, and instead of a group of inward-looking, aggressive and defensive street kids we have Mekbul who says that 'the place I love is the stage . . . I can take the audience to me and I can go to them' when he creates, and Guenet who says that when she dances she feels 'as if I am flying'.

Into the community

The argument most often made against the Adugna project has not been to question its worth to the eighteen trainees involved, but to argue that the investment has been too big for just eighteen out of an estimated 60,000 street dwellers in Addis Ababa. It is a serious question that relates to many arts and development projects, where the most evidential benefit and change is so often with the core group and where the impact on others is very hard to evaluate using traditional methods.

Until 1998 Adugna had mostly been involved in company dance training and the occasional big performance as showcase in places such as the City Hall Theatre; for the community in various *kebele* halls; for international events in major hotels; and on tour, as in the UK, when the group performed in a number of cities including a performance in London's Albert Hall. However, the intention was always to move into outreach and teaching work, and since 1998 community outreach has become increasingly central to Adugna's identity.

Although some of the group acknowledge that performance and choreography are their favourite aspects of dance, all have come to be committed to the vision of spreading their skills across the community, the city and ultimately, the nation.

> Meskerem: *I am very confident. I feel I have all the necessary skills to work and express myself to the community. I would like this to be with Adugna, but if this is not possible I can do it on my own. Adugna should go through all the*

> country and teach others about street and poor
> people. We can set up other small groups and we
> can bring about change.

Asfaw: My thinking ability has got wide. Before the
> disabled training, to tell the truth, I hated them.
> But now I want to commit myself. I want to
> dedicate my life to make a difference. It's not
> only the dance; these poor people can be given a
> chance.

These quotations demonstrate Adugna's intentions and optimism about working for change at both macro and micro levels. There is a strong sense in the dancers' philosophy that they will use dance both to liberate individual human potential and to educate their society in relation to valuing its most marginalised citizens. The ideal seeks to unite aesthetic and educational considerations as indivisible aspects of true human development.

Ongoing classes have now been running for up to three years. These include:

- two groups for Gemini Youth Club children, one for twelve- to fourteen-year-olds and one for those over fourteen;
- a Gemini kindergarten group for two- to six-year-olds;
- a group for 'hardcore' street children;
- two groups for local unemployed young men;
- a local women's group;
- the elderly citizens' group;
- classes run by individual students in their own time involving several hundred participants in all;
- a revenue-raising programme held at one of the international schools in the city which reached some 700 of the nation's most affluent children. (Yitbarak can tell very funny stories about being accosted by his old gang members when he leaves his village every morning and they ask where he is going. They are absolutely incredulous that one of their number should be teaching in such an elite institution.)

In addition, there have been a number of special projects that particularly challenge and develop the outreach skills of the Adugna members.

The Police Training Programme

Street children see the police as brutal and frightening. The police have tended to see street children as potential if not actual criminals and as useless members of society. For these two groups to work together, seeking mutual understanding and behavioural change, has been a radical development. The police project has been running since July 1998 as part of the Ethiopian Police Training programme funded by the UK Department for International Development (DIFD). Blair Davies (a retired senior British police officer), the project manager, has explained his philosophy as follows:

> The police training programme involves the use of outside agencies such as the Gemini Trust and its Adugna trainees. Through their participation the behaviour of the police is being challenged by those people they are responsible for serving . . . in this case a whole generation of street children who have been either brutalised by authority – including the police – or who have a perception about the inevitability of police brutality . . . At the Police College a safe environment is created in which the Adugna trainees are able to stand up to these same police officers who may have brutalised them or their peers or who may be responsible for managing policies and strategies that encourage – or at least do not deter – the brutalisation of street children. The workshop offers the police an opportunity to understand street children but, as importantly, it challenges the street children to understand the police. It is a hugely powerful exercise.

Personally, I always feel a sense of guilt when I simply pass a uniformed police officer in Britain, and having been beaten up by the Ethiopian police (under the previous, military, regime in the 1980s, for curfew violation) I was fairly nervous when I was taken to the Police

Training College to meet Colonel Teferedegne, charming though he was. The far more vulnerable Adugna trainees must have felt very anxious when they confronted their traditional enemies, although they hid it admirably when I worked on the first pilot project with them in 1998.

In fact, given traditional authoritarian attitudes within the Ethiopian police, Colonel Teferedegne was a very brave man to take such a radical step as inviting street children to critique police behaviour. Since the project began Adugna has utilised both dance and Forum Theatre. GEM TV has also made a video about the human rights of street children which includes issues of dealing with police abuse. Gebremeskel explains how this work has affected his confidence in relation to the police.

> Gebremeskel: *Now I can identify good and bad and through this I can approach the community and work with street kids and the police. And I talk with the police when I see them attack street children.*

Dance and theatre workshops have become a regular feature for senior officers and police cadets in the capital, and the process of implementing the project throughout the country began in 2001 when Adugna travelled to the northern city of Makele to work with a group of 320 serving officers and police recruits, and to the town of Debre Markos where they worked with some 700 constable recruits. The work is not easy for either side. Adugna members have to overcome their longstanding suspicion of the police and confront them in a mature and moderate manner. The police have to see themselves openly portrayed as corrupt and brutal (key elements in most of the pieces put together for this project) and are asked to confront, challenge and reform their behaviour in relation to communities of the poor. Nonetheless, feedback from participants has been generally favourable, and there is great enthusiasm among commanding officers for the project to continue and develop throughout Ethiopia as a tool of police training and conscientisation.

Dance with the disabled

I was fortunate enough to be in Addis Ababa in 2001 at the completion of a second short course, led by dance trainer Adam Benjamin, in which Adugna members worked with a group of eight disabled dancers. It remains rare enough in the West for such integrated groups to dance on the public stage; in Ethiopia it is revolutionary.

The dance I saw was most movingly not about disability, but about how different types of bodies could move and support each other, with crutches and calipers an essential part of the choreography. It was a dance of liberation, not only from preconceived senses of physical limitation, but also from a socially ingrained sense of uselessness which had previously crippled both sets of young people but was now patently demonstrated to be simple nonsense.

Adam Benjamin works with disabled dancers in the UK and South Africa as well as in Ethiopia. His reports interestingly echo Muldoom as he talks of disabled students being initially reluctant 'to take the space' as they clung to supporting walls. This is not surprising. If street children inhabit a place near the bottom of the social heap, they can at least be grateful that they are not in the even more appalling position of the impoverished disabled.

There is a huge danger of self-hatred for both groups, as Yidnekachew explains below, but Adugna members had also to confront their own stereotypical prejudices in regard to disabled people.

Yidnekachew: *Before, although I was a street kid I hated them and the disabled. But recently I understand this is the wrong attitude and now I try to help.*

In talking to students and to Adam Benjamin, I became aware that not only had a confident dance vocabulary quickly emerged between the two groups, but also a sense of mutual responsibility and equality. I have seen similar results in cross-community drama work, but I am tempted to speculate that the intense physicality and need for mutual physical trust brings a special bonding in dance work.

By the end of the training, the integrated group had decided to call themselves the 'Adugna Potentials'. They had performed in public and had great hope – not yet realised – of sustained work together across all areas of the mainstream Adugna programme. They had also gained tremendously in confidence and a sense of self-worth. One of the disabled dancers, Andualem Kebede, told Benjamin:

> Many disabled children are hidden in Addis. We want to be an example for them, not to be afraid or shy. We want to train them to be confident. We want to . . . reach across Ethiopia. We want to change attitudes towards disabled people in Ethiopia.

For Adugna, Andualem Amare displayed a similar pride in the achievements of the integrated group:

> We want to perform in more places. We would like to perform in City Hall where everyone can see us.

Moving outside the city

Huge, impoverished and full of social problems as Addis Ababa is, it is only one city in a country of more than 65 million people, and being the capital it receives the lion's share of innovative assistance. For a number of years, Adugna has had long-term plans gradually to move beyond the capital, both to provide training – and there is surely potential for more Adugna-style groups in this enormous and diverse nation – and to promote advocacy work on behalf of street dwellers, as well as to learn for itself more about the cultures, particularly the dance cultures, of the sixty ethnic groups which make up the population.

The trips to Makele and Debre Markos were the first such visits. Beyond the police work Adugna presented dance performances for local street youth and held a post-performance discussion. Interestingly, many had previously been reluctant to identify themselves, as they moved into the world of professional dancers, with their previous despised status as street children. But in Makele they did identify themselves as, and with, street children, and by so doing were able to communicate directly with local youth. The intention of finding local dancers to build on their own traditional dance repertoire was less successful and would probably have needed more time and the assistance of local expertise.

The second piece of outreach work took place in the town of Nazret, some seventy kilometres outside Addis Ababa. This week-long workshop with 165 young people, half of them street dwellers and half from a local school Girls Club, was supported by the police Child Protection Unit and the Forum on Street Children which brings together a number of agencies working with destitute young people.

The work with the Girls Club had been specifically requested because of perceived problems of lack of self-esteem and lack of application in female students. The group elected to work with issues of prostitution and HIV, while the street dwellers identified drug use as the issue they wanted to discuss. Once again, as with the police project (although dance was used), the focus for such issue-based work was Forum Theatre. This was the first time Adugna had run such a large-scale initiative without one of their major trainers present, and they were quite worried about the prospect. However, the Nazret young people were tremendously enthusiastic, and again the street children identified strongly with Adugna. Responses show the impact of the work: *'The things I got from you – love, happiness, self-confidence and politeness'*; *'The training was very nice but the time was short. I hope you will come back again.'*

Into the future

Throughout the last two years of their training, the Adugna students were aware that they were being prepared for an independent future, when they would have to choose if they wanted to stay with the group, and would have to begin to take control over the way they would work. When the training period came to an end at the close of 2001, the trainees were given three months' paid decision-making time.

It had already been made abundantly clear to me by the dancers during my interviews in August 2001 that most of them were totally committed to staying with the group in at least the short to medium term. This was driven partly by justified uncertainty as to how they would negotiate the outside world without mutual and external support, but partly by a very strong sense in many of the group that they had much to offer as community artists which could be best delivered under the Adugna umbrella. Among the young men there were a couple of exceptions who were keen to try their independent ability to earn a living as a teacher (Yidnekachew) and as a theatre artist working with the professional companies in Addis Ababa (Shiferaw).

At the time of writing, in 2003, the Adugna members, with the support of trainers, Gemini, and particularly the group physiotherapist, Dessalegne Damtew (who has become advisor, support and substitute parent figure to some of the group), are now all working professionally under the company umbrella, although Yidnekachew and Shiferaw are trying to work out how they might operate separately in the longer term.

Six of the group are under a year-long contract to work for Gemini/World Learning in the southern regions of Ethiopia on a project in schools, using dance and Forum Theatre to raise awareness and understanding of HIV/AIDS.

Four members of Adugna are under contract to Gemini working in Addis Ababa as dance development officers. Their brief includes running workshops on HIV/AIDS, working with disabled youth, and beginning the process of working with a new Youth Group of twelve students to train them up to become the next generation of emerging dancers.

Another four are in Paris working with their former trainer, Sylvan Prunenec, as part of his company for four months, and two are attending a three-month summer course on African dance with Germaine Acogny in Senegal.

Finally, Yitbarak is working as a full-time dance teacher at the International Sandford School, and Yidnekachew is working in support of the group's administration, while looking into setting up his own programme working with children with learning difficulties.

Things can still go wrong for Adugna. They are receiving considerable support from Royston Muldoom, Mags Byrne and the Gemini organisation, and will continue to need help for some years in terms of project planning, fundraising and administration. But the future is immeasurably brighter for all members of the group than it was five years ago.

I think their work also makes the future just a little brighter for street dwellers and other people with whom Adugna works, as they in turn are offered chances for skills training, for analysis of issues affecting their lives, for encountering an inspiring example, and for participating in the joy of the dance. The rather conservative arts institutions operating in Addis Ababa have been given a challenge which it will be interesting to see if they can respond to in opening up arts agenda; and the development community has been given the opportunity to work in a new way and to reexamine some of its approaches to development methodology and practice.

There are still concerns for me about this work. Has it drawn the dancers too far from their communities in terms of expectations and being able to fit in with a deeply conservative society? My feeling is probably not, but I am not an Ethiopian and this has certainly been a worry for some Gemini staff. Certainly the role models who have most deeply affected the dancers have been dominantly, though not exclusively, European. Should we be worried that Meseret in her quotation earlier identifies with the freedom experienced by European women, and that European contemporary dance has been the strongest dance influence for most members of Adugna? Undoubtedly it would have been better if there could have been more strong Ethiopian female role models and Ethiopian dance models to draw on, but the organisers were largely unable to find these, so it is difficult to know what alternative strategies for empowerment they could have utilised.

I said at the beginning of this chapter that I wanted to explore what it was that dance could offer that was different from other art forms. I think what I have most noticed is how the physicality of dance inspired trust and empathy between those working together, as well as how the joy of dance inspires feelings of liberation and emotional and intellectual release. What dance is less equipped for is specific analysis of particular issues, and I am still concerned that Adugna may be pushed by employing agencies into too much analytic theatre at a fairly basic level, rather than imaginative use of the liberating, transformational vehicle of dance for which they have been primarily trained and which they use so wonderfully.

I would like to see a move towards possibly more deeply syncretic work, drawing on contemporary and traditional dance and theatre forms working freely together; and I would very much like to see further integration with the disabled dance group. All these are ambitions that would require more, sensitive, training. For now I think Adugna has proved and is proving the worth of the investment in the group and the potential it has to work with a huge range of Ethiopian communities. To return to Freire, with whom I opened this essay; I am quite sure that many people, especially in the poor communities of the poorest countries, are never given the chance to live fully human lives. The members of Adugna have been given that chance. They have seized it; they value it immensely and now they are offering it on to others, so that they, too, may have the chance, not just to survive, but also to live and engage with their own destinies. In my view this is true development.

Note: Although I have consulted and interviewed widely in the course of writing this chapter, there are inevitably differences of understanding and interpretation on certain points relating to the project. The chapter as written and the views it expresses are entirely my responsibility.

NOTES

1. Paulo Freire, *Pedagogy of the Oppressed* (Harmondsworth: Penguin, 1972).
2. In Ethiopia everyone is addressed by their first names no matter what their status. This is because second names are not family names but simply the given name of the father. All quotations unless otherwise attributed are from Adugna members, all of whom I interviewed in August 2001. The eighteen members of Adugna are:

Women	Men
Assrat Mammo	Aberaham Tamene
Guenet Demissie	Adisu Demissie
Meskerem Tadesse	Andualem Amare
Meseret Yinga	Asfaw Haile
Nuria Mohammed	Gebremeskel Shewarega
Yehualawork Abebe	Getachew Abera
	Junaid Jemal
	Mekbul Jemal
	Minyahil Kebede
	Shiferaw Tariku
	Yidnekachew Essatu
	Yitbarak Wondimu

3. A *kebele* is roughly equivalent to a British ward. It is the smallest unit of government administration.

4. Public schools in Addis Ababa are so oversubscribed that despite there often being around a hundred children in a class, there is a system of 'hot-seating', or shifts, with different groups attending in the morning and the afternoon.

5. Infant mortality rates in Ethiopia generally run at 78 per 1,000; however, with multiple births this rises steeply to nearly 400 per 1,000 for children in the first year of life.

6. 'Adugna' means destiny or fate in Amharic.

7. All quotations are drawn from an interview conducted by the present writer with Royston Muldoom in June 2001.

8. The *birr* is the Ethiopian unit of currency. At the time of writing, there were 8 *birr* to the US dollar.

9. The joker is the name given to the person who facilitates inter-action between performers and 'spectactors' in a piece of Forum Theatre.

7 The Day of Mourning/Pilgrim Progress in Plymouth, USA. Contesting processions: a report on performance, personification and empowerment

RICARDO VILLANUEVA

'Plimoth Plantation – *Where history repeats itself.*'
Plymouth Township Website: http.//Pilgrims.net

22 November, 9.55 a.m., EST. Mayflower House, Plymouth Colony, New England: Twenty-nine pilgrims, survivors of their first harsh winter in America, were putting the finishing touches to their Sunday best. Shoe buckles were polished, starched aprons smoothed, muskets cleaned and oiled with puritanical zeal. Despite their festive apparel, the pilgrims' faces were sombre. Outside some 300 Wampanoags and their allies awaited them. Their chants and drums sounded an aggressive, possibly hostile tattoo. Last-minute assurances were given and received by the whites. They could show no fear. At the hour, the pilgrims cautiously filed into the street. This was the Plymouth Pilgrim Progress Procession, 22 November, 1997.

Over the past thirty-four years in Plymouth, Massachusetts, contending forces have organised and performed contesting processions, grappling over the signification and legitimacy of America's origin myth: Thanksgiving. The contending performers – *Mayflower* descendants and their followers, *and* Native Americans from the tribes belonging to the United American Indians of New England (UAINE) and their supporters – have struggled over the meaning of this national holiday, with Native Americans preferring to consider it the National Day of Mourning, memorialising the genocide of American aboriginals by European colonisers.

Later that day in 1997, the two processions inadvertently clashed when a scheduling error put them on the same street at the same time. The ensuing civil disturbance (or police riot, depending on whom you ask) resulted in dozens of arrests and scores of injuries among the Wampanoags, Pilgrims and Plymouth police involved in the mêlée. Litigation ensued over the next year, resulting in radical changes in the way Plymouth views and presents its Pilgrim and Native American past. And these changes are having rippling effects on how America itself regards its origin myth.

The parade may perhaps be among the earliest forms of group performance. It is both profession of faith and display of power, providing solace to the faithful and scourge to the wavering. However, when employed against an ideological enemy, the parade configures itself into its most empowering and potent form. Confronted with a counterdemonstration, the parade is prelude to war, and this cannot be resolved until only one parade remains: the triumphal procession, the consolidator of power and dominance, signifier of the defeat and submission of the Other.

As will be enlarged upon later, the Day of Mourning Procession began as the result of Massachusetts officials' denying Wampanoags the right to speak in 1970 at the 350th anniversary of the Pilgrim landing at Plymouth Rock. Moreover, at that time, according to the US federal government, the majority of Wampanoags did not 'exist' as Native Americans.

Lacking even this minimal legitimacy, the Wampanoags organised the first Day of Mourning (DOM) Procession, when they personified themselves as Indians, empowering themselves to claim their own identity. Moreover, they determined to change the consciousness of all Americans with respect to how America was founded and what this meant for indigenous people. And the Day of Mourning preceded and may be viewed as part of the political epiphany that unified Native Americans across the country in the American Indian Movement (AIM).

For the small, initially powerless group that engendered the DOM procession, their performance and persistence resulted in remarkable changes and provides an example to others of how significant empowerment can be realised through performance. Understandably, little has been written in the popular press or media about the DOM. In a nation that is shy at best with self-criticism, going after sacred pilgrim cows would be readership-ratings suicide. Given this, I set out for Plymouth in November 2001 to record what I could about these contending processions, made all the more perilous following the September 11 terrorist attacks and resulting rabid, eyes-rolled-back-into-the-skull patriotism. The good part? The air fare to Boston was dirt cheap.

As I clear all the jungle-camouflage uniforms and automatic weapons in Logan Airport, the only reminders of September 11 are the ubiquitous American flags. Yet here in New England, the flags seem oddly fitting among all the preserved colonial buildings. Along the southern shore from Boston, the terrain is sandy bog with mild hills. Stripped bare by a recent storm, the deciduous trees present a naked and forbidding aspect broken only by anaemic pines that line the highway. This is not a fertile land. It would not support any but the most parsimonious, and then not without hardship.

On Thanksgiving the gloomy overcast of the previous days has lifted. The severe formality of the white and black colonial town is warmed by the golden light of a fall morning. Amid the brick, plain white clapboard and church spires, I locate the Mayflower Society House, off North Street, where twenty-nine locals have changed into the apparel of the seventeenth-century English religious separatists known as Pilgrims: for some, their forebears. Unannounced and uninvited, I walk into the grounds behind the Mayflower House where the Pilgrim processioners are making their final preparations. In starched white linen and blue and black capes, they seem like moths assembling for an unfamiliar daylight migration.

I introduce myself to William Fillebrown, who says he has been in the Pilgrim Progress Procession for ten years. He says the real veteran is Gary Marks, who has participated for thirty years. I ask both Plymouth natives what the procession means to them. Gary Marks answers:

I wouldn't miss it for the world, as long as I'm asked. Because I think it represents the great odyssey of the human spirit, and a sense of perseverance the likes of which most moderns would never even learn. The conviction of these people to live and, if necessary, sacrifice themselves for an ideal, for a purpose that was beyond their own wellbeing. Not knowing about what was here including what the relations would be with Native Americans, about which Europeans had a very bad understanding. Misunderstanding who they were. And yet, they held a compact with them that lasted for fifty-three years with the Wampanoag locally, with [their leader] Massasoit and his people. But to me it's a triumph not only of the human spirit, but of a covenant relation to God that was able to sustain them through every hardship.
So is this part of your religious beliefs also?
Well, I am a minister of the Church of the Pilgrimage. He's a minister, he's a minister . . . . he's a minister . . .
So you're ministers?
Yeah, you're surrounded by them, and you're in deep trouble![1]

Their faces break into broad grins, and I am relieved as Deborah Fille-brown joins our group. She adds:

I live here in Plymouth also. I'm a minister's wife. This is the first year that I've done it on Thanksgiving Day. We did it one time last summer. It's done every Friday evening in August. And we brought our grandchildren to take part also. We had a wonderful time doing it then and said we'd like to come back and do it on Thanksgiving morning. And so they called us because they said they had need of people. And I think that what Gary Marks said is apropos. I think what the Pilgrims did, what they stood for . . . I feel a personal connection to them as well.[2]

And suddenly I realise that many of the people here are not just 'projecting' pilgrims in the way that the well-trained living-history actors do at the Plimoth Plantation. Rather, as members of the various congregations, especially the Church of the Pilgrimage, founded by the Pilgrims,[3] they are honouring the founders of their faith. The Pilgrim Progress is a religious procession! The empowerment they achieve is the consecration and preservation of a church founded in America 371 years ago. They do not claim that it is the first church in America nor the exclusive origin of the USA. But, in a land of religious diversity and dissent where so many other churches have failed or changed beyond recognition, their church still lives and adheres to the dogma and practice of its first members. Their performance, again for many, is a claim of identity and a testimony of faith. Reverend Marks adds:

> It's an incredible story that in some ways is obscured by the
> celebration of Thanksgiving. And yet ironically Thanksgiving
> kept that story alive long enough to ferret out what the details
> were. And the sacrifices made in England to get over to
> Holland. The story was lost for 200 years. Basically, there was
> remembrance of people landing here, but even *Bradford's
> Journal, Mourt's Relation* was lost for about 200 years. It was
> found in the Bishop of London's Fulham summer palace by a
> man who was doing research in an otherwise undistinguished
> book, but he realised that there were quotations from Bradford
> that were quoted nowhere else, so he began a search for it.
> And evidently it was in the Prince's library in the Old South
> Church and was taken at the time the British evacuated
> Boston in the Revolution from England. Then it was lost for
> 150 years after that . . .[4]

And I realise that in their eagerness to tell their story, they are delaying their procession. They are warm and sincere people. Reluctantly I ask if I might continue my queries later, so they can proceed.

Plymouth resident David Jehle, in charge of the procession, gives a last-minute direction. I record it:

> You are going up and on your way to give thanks to God and
> his providence for sparing the number of lives that were spared
> [the first winter]. It is in that sense a Thanksgiving. As history
> records, the group was led by a drum, and they did carry arms.

There were wild animals out there. They were not familiar
with the Indians at that point. They did not know what to
expect. They were just being prepared. This is not a military
march. The drummer would go through town to signal to
everybody that it's time for church so that they would all fall
in and march as a group just for safety reasons. And so I will
be leading with the drum. We're going to go down the hill and
by Plymouth Rock, and up Leyden Street. And when we go
up, we cross the centre of town. We're going to go right for a
little ways before we take the stairs up to Burial Hill. We'll
go to the fort site where we'll do a little re-enactment of a
church service there . . . When we get up at the top, when they
worshipped, the men and the women did not sit together. The
women will follow Cheryl Doherty and go off to the left, and
the men will follow me, and we'll make a semicircle there at
the site of the fort. We will open the service by my asking the
men to remove their hats, and we will sing a song. The
pilgrims didn't have hymn books, so they 'lined' their songs,
and so I will lead the singing. I will sing a line, and you repeat
after me. Let's sing the first one, which may be familiar to
most of you:

Bow down thine ear Jehovah, an-swer me,
for I am poor, afflicted and needy.
Keep thou my soul, for merciful am I.
My God thy ser-vant save that trusts in thee.

Very good. I may add a couple of verses, so just pay attention.
You will be happy to know that that is the more difficult of
the two songs we're doing. Then we're going to hear the
message given by Governor Elder Bruce, who is Reverend
Gary Marks. After he finishes his message, we'll sing another
song. You'll probably recognise the melody:

Shout to Jehovah all the earth,
Serve you, Jehovah, with glad-ness.
Before him come with singing mirth.
Know that Jehovah, He God is.

Excellent. Then we have a benediction. Then we have the third song, and I will remind you do not repeat that after me. I will do that one by myself. And after that we'll put our hats on, the gentlemen, and we will proceed down the hill, come through the centre of town, and back here.

Outside on the streets throngs of people are awaiting the procession. Well, not throngs. Perhaps a few hundred in all, along the whole route. It is about a fifty-fifty mix of locals and tourists in town for Thanksgiving, mostly for tours of the Pilgrim Hall, *Mayflower II*, and the Plimoth Plantation. Plymouth is not an intensely touristic town, its largest attraction having nothing to do with Pilgrims. Cranberryland is a pavilion run by the Ocean Spray company and dedicated to the joys and wonders of that fruit. Here at the Plymouth Rock temple (which will be elucidated later), the crowd grows expectant as we hear the approach of drums (or 'drum', to be precise). To paraphrase Kurt Vonnegut, we hear:

Rented a tent, rented a tent.
Rented a,
Rented a,
Rented a tent.

Soon the Pilgrims appear. Solemn and contained in a procession of twos and threes, the Pilgrims come. And the Pilgrims go. No marching bands follow. No elephants or mounted police. There are no parade floats, celebrities, sports stars, politicians or Miss Cranberry 2001, nor any other kind of beauty queen. There is only the now diminishing sound of 'rented a tent, rented a tent . . .' Next to me a five-year-old boy asks his father, 'That was it?' The father 'performs' someone very interested in a distant object out at sea.

The Pilgrim Procession proceeds as per plan, and I hike over to Cole's hill, above the 'rock' next to the Massasoit statue where participants for the Day of Mourning Procession are gathering. Even in the preparation stages, I notice stark differences in the DOM Procession. For one, no one is wearing a costume except for a fellow broiling in complete Inuit (Eskimo) togs from shaggy hood down to mukluks, and

161

I hope he is reserving his strength for when the anti-fur, deep ecology people (nearby) tire of pretending not to see him. Unlike the Pilgrim Procession, this one abounds in overt signs and banners, a sample of which include: 'Free Leonard Peltier':[5] 'We Are Not Vanishing, We Are Not Conquered, We Are Stronger Than Ever'; 'Slavery, Genocide, and Lies, This is Your Thanksgiving'; 'Homophobia, the Pilgrims' Gift'; and a flag with a photograph of the earth, presumably an ecology symbol.

Also unlike the Pilgrim Procession, the Day of Mourning partic-ipants represent every imaginable race and ethnicity, including sev-eral young Muslim women wearing their traditional headscarves, a brave gesture at that time. The age of the (about) 300 participants ranges from toddlers to well beyond seventy. As signs are prepared and banners are strung between poles, the mood is mellow, almost festive. They are happy to be here, but also feel that what they are doing is important. And, given the permanent changes in the signifi-cation of Plymouth and the Pilgrims that they have made following the 1997 riot, there is also a sense of accomplishment. Their thirty years of marching have made a palpable difference, as we shall detail later.

Today, four years after the riot, the DOM Procession has evolved into an almost venerable routine. As per an agreement with the town and police, the DOM regulates itself, DOM members with yellow arm-bands providing order and security for the speakers whom UAINE has authorised. Plymouth Town police are distant and discreet. But these precautions seem unnecessary, as all of us on Coles Hill surrender to the rare joy of a temperate Thanksgiving Day. Excluding a pair of local videomakers, there is no electronic press on scene. Up Leyden Street one local network affiliate reporter has been fussing with her makeup for nearly an hour. She is in her early twenties and seems indifferent to the events below. (Later that evening this one channel will show five seconds of B-roll of the Pilgrim Progress and DOM processions.)

Surrounding the twenty-foot statue of Massasoit cradling a peace pipe, the DOM participants gather for a prayer and blessings from Sam Sapiel, the religious leader sent by the American Indian

Movement to tend to the spiritual needs of the processioners. Eagle feather in one hand and a smouldering sheaf of sage in the other, Sapiel consecrates the gathering, asking for the blessings of the Great Spirit. Afterwards we spend the next hour listening to a variety of speakers on a raised, portable platform. A Mayan Indian talks about the troubles in Central America. There is an emissary from the rebelling tribes in Chiapas, Mexico. A representative from New York talks about the Puerto Rican separatist movement. Pleas are made for the release of Leonard Peltier and Mumia Abu Jamal.[6] There are familiar speeches about the genocide of Native Americans, ongoing poverty in reservations, continuing racism and discrimination.

I am sitting near the platform with Nan Anastasia, editor of the town's newspaper, the *Old Colony Memorial*, and town manager Eleanor Beth. It is not that the issues are not important, but this year there is a preaching-to-the-choir, 'post-modern' feel to the speeches, as if someone were recreating the 1970s for a film. We are jolted back into 2001 when Tall Oaks, a Cape Wampanoag Elder, declaims: 'I thought it was terrible when the World Trade Center Twin Towers came down. Just terrible. It's the worst thing that's ever happened in this country since they were built on stolen Indian land in the first place . . .'

There are loud cheers from the DOM participants. Tall Oaks adds: 'The only difference between Osama Bin Laden and the Pilgrims is the costume and the culture and the religion they claim to represent . . .' Wild cheers with war whoops this time. And the speeches go on, concluding with a declaration by Roland Moonaum James, who is one of the leaders of the DOM Procession:

Some ask us: will you ever stop protesting? Some day we will stop protesting. We will stop protesting when the merchants of Plymouth are no longer making millions of dollars off the blood of our slaughtered ancestors. We will stop protesting when we can act as sovereign nations on our own land without the interference of the Bureau of Indian Affairs and what Sitting Bull called the 'favourite ration chiefs'. When corporations stop polluting our mother, the earth. When racism has been eradicated. When the oppression of

Two-Spirited people is a thing of the past. We will stop
protesting when homeless people have homes and no child
goes to bed hungry. When police brutality no longer exists in
communities of colour. We will stop protesting when Leonard
Peltier and Mumia Abu Jamal and the Puerto Rican
independentistas and all political prisoners are free . . .

And then, after prayers by the statue of Massasoit, the DOM Procession winds down in front of Plymouth Rock, where for the thirty-first
time, Malcolm X is quoted: 'We didn't land on Plymouth Rock, it
landed on us.'[7] After deconstructing the Plymouth Rock myth and
generally heaping abuse on the fraud, the procession proceeds up Leyden Street, and there is a brief speech in the square where Metacomet's
head was displayed. After more prayers they also retire off the set of
signification and share a communal meal.

Lest we be misled by the surfaces of the DOM Procession, let
us remember that it *looks* like a 1970s protest march because in many
ways *it is* a 1970s protest, preserved into the new millennium by the
determination of its participants. This in itself is extraordinary when
one considers the events of the past thirty years that have divided so
many groups and causes that once marched together in the back draft
of the Black Civil Rights Movement. As protest procession, the Day
of Mourning has no equal in America in terms of both diversity and
empowerment. To understand the significance of the latter fully, first
one must appreciate the purpose and meaning of the Thanksgiving
origin myth, how it was developed, how it was manifested within Pilgrim institutions in Plymouth, and, finally, how the Day of Mourning
changed these things for ever.

The myth
'Where history repeats itself.'
My country tis of thee
Sweet land of liberty,
Of thee I see.
Land of the Pilgrims' pride,
Land where our fathers died,

From sea-e-e to shi-ning sea
Le-et freedom ring.
      (sung to the tune of 'God Save the Queen')

This tune, unlike the 'Star Spangled Banner', the American anthem, is easy to learn and sing. After the pledge of allegiance, it is the most repeated litany in our schools. It is the one song that all of America knows well.

When I was a child, each year as Thanksgiving approached, my primary grade school took on a variety of projects. Dried corn, squash and other signs of the fall harvest garlanded classrooms. We constructed murals on butcher paper representing the venerated icons of Thanksgiving: the signing of the Mayflower Compact; the Pilgrims' landing at Plymouth Rock and Squanto showing them how to plant corn; and, finally, the harvest and Thanksgiving feast of Pilgrims and Indians. This iconic triptych resolved the contradictions of the two cardinal American virtues – self-reliance and cooperation.

Thanksgiving was not just another 'curricular component' in the ponderous school year. On the preceding Wednesday the school cafeteria prepared a Thanksgiving feast, which could include anything, but, to be authentic, had to offer three foods: turkey, cranberries and pumpkin pie. The meal was unusually edible for school fare because the principal, administrators and many parents were present to witness the ritual that followed. In a ship's interior of cardboard and papier-mâché, William Bradford, Miles Standish and others in boyish forms huddle around a table draped with an oversized parchment. Behind this tableau an equal number of Pilgrim 'women' mend clothing, attend infants and prepare food, all the while casting adoring glances at the 'men'. A diminutive narrator would read: 'Seeking religious freedom, the Pilgrims left their native land and arrived off Cape Cod on November 21, 1620. There, aboard their ship, the *Mayflower*, they wrote and signed. . .'

The special meal was followed by a performance of the Pilgrim icons in the most sacred of American secular dramas. And, as if to underscore the dread significance of these observances, the very laws of universal mandatory school attendance were suspended in honour of the occasion. School was out for the Thanksgiving holiday. The only comparable event during the school year was Christmas, with its attendant choruses and Nativity play, which through the 1960s and 1970s was mounted in one form or another in most American public schools with little effective resistance from non-Christians and civil libertarians. For us children, the significance of these events could not be clearer: one explained the origin of country, the other the origin of God.

For schoolchildren of my generation, as for most American schoolchildren today, it is common knowledge that our nation was founded on Plymouth Rock. And if Washington and Jefferson were our Founding Fathers, the Pilgrims were our forefathers, and the Mayflower Compact was the direct precursor to the US Constitution. In short, Thanksgiving is the present origin myth of the United States of America and, according to Mircea Eliade, fulfils all the characteristics of an origin myth: 'It constitutes the history of the acts of the founders, the Supernaturals; it is considered to be true; it tells how an institution came into existence; in performing the ritual associated with the myth, one "experiences" knowledge of the origin and claims one's patriarchy. Thus one "lives" the myth as a religion.'[8]

If Thanksgiving instructs America's children and inhabits the national psyche, so, too, does it dominate the economy. More Americans travel during Thanksgiving than at any other weekend of the year. Between Thanksgiving and Christmas more goods are bought and sold than in the remaining three-quarters of the year combined. Thanksgiving is the foundation of the make-or-break segment of the business year.

However, as America's major holiday and national origin myth, Thanksgiving leaves much to be desired. A primary objection is the ethnocentricity of the myth, which excludes most of the ethnicities and cultures that constitute America. Secondly, and of particular importance, the myth omits the atrocious bloodshed committed by Pilgrims and other English colonists against Native Americans and the virtual annihilation of the latter's cultures after the initial relatively peaceful years at Plymouth.

The most touted quality of the Pilgrims is their virtue. Adherents point out, as we shall detail later, that unlike other Europeans who immediately plunged into the murder, subjugation and enslavement of natives, the Plymouth colony maintained peaceful coexistence with their Wampanoag allies during the first fifty years after establishing the colony. However, of the 102 original settlers (only thirty-five of whom were religious separatists, later known as Pilgrims) only twenty-six men and four women survived the first winter. Hence, as they were outnumbered and armed with cumbersome muskets that were only marginally better than native weapons, one wonders if *realpolitik* did not play a greater role than Christian virtue in the peace.

In any event, after 1620 succeeding years brought more shiploads of Pilgrims, along with their less scrupulous fellow religious dissidents, the Puritans, who embarked upon a profitable scheme of capturing natives and selling them into slavery in the West Indies. In 1636–7 New England had its first Euro-native bloodshed, the Pequot War, which introduced the natives to the concept of total war. A yet more violent war ensued in 1675 when colonists executed three Wampanoags and attempted to disarm the natives. Their king, Metacomet (King Philip), retaliated, and the bloodbath that followed has no equal in American history for ferocious desperation. Of some ninety Puritan towns, fifty-two were attacked and twelve destroyed. Several thousand colonists and perhaps double that number of natives were killed. As social historian James Loewen notes: 'King Philip's War cost more American lives in combat, Anglo and Native, in absolute terms than the French and Indian War, the Revolution, the War of 1812, the Mexican War or the Spanish-American War. In proportion to population, casualties were greater than any other American war.'[9] After being captured, Metacomet was executed and his head was placed on a pike in the Plymouth town square across from the First Congregational Church founded by the Pilgrims, this forming a powerful concluding icon for the Pilgrim-Wampanoag narrative but for obvious reasons excluded from the origin myth.

How, then, was America's origin myth constructed? After the American Revolution President Washington proclaimed national days of thanksgiving and prayer in November 1789 and 1795.[10] Perhaps the most influential force pushing for a national day of thanksgiving was Sara Joseph Hale, editor of the *Ladies' Magazine*, who wrote numerous editorials between 1827 and September 1863, urging a uniform national day of thanksgiving. Her last editorial on the subject stated:

> Would it not be a great advantage, socially, nationally, religiously, to have the day of our American Thanksgiving positively settled? Putting aside the sectional feelings and local incidents that might be urged by any single State or isolated territory that desired to choose its own time would it not be more noble, more truly American, to become national in unity when we offer to God our tribute of joy and gratitude for the blessings of the year?[11]

Partly as a result of Hale's editorials and obviously necessitated by a divided nation's need to find a unifying ritual, President Lincoln proclaimed, on 3 October 1863, the last Thursday in November a national Thanksgiving Day. (Historians generally connect this proclamation to the Battle of Gettysburg, 1–3 July 1863.) Still, Thanksgiving had no association with the Pilgrims in the popular imagination, as evidenced by the Condé Nast Thanksgiving 1864 cover of *Harper's Weekly*, illustrating the figures of Uncle Sam and Columbia serving turkey to people from various cultures around the world seated together at one large table. (Nast was the artist who originated the persona of 'Uncle Sam'.)

Meanwhile, Pilgrim mythology was progressing along its own trajectory. The first elaborations no doubt began with the descendants of the Plymouth Separatists (technically members of the Church of Scrooby, Nottinghamshire, England) who did not claim exclusive use of the 'Pilgrim' sign until perhaps the 1880s. (Before this, 'Pilgrim' was familiar local usage for any early Christian in New England.)

The landing at the rock enters the record in 1741 in a narrative related by Elder Thomas Faunce. The descendants of both John Alden and Mary Chilton claimed their ancestor as the Neil Armstrong of 'the

Plymouth landing', although historians examining *Mourt's Relation* (an account of the colony's first years written in 1622) decided that the first landing occurred several miles north of the boulder that became known as Plymouth Rock.[12]

Historical verisimilitude bowed to the powerful need for a tangible symbol of the Europeans' first contact with the new continent. The rock filled this niche satisfactorily, so that by the time De Tocqueville toured the colonies, he encountered prized fragments venerated as relics among newer American towns.[13] Similarly, a holiday (now long abandoned) known as Forefathers' Day and commemorating the 'first landing' was celebrated on 22 December 1769 in New England and spread nationally thereafter.

In 1843 a ballad written by one Moses Mullins appeared in the *New York Rover*, telling the story of a love triangle between the young John Alden, the middle-aged widower Miles Standish and the maiden Priscilla Molines. This was eclipsed by Longfellow's 1858 *The Courtship of Miles Standish*, which was said to have sold 10,000 copies in London on a single day.[14] Longfellow's narrative is pegged on the conflict between duty and desire, namely John Alden's obligation to convey the amour of his inarticulate friend, Miles Standish, to Priscilla, whom Alden also secretly admires. Priscilla detects this and reciprocates. When Standish learns that she prefers his friend, his outrage and pain change into a murderous bellicosity directed against the natives. Throughout the poem idealised images of the colonists are juxtaposed against demonised views of the Indians.

If Longfellow's narrative evidences a casual acquaintance with then contemporary historical knowledge about the Pilgrims, his descriptions of 'the rock' indicate that he had not bothered to make the short journey from Boston to Plymouth to view the boulder. Had he done so, the sham would have been obvious. First, the stone is far too small to have been used as a landmark for navigation. Second, when landing a wooden boat on a mostly sandy shore, the very last place one would wish to land would be on a rock. Nevertheless, Longfellow writes: 'Down to the Plymouth Rock, that had been to their feet as

a doorstep/Into a world unknown, – the corner-stone of a nation!'
Several stanzas later the master of mixed metaphor has swelled the
stone into a Gibraltar: '. . . but Alden lingered a little/Musing alone on
the shore, and watching the wash of the billows/Round the base of the
rock . . .' Concurrently, like the myth, the designated 'rock' itself was
on its own eccentric trajectory. In 1774 the boulder was split in two
when members of the Forefathers' Association attempted to move the
'altar of liberty' on to a wagon. In 1807 the upper half was hauled up to
the town square, later becoming part of a wall. Here, like Stonehenge,
the rock began to lose pieces to the souvenir hunter's hammer, so in
1834 the rock was moved from that ignominious location to a pro-
tective cage by Pilgrim Hall. During this trip it acquired yet another
fracture. However, according to an entry in Thoreau's 1851 _Diary_,
the cage offered inadequate protection from tourist hammers, and the
town installed additional safeguards. Sixteen years later the stone was
joined with its lower half, combined with the bones of early colonists
discovered during the construction of a sewer, and moved to a protec-
tive canopy. By 1880 '1620' had been carved into the rock, replacing
the earlier rendering in paint.[15]

However, thus far the Plymouth Pilgrims and the American
Thanksgiving were independent signs. This all began to change in
1889 with the publication of Jane G. Austin's novel, _Standish of Stan-
dish_. According to Peggy Baker, director of the Pilgrim Society, historians generally consider the description of Thanksgiving in this romance
as the catalyst for a movement, mostly played out in women's maga-
zines, to 'Pilgrimise' Thanksgiving. The differences between the narratives are great. Longfellow's prose poem includes no Thanksgiving. Austin's story is told from the women's point of view, particularly Priscilla's, with the men's affairs forming the background. The
Thanksgiving chapter, for example, is largely concerned with how
Priscilla and three other women surviving the first winter manage to
improvise all the dishes necessary for three days' feasting for ninety
Wampanoag and twenty-six Pilgrim men. The women's heroic success
in this seems to nourish the ensuing amity between the two cultures,
as evidenced at the conclusion of the gathering when Austin writes of

'the closing ceremonies with which the governor bade a cordial and even affectionate farewell to the king, the prince, their nobles, and their following'.[16]

Two main influences seem responsible for the shift in the privileged meaning of Thanksgiving. First, by the 1880s all organised resistance from Native Americans had ceased and it was, astonishingly, transformed into romance, beginning with Buffalo Bill's Wild West Show, which overnight turned demonised Indian leaders, such as Sitting Bull, into popular entertainers. And by 1911 this nostalgia was combining with a growing sense of guilt, perhaps explaining how 'Ishi', the last of a surviving band of Yana Yahi Indians (and said to be the last 'wild Indian in North America') could wander into a small northern California town and become one of the most beloved, feted personalities of his day.[17]

Second, an unprecedented influx of immigrants from Southern, Central and Eastern Europe, peaking at 8.8 million in 1900,[18] stimulated waves of xenophobia and nativism among Americans of Anglo-Saxon and Northern European descent. This resulted in a system of indoctrination for immigrants dubbed by historians as the 'Americanisation Movement', which found the hybridised Pilgrim Thanksgiving myth ideal for immigrant literature and grade school primers. As stated previously, the myth demonstrated independence and cooperation, but below this surface its deeper structure presented inclusion under an umbrella of white Anglo-Saxon Protestant origin and dominance.

Having fulfilled its role in the Americanisation of the immigrant masses, the Pilgrim Thanksgiving next became the starting-gate for the Christmas (buying) season as the Macy's Department Store Thanksgiving Day Parade. And, lest the reader overlook the importance of this stimulus to the American economy, it should be noted that in 1939 President Roosevelt moved Thanksgiving one week forward at the behest of merchants to boost the economy, only to have to return it to the original last Thursday in November in 1941 as a result of popular protest – which suggests that the holiday had stabilised a sign and now had its culturally conservative defenders.

Plymouth town today

. . . there are plenty of people who use Plymouth as a bedroom community to commute to Boston and would be hard pressed to tell you who the Pilgrims were.

Peggy Baker, director of the Pilgrim Society[19]

'America's Home town'

Plymouth town motto

According to the 2000 US Census, Plymouth County has 461, 098 residents, more than half of whom commute outside the county to work. The overwhelming majority are white, followed by 21,736 African Americans, 2,204 Asians, and 0 American Indians.[20]

If we look at the Native American population, the United Native Americans of New England (UAINE) asserts that there are some 4,000 Wampanoag people in various tribal groups scattered from Plymouth down to Cape Cod and Rhode Island. Of these, only the 900 members of the Aquinnah Wampanoag (Martha's Vineyard) have been recognised by the US government (as of 1987).[21]

The principal colonial iconic topography of Plymouth town begins with Burial Hill, which is surmounted in elevation only by the steeples of the First Congregational and First Unitarian Churches, direct descendants of the Church founded by the Pilgrim Separatists. Burial Hill is consecrated to the remains of Governor William Bradford and the other Pilgrim dead. Below the hill and between the churches is town square, where the Pilgrims displayed the head of Metacomet (King Philip) after the conclusion of King Philip's War. Main Street encloses the bottom of the square, and at North Street is the location of the Mayflower Society House and gathering place for the Pilgrim Progress Procession. Farther north off Chilton Street, we encounter the Pilgrim Hall Museum. If we descend from the square down Leyden Street towards the harbour, we will pass the Plymouth National Wax Museum and find ourselves on Cole's Hill, which is dominated by a colossal statue of Massasoit. He stands at the place where the Day of Mourning Procession gathers. Below Cole's Hill on the waterfront and across Water Street, we find the present location of Plymouth Rock in a neo-Greek temple.[22] The smaller-than-life statue of William

Bradford is installed just south of the temple. (One cannot escape the apprehension that the little man is in for a rude shock should he ever gaze up Cole's Hill at Massasoit.) Just north of the temple lies the *Mayflower II*, a full-scale reproduction built in Bristol and sailed to America on her own keel in 1956. Plimoth Plantation (its directors prefer the seventeenth-century spelling), a recreation of Plymouth Colony during the first years, is two and a half miles south of town.

Plymouth hosts three permanent non-profit research and educational institutions dedicated to Pilgrim history and myth (the Plymouth National Wax Museum is a for-profit tourist attraction). Peggy Baker has been director and head librarian of the Pilgrim Society (which operates Pilgrim Hall Museum) since 1991. The society was formed in 1820, and the museum – claimed to be the oldest in America – opened in 1824. As she explained to me:

> We are a non-profit educational institution whereas the museum is not. So we have a different mission and a different means of operation. As a non-profit, we're transparent; we have to file annual reports. We are accountable. We hold out things in trust to the public. And so we have to operate along those lines. And our mission has always been concentrating on the Pilgrims. That's who we are and what we do, and we use the original seventeenth-century artifacts to tell that story. [By contrast] the Plantation is living history. They don't have the artifacts. And they have widened their mission to include the entire seventeenth-century experience (including Wampanoag culture). Our mission is much more focused.[23]

Caroline Kardell, a *Mayflower* descendant, has served as historian general of the Mayflower Society since the late 1980s. As she told me:

> The Mayflower Society is only made up of people who can prove descent from passengers on the *Mayflower*. The Pilgrim Society of which I am a trustee and a life member also is made up of people who came over not only on the *Mayflower* but [also on] succeeding boats because there were several boats of

Pilgrim women and children who came over after the
Mayflower; and also it's made up of people who are interested
in Pilgrims specifically and Plymouth in general . . . In order
to do lineage papers, we have to have access to all our
reference materials. This is where we do our work. The vaults
contain the lineage papers of everybody who has ever joined
since 1898 when we were formed.[24]

The Mayflower Society asserts that 'tens of millions' of Americans
are *Mayflower* descendants, although only some 20,000 have actually
become members since 1898, with about 5,000 active members currently. Kardell emphasised that neither the Mayflower Society nor
the Pilgrim Society promotes racial purity, pointing out that a former
president of the Pilgrim Society, Reverend Peter Gomes, is an African
American who was raised in Plymouth and was involved in the society
from boyhood. Kardell added:

> Our secretary general, Barbara Bell, who died just two years
> ago, was a direct descendant of one of [King] Philip's wives. He
> had three or four wives. And she had an Indian
> great-great-grandmother . . . Somehow or other, one of her
> ancestors married a nice Indian girl. And she was very proud
> of that. She thought it was great that she was both Pilgrim and
> Indian.[25]

Begun in 1947 by local Harry Hornblower and the Pilgrim Society, the Plimoth Plantation sought to recreate life in the early colony
by accurate reproduction of period living and working spaces and by
staffing these with performers well trained in the dialects, customs
and beliefs of the period. Over the past fifty years, as new historical
insights about the early colonials have emerged, the Plimoth Plantation has adjusted its exhibits and presentations to reflect these. For
example, in 1970 a research library was established with opportunities for working scholars, and in 1973 (after the initial DOM processions), the plantation initiated its Native American Studies Program
'directed, researched, and staffed by Native Americans', which also
interprets Wampanoag and related Indian cultures to visitors.[26]

Moreover, in recent years Plimoth Plantation has not demurred from presenting the less savoury aspects of colonist–Indian relations. For example, a 2001 exhibit entitled 'Irreconcilable Differences' traced the relations between Pilgrims and Wampanoags from initial Euro-settlement through King Philip's War, including such distressing facts as:

> *August 9, 1676*: Governor Josiah Winslow approves the sale of 110 Natives to be sold as slaves out of the colony.
>
> *August 12, 1676*: Philip and his forces are surrounded in a swamp at Mount Hope. A Pocasset Native named Alderman shoots and kills him. His body is quartered. The war is over although 'mopping up' operations continue over the next few months.
>
> *Fall 1676*: Debate rages among colonial religious leaders concerning the desire of some to execute Philip's nine-year-old son. Although fearful of his possible actions as an adult, the colonists compromise by selling him into slavery.[27]

Also in 2001, Plimoth Plantation, its Native American Studies Program and the National Geographic Society published a children's book emphasising the Native American view of, and role in, Thanksgiving. It declared: 'Taking a new look at Thanksgiving means putting aside the myth. It means taking a new look at history. It means questioning what we think we know. It means recovering lost voices – the voices of the Wampanoag people. True history includes the voices of all its participants. Read, listen, and think about our shared history.'[28]

As we can see, the privileged signification of Thanksgiving among Plymouth's Pilgrim institutions has changed over the years, especially compared with contemporary American high school and elementary school texts. Certainly much if not most of this change should be attributed to the struggles of people of colour in America in the 1960s and 1970s. In terms of Thanksgiving and America's origin myth, the most particular site of struggle has been the contending Day of Mourning and Pilgrim Progress Processions.

The Pilgrim Progress/Day of Mourning processions: a brief history

'Pilgrims in the morning, Indians in the afternoon: how do you feel about the processions today?' I asked a Plymouth matron standing in front of her colonial home on Leyden Street. Her eyes became merry, and she smiled as she replied, 'I'll tell you what, it's what makes America great.'

The older procession is the Pilgrim Progress. According to Kardell, 'The Pilgrim Progress, they celebrated it in 1921 because they weren't ready in 1920 when they had the big 300th anniversary celebration. They were still busy removing all the piles of coal and prettying up the wharves because it was a working seaport.'[29] The Day of Mourning Procession did not begin until 1970, this resulting from developments earlier that year associated with the 350th anniversary of the Pilgrim landing. The Massachusetts Department of Commerce invited Wampanoag leader Wamsutta Frank James[30] to speak at the celebration, but it required him to submit an advance copy of his speech. James' speech stated in part:

> Today is a time of celebrating for you . . . but it is not a time of celebrating for me. It is with a heavy heart that I look back upon what happened to my people . . . The Pilgrims had hardly explored the shores of Cape Cod four days before they had robbed the graves of my ancestors, and stolen their corn, wheat, and beans . . . Massasoit, the great leader of the Wampanoag, knew these facts; yet he and his people welcomed and befriended the settlers . . . little knowing that . . . before fifty years were to pass, the Wampanoags . . . and other Indians living near the settlers would be killed by their guns or dead from diseases that we caught from them . . . Although our way of life is almost gone and our language is almost extinct, we the Wampanoags still walk the lands of Massachusetts . . . What has happened cannot be changed, but today we work toward a better America, a more Indian America where people and nature once again are important.[31]

Disinvited, James and other Native Americans then organised the first Day of Mourning (DOM) Procession. Shirley Mills, 72, has been participating in the DOM Procession since 1971. A Native American who married into and was adopted by the Wampanoag tribe, Mills recalled:

> My mind goes through many phases when I'm walking. I think back to the days when they used to put the police dogs on us when we walked. Those early Seventies, we had a hard time. That's when the Pilgrim Parade of Progress, that's what they used to call it, was going on . . . The images are still burned in my mind, the Pilgrims marching with the rifle in one hand and the Bible in the other. And there they were getting the police to put their dogs on us, and we weren't doing anything. We weren't hurting anyone. We were just simply walking and going to the different sites much like we did today, but we didn't have any plaques or anything. We would just go to the different places, say prayers, like where King Philip's head had been on that stick for so long. Just different things like that which go through my mind; I just reflect on that. [I remember] all the people who joined us over the years and how exciting it was when they used to go on the *Mayflower* and all those people from cross country coming here. As a result of that, I ended up joining the American Indian Movement. So a lot of my thoughts intertwine with UAINE and AIM. I met all those people, and it was very good for me because as a result I got to Sundance out at Rosebud [a Lakota Sioux Nation reservation] because we had a spiritual leader in common . . . and it was just a wonderful experience.[32]

Mills's colleague and companion is Sam Sapiel, who explained:

> I've been down here about twenty-six to twenty-seven years. I got here a year late, a couple of years late. Things had already started. I used to travel up north with the traditional people . . . The American Indian Movement came into existence, and

they put a chapter in Boston. So [Shirley] and other people asked if I could come down and help them do spiritual things. And I said, yeah, I will. So I have been here for twenty-seven years . . . My Indian name is Gehnuth. It means fish pickle. My other name is Aselma. I can't tell you what that means because I'm still in that stage of learning a lot of things . . .[33]

Sapiel leads prayers and ministers to the spiritual needs of the DOM processioners, although he states:

I don't declare myself as a medicine man.[34] I feel good [about my role in the DOM Procession] . . . I feel great because I'm doing something for my people, all of my people that are here and the ones that support us. I feel good about it all because I want to be with them. Hey, I could be home having a good Thanksgiving dinner watching some ball game. I would rather be with the people. That's my job, to be with the people, and I enjoy it. That's why I come down here from the North to help the American Indian Movement and my people here. They wanted some kind of a spiritual leader, so I volunteered to come down. I've been here ever since . . . Twenty-seven years in this area, about twenty-four to twenty-five years in the parade.[35]

Various acts of subversion or vandalism, depending on one's point of view, have taken place in Plymouth in association with the Day of Mourning. Protesters have splashed red paint on Plymouth Rock and dressed the Governor Bradford statue in Klu Klux Klan robes. In 1995 UAINE buried the rock with sand. Although there had been some minor altercations between processioners and police, over the thirty years the processions have run concurrently (albeit ideally at different times on Thanksgiving Day); trouble did not occur until 1996, when, as Nan Anastasia, editor of the *Old Colony Memorial* newspaper, related:

There was another year when, after the march into the church, the church kind of disinvited the Progress from actually going to the Union Service afterwards. The time of the Progress was changed to one o'clock. It's usually held in the morning at ten o'clock. That meant that it clashed with the Day of Mourning, which is held at noon. And that's the year there was sort of a stand-off on the street. That was the year before the arrests . . . There was a lot of talk in the town after that, and some of the people say the police shouldn't have backed down and called for more force. The year following that . . . there were more arrests. There was a march through the streets for the Day of Mourning, and the police tried to stop it.[36]

Peggy Baker generally agrees, but places some blame on the UAINE:

The year before [the 1997 disturbance/riot], the Native American Day of Mourning, there had been a change in the time of the Pilgrim Progress, and the two events collided. And the police turned back the Pilgrim Progress. And then they were severely criticised for that. The Pilgrim Progress has been going on for a long time. They had done their little permitting business; they were all legal. UAINE had not. And so I think that perhaps the police were on edge.[37]

Accounts of the arrests in 1997 are widely varying, with some calling it a provocation by non-native outsiders, others a civil disturbance, and others still an unprovoked police riot. According to Kardell:

That was when the police overreacted. However, the children and adult women in that parade were scared for their lives because the Indians were very threatening. You wouldn't believe the number of people who come here in saffron robes, and who are definitely not Indians, and people from all over the cities who were brought down at the beginning of this . . . and there are white Americans who join them, you know, the radicals who believe the revisionist history.[38]

Mills recalled:

. . . I think that was the year they didn't want us to go in the church. I remember that first stop we made at that big church, they didn't want us to go in there, and then it turned out the minister came out and said yes, these people are allowed to come in here. After that my granddaughter was kind of upset. She wanted to go home, so I went home with her. Sam [Sapiel] stayed because he had the drum . . . He heard all this noise, marching around the corner, and he went to see what was happening, and they told him they don't want us in the street. They want us on the sidewalk. So he said, let's conform and go on the sidewalk. And then without any other thing happening, the police just grabbed him, and I could see all that on tape because someone was taping the whole thing. Unbelievable what people went through.[39]

Nan Anastasia covered the 1997 processions for her newspaper:

Oh, I was there. People were arrested. I believe they were all released that day, but they were arrested. There's definitely different viewpoints of what happened. And there was no place on the street where you could see everything that happened that day. The Day of Mourning took place as usual. They started to march up Leyden Street. A police captain asked them to get off the middle of the street and move to the sidewalks. There was a confrontation, and the arrests started, and from there it got very confusing. There was some pepper spray used to subdue some of the people. There were some claims that people were injured by pepper spray. One police officer had an asthma attack and also had a knee injury, which he is still recovering from. I didn't see anyone injured. I didn't see anyone bleeding. There were some very dramatic photographs, but it didn't look anything out of the routine for when people get arrested. It's always an upsetting scene.[40]

At the time, UAINE was making a video of the Day of Mourning Procession with help from People's Video, a community video non-profit group from New York. According to People's Video representative Sue Harris, 'a number of people were detained and beaten by the police.

The United American Indians of New England sued the City of Plymouth and used the video as evidence.'[41]

Viewing the video, one sees various people passively resisting police instructions to move off the street, this amid generalised jeering. As the police begin making arrests, the force they use does not seem inappropriate. The video appears to confirm Anastasia's account. However, Mahtowin Munro, Wampanoag co-organiser of the DOM Procession with UAINE leader Roland Moonaum James (son of Wamsutta Frank James) adds that the video 'did not capture some of the worst cop abuse'.[42]

Charges by the City of Plymouth and counterclaims by the UAINE were dropped on 19 October 1998 when an out-of-court settlement was made in negotiations between UAINE representatives, the American Civil Liberties Union and the Plymouth Selectmen. (Plymouth retains the New England Selectman form of town government rather than the mayoral-city council system of most American cities.) Terms included the town paying $135,000 dollars into a fund to promote education about Wampanoag and Native American culture. The town also acknowledged UAINE's right to conduct a Day of Mourning Procession in perpetuity. And, finally, the town agreed to install a plaque on Cole's Hill that recorded the Wampanoag view of Thanksgiving and one in town square marking the location of Metacomet's severed head with the proviso that the text was approved by the Massachusetts Historical Commission. UAINE submitted the following:

> Since 1970, Native Americans have gathered at noon on Cole's Hill in Plymouth to commemorate a National Day of Mourning on the US Thanksgiving holiday. Many Native Americans do not celebrate the arrival of the Pilgrims and other European settlers. To them, Thanksgiving Day is a reminder of the genocide of millions of their people, the theft of their lands, and the relentless assault on their culture. Participants in a National Day of Mourning honor Native ancestors and the struggles of Native peoples to survive today.

It is a day of remembrance and spiritual connection as well as
a protest of the racism and oppression which Native
Americans continue to experience.

(Plaque on Cole's Hill)

After the Pilgrims' arrival, Native Americans in New England
grew increasingly frustrated with the English settlers' abuse
and treachery. Metacomet (King Philip), a son of the
Wampanoag sachem (leader) known as the Massasoit
(Ousameqin), called upon all Native people to unite to defend
their homelands against encroachment. The resulting King
Philip's War lasted from 1675–1676. Metacomet was
murdered in Rhode Island in August 1676, and his body was
mutilated. His head was impaled on a pike and was displayed
near this site for more than 20 years. One hand was sent to
Boston, the other to England. Metacomet's wife and son, along
with the families of many of the Native American
combatants, were sold into slavery in the West Indies by the
English victors.

(Plaque in Plymouth town square, also called Post Office square)

The Massachusetts Historical Commission did not so much approve
the text, said Plymouth Town manager Eleanor Beth, as admit that it
was *not* historically inaccurate.[43] And hence the plaques remain today
in the town square and beneath the statue of Massasoit on Cole's Hill
above Plymouth Rock and *Mayflower II*.

Post riot, post settlement, post September 11, the Day of
Mourning processioners have no intention of abandoning their obser-
vance/protest. Realising this, Plymouth residents express mixed feelings. Says Kardell:

I resent that they do it here because we were not like the
Spanish who tried to wipe out the Indians . . . They have
agreed to hold off their stuff until after noon time, until all of
the Pilgrim things are done and the Pilgrims have gone home
to eat dinner. Before, they interrupted the parade, and they

scared children. They had children crying and screaming . . .
They're starting to cool down a bit. Oh, I hope so.[44]

Baker says the reaction of most town people 'is widely varying': 'Some
people find it incredibly annoying because it's taking a feel-good day
and taking away some of the feel-good. Most of us say, "Fine, it's a
free country."'[45]

And those with mixed feelings about the DOM Procession
include some Native Americans. One member of the Mashpee
Wampanoag tribe, who asked not to be identified, explained:

At the first Day of Mourning, the people were with it. They
were behind the message when Frank James was denied the
right to read what he had to say in 1970. But since then it has
grown to include other people: gays, lesbians, steelworkers.
It's gotten away from the original idea. Don't get me wrong.
While most [Wampanoag] people would support most of what
they're saying, they can't support the whole group now. It
needs to get back to its original purpose.[46]

Yet, amid this contestation, there does appear to be a genuine desire for
reconciliation. Asked if he thought the Day of Mourning Procession
might over the years change into a ritual that was more consecrating
and less broadly political, Reverend Marks responded, 'Yes. And then
I could join them. And in fact I would like to join them.'[47]

How would Shirley Mills feel if Reverend Marks dressed in his
Governor Bradford costume and other 'Pilgrims' joined the Day of
Mourning Procession? 'If [Pilgrims] came, it would be unifying. I think
it would be the most healing thing that could happen. I just hope I live
long enough to see that.'[48]

NOTES

1. Interview with Reverend Gary Marks in Plymouth, Massachusetts, 29 November 2001.
2. Interview with Deborah Fillebrown in Plymouth, Massachusetts,
29 November 2001.

3. According to Nan Anastasia, editor of the *Old Colony Memorial* newspaper in Plymouth, both the First Parish Church and the Church of the Pilgrimage claim to be the direct descendant of the church of the pilgrims. There has been an ongoing, sometimes bitter, dispute between them since a split in the nineteenth century. Both churches are located in Plymouth Town Square.

4. Marks interview. *Bradford's Journal, Mourt's Relation*, was written by Plymouth Colony Governor William Bradford between 1630 and 1647. It records the history of the Scrooby Separatist Congregation (later known as the Pilgrims) from Nottinghamshire, England, from when they settled in Holland in 1608 through the first years of their colony in the New World from 1620 through 1647. Lost for 200 years, the manuscript was rediscovered in the Bishop of London's library in the 1850s and returned to America in 1897. It is currently housed in the Massachusetts State Library in Boston.

5. Leonard Peltier was accused and convicted of killing a federal agent in a shootout between members of the American Indian Movement and US Federal Bureau of Investigation agents at the Wounded Knee Hamlet of the Sioux, Pine Ridge Reservation, North Dakota, on 26 June 1975.

6. Mumia Abu Jamal is a radical African-American Activist and former member of the Black Panther Party who was accused and convicted of shooting a police officer in Philadelphia, Pennsylvania, in 1978. Many people consider Jamal and Peltier to be political prisoners.

7. From Malcolm X and Alex Haley, *The Autobiography of Malcolm X* (London: Hutchenson, 1966).

8. Mircea Eliade, *Myth and Reality* (New York: Harper and Row, 1963), pp 18–19.

9. James W. Loewen, *Lies My Teacher Told Me* (New York: Simon & Schuster, 1995), pp. 75–97.

10. Stephen G. Christianson, *The American Book of Days*, 4th edn (New York: H. W. Wilson Company, 2000) pp. 794–7.

11. The *Ladies' Magazine*, with a circulation of 150,000, was America's most popular and influential women's periodical.

12. The boulder, of dedham granodiorite (related to granite), was probably a fluvial deposit formed after the last Ice Age some 10,000 years ago.

13. James Baker, 'Plymouth Rock' and 'The Adventures of Plymouth Rock' (Plimoth on the Web, http://www.plimoth.erg/library/landing.htm).

14. Van Wyck Brooks, *The Flowering of New England* (London: J. M. Dent & Sons, Ltd., 1937), p. 509.

15. Baker, Plimoth on the Web.

16. Jane G. Austin, *Standish of Standish: The Romance of Miles Standish and Mistress Molines* (Boston: Houghton Mifflin & Co., 1889), pp. 276–87.

17. Theodora Kroeber, *Ishi in Two Worlds, A Biography of the Last Wild Indian in North America* (Berkeley and Los Angeles: University of California Press, 1961), pp. 121–46.

18. Vincent Parrillo, *Strangers to These Shores: Race and Ethnic Relations in the United States*, 6th edn (Boston: Allyn and Bacon, 2000), p. 171.

19. Peggy Baker, email correspondence, 15 October 2001.

20. The US Census further categorises the Plymouth County, Massachusetts, 'whites' into Irish-American (160,457), Italian-American (86,598) and Anglo-American (80,025).

21. The US Census Bureau, the US Bureau of Indian Affairs and the UAINE do not agree on Wampanoag tribal status or membership.

22. The 'temple' was erected in 1921. One might add that the 'rock' has resided at or near all the sites mentioned in Plymouth at one time or another.

23. Interview with Peggy Baker in Plymouth, Massachusetts, 28 November 2001.

24. Interview with Caroline Kardell in Plymouth, Massachusetts, 28 November 2001.

25. *Ibid.*

26. Anon., 'Plimoth Plantation, the Living Museum of 17th Century Plymouth', Plimoth Plantation, brochure collected in Plymouth, Massachusetts, 28 November 2001.

27. From 'Irreconcilable Differences', an exhibit at Plimoth Plantation, Plymouth, Massachusetts, 2001.

28. Catherine O'Neill Grace and Margaret M. Bruchac, *1621: A New Look At Thanksgiving* (Washington: National Geographic Society and the Plimoth Plantation, 2001), jacket.

29. Kardell interview.

30. Wamsutta Frank James died last year. His son, Roland Moonaum James, has provided leadership for the DOM Procession with Mahtowin Munro.

31. Frank Moonaum James, speech at the first Day of Mourning Procession, 1971. Some assert that the first DOM procession took place on Thanksgiving Day 1970.

32. Interview with Shirley Mills in Plymouth, Massachusetts, 29 November 2001.

33. Interview with Samuel Sapiel in Plymouth, Massachusetts, 29 November 2001.

34. Sapiel is a respected Native American spiritual leader. The difference between this and 'medicine man', or even the question of whether one can declare oneself a medicine man, is problematic and outside the scope of this study.

35. Sapiel interview.

36. Interview with Nan Anastasia in Plymouth, Massachusetts, 28 November 2001.

37. Baker interview.

38. Kardell interview.

39. Mills interview.

40. Anastasia interview.

41. Sue Harris, email correspondence, 23 November 2000.

42. Mahtowin Munro, email correspondence, 29 November 2000.

43. Interview with Eleanor Beth in Plymouth, Massachusetts, 29 November 2001.

44. Kardell interview.

45. Baker interview.
46. Interview with unidentified Mashpee Wampanoag in Plymouth, Massachusetts, 28 November 2001.
47. Interview with Reverend Gary Marks in Plymouth, Massachusetts, 29 November 2001.
48. Mills interview.

8   South Asia's Child Rights Theatre for Development: the empowerment of children who are marginalised, disadvantaged and excluded

MICHAEL ETHERTON

Sunday, 18 March 2001: fourth day of the Doti TfD Training Workshop
Performance in a farmer's compound in Uchakot village, 2.00 p.m.

We are two-thirds of the way up the mountain, about 200 metres below the Bazaar on the ridge. We have turned a farmyard of old stone buildings on three sides into a makeshift 'theatre' for this warm Spring afternoon's performance. The fourth side is a spectacular view of the high Himalayas. Uchakot is a poor village, divided between Brahmins and Dalits –'Untouchables'.

In the afternoon sunshine the children are seriously into performing the plays they themselves have improvised over the past three days. There is also an improvised play that some village leaders have created as part of the TfD Workshop. An audience of about two hundred villagers – men, women and children – surround the performers, engrossed in the plays. On one side of the impromptu stage there is a black drape and two life-size puppets pop up from time to time to interact with the children and the audience about the issues which the plays are presenting.

Everyone is enthralled, amazed – including we facilitators – that children aged between twelve and fourteen years, Dalits and Brahmins together, could in three days so successfully command the attention of this village audience, so delight them, challenge them; communicate with them so well. This achievement – the substantial issues of the plays, determined by the children themselves, as well as their new-found ability to improvise and act so convincingly in their roles – seems to have been plucked out of thin air, a spontaneous celebration of people and situations closely observed.

This is a diary entry I made during the last Theatre for Development (TfD) training I helped organise in Nepal just before I left South Asia. The workshop took place nearly three years after our first experimentation with Theatre for Development in the context of children's rights. By the time of the workshop, my South Asian colleagues – from India, Bangladesh, Pakistan, Nepal and Sri Lanka – were extending the work in their various countries in a number of different ways, ways which I will attempt to describe.

The first TfD Training Workshop: Dhaka, Bangladesh, May 1998

In May 1998 I began work with two Bangladeshi colleagues, Asif Munier and John Martin, who both worked for Save the Children in the Bangladesh Development Programme. They, like me, were development activists with a background and continuing interest in radical branches of professional and academic theatre. There was no grand design. The first workshop was thought of as a one-off training for a mixed group of Save the Children project officers, some Bangladeshi non-governmental organisation (NGO) staff and a small group of post-graduate drama students from Dhaka University. Children were to be included but were not the main focus.

We were precipitated into a political conflict that resulted in a marvellous focusing of minds and great learning. We had gone through a training process in Dhaka with the group of adults who were all interested in seeing how theatre might be significantly combined with development initiatives. In order to practise using the process, we all went up country to a remote village to work with the adults and young people in that community. There was an unexpected and enthusiastic reaction, over the first twenty-four hours there, to what we were proposing to do. Young girls, teenage boys and young adults all came forward eagerly to involve themselves in developing plays for performance and discussion.

We were delighted. Dramas began to be developed around issues identified by the different village groups with their Bangladeshi facilitators. For example, a small group of women had tentatively come together, hoping, through making their own plays, to find their collective voice. Another group was made up of young girls who bitterly resented early marriage. Camaraderie grew among the various groups who were developing improvisations. Then, quite suddenly, the people in the independent Bangladesh NGOs who were hosting our workshop received threats of violence from some rich young men in powerful village families. They accused us of undermining the 'cultural values of Bangladesh'. We had clearly come up straightaway against the powerful vested interests in the village.

It took us by surprise, because this was an initial experimental training exercise and we were not immediately in a position to deal with such a confrontation in a positive way. Not one of the participants, nor the NGO representative, nor the trainees from Dhaka, nor the villagers, wanted us to leave. However, it seemed to me necessary to complete the training before engaging in the real thing. One purpose of this TfD initiative was to enable adults and young people together to learn negotiation skills and conflict resolution. We decided to complete the training in Dhaka, in the slum communities there.

Before leaving, I agreed to a meeting that the village elders had requested. It was their adult sons who were intimidating us. The NGO representative convened the meeting. I had with me, fortunately, a summary of the Islamabad Declaration of Children's Rights in South Asia, of which the Bangladesh Government was a co-signatory. It had been agreed by all South Asian heads of state to adapt the UN Convention on the Rights of the Child to a specifically South Asian context. It contained an unambiguous endorsement of the articles on children's participation: their right to be heard, their right to express their views in media of their choosing, their right to assembly.

The meeting was initially tense. Accusations were reiterated, but we were able to demonstrate that everything the children were doing in the workshop was within their rights and in accordance with the law of the land. The elders eventually apologised for their sons' behaviour towards us. Save the Children subsequently went back to the village much later and continued to work with the groups of young children. The workshop had been a complicated political and aesthetic experience. It wasn't 'safe', unlike many theatre and development interventions, which tend to avoid challenging existing hierarchies and power relations.

The workshop also challenged everyone's perceptions of 'good theatre' and 'good drama'. It wasn't didactic street theatre, laden with messages. There was no author or written script and actors did not have to memorise their lines. The plays' collective creation extended to the audiences, who could further modify the unfolding fiction better to reflect a shared experience. Making a good play did not take a lot of time. It was an exciting process. It could lead groups into analysis and useful negotiation.

It was extraordinary that even the first training workshop with children and young people very quickly moved from a focus on their basic *needs* to focusing on the consistent and pervasive infringement of their basic *rights*. The reason for this shift lay in the use of a particular form of activist theatre that places an emphasis on improvisation, audience involvement and collective creativity. It rests on the assumption that dramatic fictions are very powerful, seemingly with a life of their own. In a holistic way they are often seen to be more truthful and accurate about the human condition than factual analysis. This truthfulness takes us to the heart of children's rights.

However, the idea of using theatre and drama was first seen as good practice in development, encouraging not only adult participation in the communities but also the participation of the children. It coincided with a growing dissatisfaction in parts of Save the Children with the ways in which adults were tackling child rights. It also coincided with a perceived lack of skills in working with children and young people among project staff and local partner organisations.

Many needs-based development initiatives are dominated by donors and aid agencies, large and small. The donors come to communities with predetermined agenda, commitments and analyses. It is much easier to provide schools and clinics and food-for-work than it is to challenge power relations and oppressive attitudes towards disadvantaged sections of the community. Children, women and poor people constitute the disadvantaged and powerless in society. Donors believe that their first concern is to fulfil their material needs. However, it has been part of my experience over the past four years in South Asia that when poor and powerless young people can be heard, they usually want to decide for themselves what they want changed. Once they are given a voice, they alter the agenda for action and change. NGO activists, who work with children in an open-ended way, find themselves struggling to keep pace with them.

In all these countries the pattern has been to train adults in TfD and facilitation skills, so they are then able to train children and young people. The children go on to use the TfD skills to communicate their perspectives to adults in positions of power and authority, and to start to negotiate with them for change.

Helping to secure the rights of marginalised and
disadvantaged children and young people around the world
Development activists are now moving into the much more radical notion of children and young people co-opting adults around their agenda, rather than adults getting children to participate in adult agenda. This process, initiated by Save the Children UK, is a part of a much wider movement among children, not only in Asia but worldwide. It is currently referred to as the Global Movement for Children but may in future simply be known as the Children's Movement. Globally it has noticeable parallels with the growth of the Women's Movement.

One of the rights of children and young people which is more often denied than upheld is their right to participation and representation, to express their views and to be heard. The kind of Theatre for Development we have been evolving with children and young people specifically addresses this right.

The Convention on the Rights of the Child (CRC) was adopted by the UN General Assembly on 20 November 1989. Governments in countries that have ratified the Convention are legally required to report to the Committee on the Rights of the Child on the passage of legislation to ensure compliance with the Articles of the CRC. The CRC has for a decade been the basis for activism by adult organisations around the world to secure global recognition and understanding of the Rights of the Child.

The Articles of the Convention that specifically address children's right to participate in making decisions affecting them are Articles 12, 13 and 15. Article 12 covers the right to form views and opinions in matters affecting them and for those views to be heard. This also extends to judicial and administrative proceedings affecting the child. Article 13 extends the right to receive and impart information, and to do so through any media. Article 15 covers the child's rights to freedom of association and lawful assembly.[1]

The significance of theatre for Child Rights

Theatre has a particular significance for Child Rights. By 'theatre' I mean young people creating their own dramas through collective improvisation. This kind of theatre is increasingly seen as one of the most important ways by which children and young people communicate with each other as they seek to build a constituency among their peers. They also find it a good way to communicate with adults over matters that collectively concern them. This is because the power of children's imagination is considerable and fiction gives expression to it. Stories are a convincing way of understanding our lives, both for adults and for young children.

Children love stories even when they are very young. As they grow, emotionally and physically, the stories they listen to change. Stories *told* to them, accompanied by pictures, give way to stories *read* by them in words, in books. Today children absorb a huge range of fiction by a mixture of reading books and watching television. However, beyond this passive process, children's active creativity and their mimetic skills are also highly developed, much more so than they will be later, when children become adults and so fall prey to the preoccupations of the adult world. Children can imagine their own stories. They will accept the terrors and possibilities of what Eric Bentley called the 'life of the drama', through their collective improvisation. This kind of collective creativity, expressed through open-ended dramas, can enable children and young people to explore with their audiences the moral dilemmas, enigmatic behaviours, ironies and contradictions that are all the stuff of human society. TfD is a dramatised expression of a shared humanity, in this case by children in communities in many different countries around the world. It leads directly to the heart of Child Rights. I am constantly inspired by very poor children's collective ability to express what is good, what is bad, what is right and fair, an understanding that transcends their poverty, disadvantage and exclusion.

The three Articles of the CRC legitimise training children and young people in this kind of Child Rights TfD process. This means enabling children to create their own plays collectively, and to perform them to audiences of their own choosing. In the TfD process these plays are deliberately inconclusive. They are without contrived endings. Being open-ended, the dramas lead on to negotiation and strategies for change. If children and young people choose to express their views through this kind of theatre (or, indeed, through any other kind of collective creativity, such as art or music or dance or film) in accordance with these Articles, they are exercising their rights.

We found that the training of adults in a rights-based TfD process functioned on two levels. The first addresses the creative and expressive level of adult participants themselves and concerns their own experience. The second requires the adults to learn how to facilitate the training of children and young people in a similar TfD process in which the young people are encouraged to work out their own views, their own manner of expressing them and their own choice of audience. For development workers and theatre activists who are accustomed to telling adults and children what to do and how to do it, albeit very politely, this is a radical departure.

The response of young people, and indeed children from eight to twelve years old, is amazing. Not only are they collectively able to make funny and perceptive plays, but girls and boys who were previously tongue-tied in front of adults find themselves commanding the rapt attention of large adult audiences. They have also found that they have the ability to organise themselves and acquire information and knowledge that they consider important in their difficult lives. It is the unexpected perceptiveness of children and young people that impresses the adults who have facilitated their training in TfD. They see issues differently from adults. This fresh view of a problem also brings forth new and possibly more effective ways of dealing with it.

This work in South Asia has become TfD *by* the children and young people. It has the following essential characteristics:

- it is without an adult agenda;
- it defines rights and addresses violations through the children's own collective expression of these;
- it results in increased self-esteem and confidence among children, especially among girls, who often begin with very little or none;
- it leads to children's and young people's strategies for lobbying and advocacy for the changes they want to see made;
- it provides platforms for endorsement and wider representation;
- children and young people themselves subsequently sustain the process.

Asia's 400 million marginalised and powerless children

The huge populations of China and India are understood in other parts of the world only as abstract numbers. They can provoke a leap of the imagination only when significantly disaggregated by age, gender and the kinds of exploitation suffered by hundreds of millions of young people under the age of eighteen.

India is worse than China in that it has proportionately – and probably also in actual numbers – more children under eighteen, and more girls and boys, suffering myriad deprivations. Young girls are trafficked, sold into prostitution across borders. Hundreds of thousands of boys and girls work in hazardous and exploitative work, forced into it by the poverty of their parents who connive at the violence meted out to them by the adult world of which they have so early become a part. Across the whole of the Indian subcontinent, girls especially are daily subjected to violence: first in their own families and then in the families of their husbands whom they have been forced to marry too young. Schools are dangerous places for both boys and girls: young bullies take violent teachers as their role models and terrorise other children. The streets initially offer an escape route and survival, but at the price of prostitution, early death from HIV/AIDS and a rapid slide into criminality and addiction.

Donors and aid agencies, big and small, international and local, have for the past thirty years sought to provide for the needs of families in poor communities: alternative schooling, clinics, income-generation schemes for women, irrigation schemes and land reclamation, improved agriculture for the children's parents. The donations are large; governments are grateful, and willingly give up their own responsibilities to provide for all their children. The donations then run out.

The impact of these interventions on children has been marginal. The systems of state provision of care, protection, justice, education and health hardly change for the poor, and certainly not for their children. They number hundreds of thousands, yet they are invisible both to outsiders and to the burgeoning middle classes (and their youngsters) in the countries of South Asia.

Some NGOs have decided to address these children's and young people's lack of freedom, their lack of choices, lack of a voice and inability to communicate successfully with their more affluent citizens and governors. Arguably, the organisations are already achieving a greater impact than the millions of dollars from abroad. On the other hand, in many separate parts of South Asia, but especially in India, Nepal, Sri Lanka and Bangladesh, children of eleven and twelve years old, as well as teenagers, are organising themselves on their own collective initiatives. Children's organisations, set up and run by children, are tackling the discriminatory attitudes and practices of adults. This shifts the focus away from the more usual 'wish lists' of children that adults cannot possibly fulfil. It brings into focus the failure of the present system of governance.

A few examples will indicate the range of initiatives. Working children in different parts of India and Bangladesh are forming their own trades unions.[2] Rural children in poor communities have formed their own village development committees (Bal Panchayats) and have achieved institutional recognition for them. Girls and boys in Sri Lanka held the First Sri Lankan Children's Parliament in September 2001. Ladakhi children have formed their Children's Committees for Village Development (CCVDs). These are making an impact on adults' priorities for improving their village communities. Autonomous Children's Clubs have developed by themselves all over Nepal. Children in custody in Dhaka, Bangladesh, have been helped to organise themselves to fight for their basic human rights in detention and in adult jails.

Only after Save the Children UK in South Asia had begun to develop the Theatre for Development training workshops with children and young people did we realise that we were becoming part of something much bigger. We knew we were part of a wider Save the Children Alliance initiative around children's participation in civil society; we now found ourselves to be part of a global movement of children, much bigger than Save the Children or UNICEF. In different parts of the world, a lot of people – adults, children, teenagers – are contributing to a movement that is becoming visible, and being defined by children and young people.

Similar initiatives have emerged among children's groups, independently, in different parts of the world. A 'Children's Movement' is increasingly compared to the women's movement: there *are* similarities, particularly in the way in which both movements focus on the struggle for greater equality and recognition of their legitimate status as women or as children. Children, too, have rights. However, there are obvious and significant differences: children grow up and cease to be children. Gender inequalities within the Children's Movement need to be tackled within the wider context of the rights of children generally.

At the UN General Assembly Special Session on Children, in May 2002, children amazed world leaders and diplomats by starting to claim their right to participate in policy decision making that affected the lives of children and young people around the world.[3]

Three key events in the regional expansion of Child Rights Theatre for Development

Karachi, Pakistan, TfD Training Workshop, August 1999

We had invited two people from Pakistan to the first Bangladesh TfD Training Workshop. They came from a local NGO in Karachi, the colossal city in the south of Pakistan in Sindh Province, and were involved in using theatre extensively with slum children. Following the impact of this first Bangladesh TfD Training Workshop, there came a commitment from the Save the Children's programme manager in Sindh, Sadia Ahmed, to develop a TfD event in Karachi. Sadia herself had not come to the Bangladesh training workshop in Dhaka described earlier, but had started to fund the work of a small Karachi NGO which experimented with using theatre in plays with messages about the Convention on the Rights of the Child (CRC). Sadia's TfD Training Workshop eventually took place in August 1999.

Children in three of Karachi's worst slums (*kachchi abadis*) developed a wide range of performances. These performances led into intense discussions with some of the communities in those areas. It was a bigger event than the first trial workshop in Bangladesh. In addition to some Pakistani project staff from Save the Children UK, the training involved a number of Pakistan's NGOs and community-based organisations (CBOs), most of which received development grants from Save the Children UK. This donation-dependent relationship, often described – inaccurately – as a 'partnership', is one of the key problems of an international organisation trying to develop Child Rights initiatives with local NGO 'partners'.

The problematic nature of promoting children's rights when the international non-governmental organisation (INGO) is funding the local organisation is part of the wider issue of the relationship between powerful donors from affluent countries and local activists engaged in civil society and governance in impoverished states. It is economically easy but emotionally difficult for countries with strong economies to insist that by virtue of their economic might they already occupy the high moral ground and can dictate the rights agenda to economically poor states. It echoes missionaries in the earlier European colonial dispensation and is even more problematic when the focus is on children's rights.

There was significant consultation in the pre-planning phase in Pakistan. Expectations were raised for the outcome of the training among development workers and rights activists, of whom a number were based in Karachi. Their work among very poor and marginalised groups was particularly difficult in the febrile political atmosphere of that tense city.

Asif Munier, John Martin and I did a great deal of planning around how we would tackle any problems which might arise when young people started articulating their rights. This was because of the threatening confrontation, described earlier, with the rich and powerful young men in the rural community in Bangladesh that TfD training had generated. Karachi was a much more dangerous place than rural northern Bangladesh. In particular we wanted to be able to deal with challenges in a negotiated and productive way in the Karachi *kachchi abadis*. Sadia Ahmed took the initiative to undertake a risk analysis with her colleagues in the local NGOs and CBOs, and this established a significant framework for the work. It was dependent on the political standing of the CBOs and their existing mediating role within the slum communities.

I have vivid images of the various training events in Karachi. After the initial training of the adults, we went to widely dispersed slums across the sprawling conurbation. The partly trained adults now had the opportunity to work with a wide age-range of children, youths and young adults, among the very different ethnic groups that make up Karachi. I was in the largely Baluchi *kachchi abadi* of Lyari that incorporates what was the original city. We worked with young men and young women together. I had assumed that because of the Islamic sensibilities of the tribal Baluchis we would have to work with separate groups of men and women; and indeed we had planned to do so. But the young men and women chose to work together. It was a surprise.

We had also decided to work with younger children, to see how this particular sort of TfD concerned with Child Rights might appeal to six- to eleven-year-olds. The adults who had gone through the initial training had developed a methodology of facilitation that had no overt or hidden agenda. This absence of any kind of moral judgement enabled the participants to explore and analyse collectively the issues they felt most affected them. They were able, after a few days, to express to a wider public and audience what made their lives so difficult and denied them their future. My Nepali colleagues, Karna Maharjan and Macche Narayan, who are video documentary makers and who worked with me in Kathmandu, joined us in Lyari to film the process of the workshop.

In all of the three scattered locations, the dominant concern was the prevalence of drugs, a pervasive hard drug culture in the *kachchi abadis* that directly affected children as young as four years old, even if they themselves were not drug-takers. This was our second surprise: we had not expected drug-taking to be so prevalent across Karachi.

'Oh no!' remarked Sadia Ahmed, the Sindh programme manager. 'Not drugs! Please not drugs! Save the Children won't allow us to tackle the drugs problem!'

The CBOs we were funding echoed this view: 'We don't tackle drugs. Our funding doesn't allow us to do that.' There could be no question that the donor was influencing the agenda.

The young adults were deeply committed to the drama they had created. They were amazed that they had collectively created this powerful theatre piece. The audience to which the young adults in Lyari chose to show their drama about drug-taking, for comment, criticisms or endorsement, was in fact made up of about forty drug addicts and pushers in the immediate community. How did this happen? The group had asked me to look at their play after they had worked on creating it together for a couple of days. It was indeed powerful. But was it accurate? I was particularly interested in the status of the irony and paradoxes that the play brought out. I asked them if any of them were in fact drug addicts.

'None of us are addicts,' said one young man, slightly emphasising the last word. 'Then how do you know if what you are saying in
your play is accurate?' I asked. 'Well, we don't,' was the general reply.
'Couldn't you try and find out?' I asked. 'Though I haven't any idea
how . . .' 'Let's get them here as our audience!' someone suggested.

It seemed something impossible to me. 'Could some of you get
four or five to come and look at your play?' I asked. 'They'd have to
come here after lunch for an hour.' 'Oh, I'm sure we could get more
than four this afternoon,' they said.

Forty or so men, all addicts or pushers, gathered at about three
o'clock in the afternoon in the small hall of the CBO which was hosting us. The drama was followed by an intense interaction between the
creators of the drama and the audience. The discussion went on for
an hour. 'This is the first deep and honest drama about our lives,' one
member of the audience commented, and others agreed.

Every night all the facilitators had to go on the bus back to
our hotel in Karachi because we were not permitted by the authorities to stay in Lyari. My lasting image is of the excitement of the
facilitators of this particular group on the bus after this extraordinary afternoon. They were totally overwhelmed by the insights of
the interaction. First, the quality of the drama created, after just four
days' training in improvisation, was very powerful. They kept going
over the ironies, the detailed and accurate observation, and the sudden
denouement.

Second, not only were young men and women working together
behind closed doors, they were prepared to perform together in front
of a wider group within their community (the forty or so addicts and
pushers). For the facilitators, the intensity of the presence of this group
had been almost too difficult to bear.

The performers and audience allowed Karna Maharjan, a filmmaker from Nepal, to film the performance and subsequent interactions. Not only has this extraordinary event happened – quite unexpectedly – it has also been recorded professionally on videotape and
can, even now, be 're-viewed' quite literally. Indeed, my only images
of the event are those images captured on the video, as I was not
present at the performance – I was working around the corner in Lyari

with another group of trainee facilitators. These were the facilitators working with sixty-five small children.

This also has its powerful remembrance. Within a short day this group of children had, with their adult facilitators, made up their own stories, and, with a compelling naiveté, enacted them directly. This, too, is on videotape. The children's overwhelming experiences of the drug culture in their lives pervaded this event as well. Nine-year-olds acted out addicted adults with such acute observation and verisimilitude that it can have come only from repeated observations of adults and young people in their immediate neighbourhood, and indeed within their families. The plays also showed the ways in which children related to the addicts. The children's stories unfolded in animated performances during which they were surrounded by about a hundred other children and adults. These Lyari folk had gathered in the concrete backyard of the little school.

The children's plays told a clutch of different tales. One story was about the addict's need for a friend and what this friend was required to do. He had to be around so that he could always pick him up in the dusty lane and save him from further humiliation. Another tale from a group of very young streetwise girls suggested that addicts deserved to be baited and teased by gangs of children. Another hinted at a darker violence surrounding the everyday activities of going to school, shopping, travelling on a bus. Witches, magic and animism hovered around the edges of a strident if not quite fundamentalist Islam.

However, the atmosphere of the afternoon was not at all dark. In the bright sunlight it was vivid, full of songs and excitement. The most memorable song was the patriotic children's song in praise of Pakistan. Our day's playmaking took place on Pakistan Day, and on this day most middle-class children are forced to school and into singing this song in reluctant school parades. Our slum children, by contrast, had asked us to 'play' with them on this day and had come to the school, which was closed, voluntarily. In the creative atmosphere of the compound, they sang the song of their own choosing – jazzing up the rhythm and bringing the audience in as a vigorous chorus. Some of us thought that these children in particular had little reason to praise the Pakistan state.

The following day there was a spontaneous 'festival' of TfD plays in the concrete shell of a community centre. The construction of this two-storey building had been halted for some time by factional strife within this part of Lyari. The CBO had been given permission to use it for the afternoon and we had managed to get buses to bring the children and young people to Lyari from the other slums where they had been involved in similar outbursts of creativity. It had seemed to me an exciting idea and a bonus for the workshop, riding on the coattails of our success, something we had not planned on doing at all.

Spontaneous happenings that emerge out of a collective creativity are often empowering for adults, although there is always an element of risk. That element of risk should be kept at a minimum in work of this kind when it is with children. Even if it is empowering for some of the children, others could find it discouraging. Some of the Karachi children got a lot out of this impromptu coming together to see each others' plays. But others did not, perhaps because they felt that they had lost control of something of which they thought they were in charge. This sudden mini-festival was an adult-inspired event, and although the Lyari children had shouldered responsibility for organising it, those children and young people from other *kachchi abadis* felt that they were coming to someone else's party. A further problem was that the festival tended to suggest that the performance was the main thing. The central idea of Child Rights TfD is to emphasise the neverending process of improvisation and analysis.

In addition, this last, exciting experience was – suddenly – too big too soon. The intense creativity of the previous four days had been such an empowering experience for all the young in their own communities that it was exhausting to think that there might be further heights of collective and personal achievement outside their slums.

What was the follow-up to this event?

The adults involved have done the following things:

MICHAEL ETHERTON

- the young adults' drugs play was, at the request of the drug addicts in the audience, made into a fiction film for relay on the community television station;
- videomaking involving children has been developed by Samina Sardar;
- further key training workshops have been held for adult facilitators in the NGOs and some CBOs, mainly on the initiative of Action for the Rights of Children (ARC), an umbrella Child Rights NGO coalition and a key activist in ARC, Sadia Khan;
- Sadia Ahmed, the Save the Children Sindh programme manager, who had so professionally organised the Save the Children initiative in Karachi, followed up by leading a TfD Training Workshop in rural Nepal with very poor children.

I believe that young people have done more. The TfD children's rights process has been developed, with children, in the Thar Desert in Interior Sindh; and there have been two well-documented instances where young people have used TfD in jointly advocating Save the Children projects. One of these was an evaluation of an HIV/AIDS project with children in Lahore. The other was in the final evaluation of a large British government-funded project in Punjab to tackle child labour in the international football-stitching industry. Other initiatives have followed the original workshop; these developed TfD with children and young people in quite different ways.

This gave rise to a lively debate in print and through email throughout 2000, one aspect of which was to question the role of Save the Children UK in nurturing this kind of work while funding NGOs and evaluating their projects. The problem had surfaced even during the workshop in Lyari. Some perceived a potentially strong conflict of interest. On the one hand, the international NGO had an established role as an agent for disbursing aid and monitoring the development projects of local NGOs. On the other, it wanted to use the local NGO or CBO to gain access directly to children in 'their' community and encourage the active and perhaps critical participation of children and young people in claiming their rights.

page number204

An international agency like Save the Children would say that the dilemma was not the one discussed in the exchanges. It was between its responsibility towards adult stakeholders – donors in the UK and local NGO implementers – and their mandate to support children and young people directly.

The question remains about the extent to which this TfD process has empowered children who have been involved in it in different parts of Pakistan. This kind of TfD around children's rights has gone much further than any of us expected.

The most significant problem raised was one relating to the INGOs. It is the inability of NGOs to deal with the children's widely representative views and concerns if they contradict the established agenda of the NGO or INGO. International organisations are often unable to help children and young people tackle their most pressing problems.

India: Ladakh TfD for Advocacy in Education Training Workshop, September 2000

The training workshop in Ladakh was part of the follow-up to TfD work around children's empowerment in India. It came after an initial training in Nepal and a number of more specialised workshops in Bangladesh and Nepal. Although all these events developed interactions with children and young people in many different ways, the Ladakh training workshop proved to be of critical significance for young people's advocacy, both inside Save the Children and more broadly within children's groups and organisations. We were able to focus, with children and young people, much more coherently and effectively on lobbying and advocacy. The achievement was the way in which the young people made us refine the TfD 'process' around *advocacy*.

The workshop involved thirty Ladakh and Kargil adolescents and nine primary school teachers, working together as equals. There were also a number of Indian TfD facilitators, three of them from Ladakh, who had been trained in earlier workshops and who were already working with many of these teenagers to enable them to engage in civil society.

As a team of facilitators, we experimented together with the aesthetics of performance in tandem with the ways in which children analysed problems. The improvisations evolved over a few days from plays focusing on the microanalysis of problems in various schools to plays that reflected a much broader macroanalysis of problems in the education system. In the process we discovered powerful new communication tools for lobbying. This highlighted significant new responsibilities for Save the Children and the nature of children's participation in citizenship and governance.

We started to use the technique of painting collectively, on large sheets of paper, which enabled children and adults together to depict their own concepts of the issues confronting them, in a holistic visual way. Young people, who have not yet fully mastered reading and writing, seem to us to be especially eager to have a means of instant, comprehensive communication. There is some hesitation at the beginning of the exercise – for about fifteen minutes or so – and then the images begin to fill the posters. The images are of their experience and their ideas; and the oral description of what they have collectively drawn further develops the communication.

Teacher violence in Indian schools, including schools in Ladakh, emerged as one of the main reasons why children, girls especially, drop out of school. At one point when we were all sitting on the floor together discussing the pictures on the posters, two Islamic girls from Kargil, both aged about fifteen, felt empowered to tackle the primary school teachers. The girls asked the teachers if they thought that the children who came late to school should be beaten.

'Yes,' said the teachers. 'Definitely.'
'Why?' the girls asked.
'To make them come on time, of course.'
'And if they keep coming late, they should be beaten even harder?'
'Of course.'
'Do you have a lot of children coming to your schools late, a lot of the time?' one of the girls asked.

The teachers all agreed that it was a big problem.
'Well,' said the other girl, 'to us the beating doesn't seem to be working. It's meant to make the children come on time. And they don't.'

The teachers in the workshop appreciated the logic, despite themselves. There was a frisson among the thirty young people and fifteen adults on the floor in the room.
The girls then went on:

'Do you think that teachers who come to school late [actually a major problem in Ladakh schools] should be beaten?'

The teachers had no answer. A furious but friendly discussion erupted between the teenagers and the primary school teachers, which was eventually steered by some of the young people, unprompted, into how children and teachers could be convinced that they needed to come on time, without recourse to any kind of punishment.

There were similarly sensible and rational discussions around other problems in the education system in Ladakh. The character of these discussions also marked the improvisations being developed into four extremely funny and acutely observed plays. The young people's perception of the problems in a range of issues disturbed some of the adults.

One of the fifteen-year-old boys at the workshop asked us, as we were preparing to perform before Ladakh's education officials, 'If we are saying something that adults don't like and don't want to hear, will [Save the Children UK] still support us?'

What the young people wanted to be clear about was just how solid the support from the adults working with them was for their views. They did not want us to agree superficially with them. They wanted us to be completely honest about the issues they were raising. We could not unanimously answer them in the affirmative and the young people decided that the time was not quite right to engage with the education officials. Instead, they thought that their next move might be to try to build a wider coalition among school-going children, out-of-school children and teachers. They said that they would need to do this before engaging with senior government administrators. And they were right.

This workshop had broken significant new ground in the way Save the Children UK tackled the interlocking issues of children's and young people's participation in governance and civil society, advocacy and rights. The breakthrough was irrespective of any particular methodology or process, although the combination of creativity and analysis in this particular form of TfD echoed the needs of young people.

Following on from the Ladakh workshop, some South Asian colleagues developed a Child Rights TfD Training Manual, which they have produced both as a CD-ROM and as a hard copy in four languages. This manual, in English, is now being used and developed in some countries in Africa, in Save the Children's projects.

Nepal: Doti, Far West of Nepal, March 2001

The particular TfD process that I have been describing has gone further in Nepal than in other countries in the region. Children and young people there have developed new skills, and have gained in confidence in organising themselves and tackling issues in some innovative and significant ways, ways that have generated change and will continue to do so. This is their definition of claiming their rights. Many of the children we have worked with are familiar with the Articles in the Convention on the Rights of the Child. However, they are now themselves defining much more precisely the relevance of the CRC both in terms of their own lives and, more significantly, in terms of the lives of the rest of the children in their group and in wider communities.

The TfD process in Nepal and other countries in South Asia contributed to this achievement. In each of the countries, it has not been the only approach to children's participation in civil society. In Nepal it has been systematically integrated at all levels into the broader programme developed by Save the Children staff and young people together, and there has been a comprehensive and deliberate process to empower children and young people.

The first group of TfD Training Workshops in Nepal took place in late 1999. Children and young people in what are called Save the Children's 'project impact areas' have increasingly taken over the work. A good pattern of interaction with adults has started to develop. Some of the adults involved in this interaction are the newly trained Nepali facilitators who have moved the process more and more into advocacy. Other adults with whom the Nepali children have started negotiating are district officials and central government officials. At the same time, the Nepali facilitators have been keen to extend the process into other more remote places where Save the Children and local partner organisations were working to find ways to enable young people and adults together to generate change on a wide scale. The Doti workshop in the far west of Nepal in March 2001 was my last TfD Training Workshop in South Asia before leaving the region. A description of one of the performances began this chapter.

When we started TfD in South Asia three years ago, we began by training adults and then had adults work with children. The work increasingly became much more child-focused, with a developing emphasis on training children as facilitators. We included teachers in the workshops as equal participants with the children and young people. This time we decided to include the vice-chair from the Village Development Committee (VDC), the headmaster of the secondary school and the director of the development CBO in the district, and to train them alongside the children. The condition was that the adults had to attend full time and be fully involved.

Adults, children and young people, working together, create a marvellous atmosphere of sharing. They share ideas, experiences and each other's perspectives. This gives the children, especially, a huge amount of self-esteem. It succeeds precisely because it draws out individual creative potential. There is also a growing awareness of the collective ownership of this creative potential. 'I didn't know we could do this! I didn't know I had this in me!' Differences in age, gender, status and caste tend to be subordinated to this sense of collective creativity.

This workshop took place in Uchakot Bazaar, where Save the Children UK is working with children around issues of discrimination and violence. The participants in this workshop were a group of eighteen children aged between twelve and fourteen years old: ten girls and eight boys, half of them Dalits and half Brahmin. Irada Gautam and Rajendra Tuladhar, the Nepali organisers of the workshop, want to get Dalit girls into schools, and they want them to find the education so interesting and useful that they will remain there. The Dalit children in the workshop had had little formal education: some had been in school for only a year, perhaps two years, and two girls had never been in school at all.

It was a new initiative for us to deal with ideas of negotiation and representation with such rural and disadvantaged younger children. We could only do this because it is an integral part of the process of enabling them to realise their creative potential.

Nepal: puppets against the caste system
We therefore developed further tools and exercises specifically to help children from poor and disadvantaged backgrounds facilitate discussions with adults in the community. Puppets became central to the process. We wanted to use puppets in new ways to equip children with participatory tools for working out problems and solutions. This, for me, was a technical innovation in the TfD work we had been doing over the past two years in various countries in South Asia.

Children – and adults – all around the world make puppets and make up dramas for them. There is also an adult profession of puppeteering, and there are significant Asian puppet performances in the mainstream of a number of Asian theatre traditions (from the 'high art' Bunraku in Japan, through Vietnamese water puppets to the folk art Rajasthani puppet tradition in Rajasthan, India).

We were able to develop an innovative form of TfD puppeteering through one of the co-facilitators, Ram Lal, a puppeteer from Rajasthan in North India. He had been professionally trained in the Rajasthani tradition: his father's lifetime's work was as a Rajasthani puppeteer. Ram Lal has extended this tradition with inspiring innovation into development, and with us he was extending it into rights. His personality combines creativity and communication with selflessness. More often than not, someone with a vivid character like

Ram Lal could be expected to dominate the creative process. Ram Lal somehow never does. He inspires everyone – children, young people, adults – to explore their own creative potential. It is an enriching experience working with him. He showed me the power of a robust but genuine humility.

The puppets consist of a painted papier-mâché face which is a little smaller than a human face, with a movable mouth, a costume and a papier-mâché arm and hand. The puppet's other (very expressive) hand is the puppet operator's own right hand, while the left hand works the head and mouth. The puppet is sometimes held beside the puppet operator, sometimes above his or her shoulder while the operator is hidden behind a low screen.

So far, this is conventional puppetry. What is different is the ways in which the puppets are used as part of the process of *analysis* as much as part of the actual *performance*. In Doti the puppets continually challenged both actors and audience, asking them why the plays were unfolding in the way they were. During the performances the puppets were endlessly reassuring for the young performers, playfully arguing with them, sometimes challenging them in exaggerated parody. This gave the shy children confidence.

We used the puppets within the process itself from the first day of the workshop. It was a means of engaging both children and adult participants in the process, and more actively in the discussions and analysis, particularly in helping them explain ideas, or scenes in their plays.

Initially Ram Lal was the puppet operator. He experimented with the puppets' interrogative role within the analytical part of the training. Then he trained the young local adult facilitators to take over this new enabling role. Using the puppets in the performances in front of audiences flowed out of this interrogative role. He also wanted to get the young people to make the puppets themselves.

The work with puppets in Uchakot Bazaar brings the issue of language, which is significant in all the training workshops, into sharp focus. I am rarely able to work with children in English, but I have never found this to be a problem, provided there is constantly careful interaction with a number of people who are translating. I always try to ensure that whoever translates also participates in the training or is one of the facilitators. Translation then becomes a continuous shared activity and the process of translation is used to clarify new ideas which otherwise might remain hidden behind strange terminology. Good drama also communicates very well physically, beyond verbal language. We spend a lot of time with children showing, for example, how eyes can establish status and how pauses and silences, as well as big and small gestures, all contribute significantly to powerful communication with audiences.

Ram Lal, who is from India and whose mother tongue is Hindi, could not speak the dialect of Nepali in Uchakot. Most of the children could not speak Hindi and in addition a few of them could not speak even standard Nepali. But Ram Lal communicated brilliantly with everyone in the village and on the workshop. He has the child-like ability, which I find that most good TfD practitioners have to a greater or lesser extent, to pick up key phrases in the languages surrounding him. His skills in physical communication are highly developed. However, I have observed that in this kind of TfD, with shared linguistic interaction going on all the time, and in a context of collective physical creativity, communication between people using different languages seems effortless.

Nepal: children and digital video filmmaking

Karna Maharjan, who had filmed the TfD process in Karachi, continued to develop the interactive use of digital video within the many TfD workshops that followed. He has also developed a complementary process in training young slum children in Nepal in digital video, but this is now a process that has veered away from TfD. This new initiative has come about because some children and young people asked us to help them in developing skills in filmmaking for negotiation with adults, in order to complement their work using TfD in lobbying.

The purpose of training poor children in digital filmmaking was focused initially on the technical skills required in active documentary filmmaking. We also wanted to work out with the young people the values and ethics that ought to be inherent in the way they made their documentaries. This should be part of a coherent follow-up programme with the children in South and Central Asia. Finally, we needed to document this workshop as a first step in developing the expertise and parameters in this new area of young people's advocacy. We expected:

- at least two short films made (planned, shot and edited) by the children and young people, in two groups;
- a report in draft within two weeks of the close of the workshop on the values and ethics in training young people to make digital videos;
- the children who would be trained in this workshop to go on to make short videos and then use them to negotiate successfully with adults in authority for changes on issues they consider important in their children's organisations.

It proved to be a highly successful training workshop. It achieved more than even our ambitious programme. A group of ten children has acquired significant skills in using cameras to record individual testimonies from people whom they had not previously met. The children already have skills in developmental approaches to social change. The combination means that they have a unique set of skills for lobbying and negotiation.

These skills, and this potential, carry with them significant responsibilities. The children will discover in the years immediately after this workshop that their exemplary filmmaking skills and access to a digital video camera are highly marketable. They need to accept fully that their abilities in filmmaking, as they get better and better, should benefit not only them but also their disadvantaged peers. They have a responsibility towards the subject of their filmmaking, and by extension to the people whose lives and problems they film.

We addressed the question of responsibilities in a practical way, under that segment of the training we called 'values in filmmaking'. We approached the subject through the question, 'Who owns the film you have made?'

When we first asked it, one or two of the children, aware of their duty towards INGOs, promptly answered, 'Save the Children!'

'Yes,' we replied. 'Do you think so? Who is making the films?'
'Of course, we are,' some of the boys and girls replied.
One of them added, 'It's our film! We own it.'
'Yes,' we replied, 'that's true. But what about the people you have been filming? The vegetable seller? The woman in the little photography shop who cried on your film?'

One of the boys interrupted us, 'Of course, the people we filmed own the film. Of course they do.'

Not all of the boys and girls were in agreement, and we left the issue undecided for the moment. After the editing we returned to the question and the earlier discussion. Now they were unanimous that the film was owned by the people whom they had filmed.

'So we'd better put their names on the films, then, hadn't we?' I asked.

There was a long pause. Then, 'We don't know their names . . .' one of the girls said.

There took place a marvellous discussion on responsibility in filmmaking.

The children undertook to find out the names of the people they had filmed in the town's slums. They also thought that they should screen the films in the first instance to the people who were the subjects of their film. They agreed to ask them the question, 'May we show this film of you to other people?' and to abide by the answer given.

These growing skills in filmmaking – in the broadest sense – are put at the service of their group, children's organisation or community. The groups themselves decide what small films need to be made; what their responsibilities are in doing so; and how they will subsequently use these films.

Hopes for great happenings: the global Children's Movement
One of the main areas of debate within theatre activism, including TfD, revolves around the question of what its overriding purpose is

in relation to wider economic and social development. Some political theatre activists see NGOs negatively, whether these NGOs are international, national or local. They are seen as part of the development industry, a destructive economic force that continues to marginalise individuals and communities. NGOs promoting TfD, therefore, are seen as having the ultimate purpose of promoting compliance in the existing world order. An independent theatre, by contrast, enhances the collective cultural will and the desire for profound change in the world order.

On the other hand, INGOs themselves see no future in TfD if all it does is produce more and better political theatre. They would embrace theatre if it produced significant social change.

I have spent the latter part of my working life involved in both camps, seeking a combination of theatre and development that demonstrates a positive impact on the lives of severely disadvantaged people. In the opening years of this millennium, it has been rewarding to find myself involved in the global Children's Movement. I think children's and young people's TfD – and digital video – have a part to play within the gathering momentum of this movement. I would not have been able to take part in the wider global movement had I not been working for Save the Children for the past five years. This has been the time when we realised that rights are significant for disadvantaged children and young people when they themselves are able to define them and their infringement.

There are now many organisations in civil society exploring new collaborative ways of working with the most disadvantaged and socially excluded children in their countries. This collaboration is not without risks. Antagonism to that collaboration can build up in different quarters of adult society. But it has already proved to be the path to the future, both for the children and for the NGOs themselves.

TfD itself is a method and a process that the young people say enables them to deal with those in authority. The method is collectively creative, based on learning skills in improvisation, analysis and effective communication. The process is contained in a set of tools and exercises that leads children and young people into negotiation with adults in positions of power. TfD, then, is itself a process of empowerment of socially excluded children and young people. Save the Children gave me and my colleagues the space to build up this experience, because of a growing sense of change in the relations between the powerful adult world and marginalised children and young people.

Acknowledgement

All the South Asians and Save the Children colleagues I was privileged to work with from 1998 to 2001 enriched my life and I thank them for enthusiasm and commitment. My special thanks to Asif Munier for taking the work forward and for his help in compiling the Notes. I am also very grateful to John Reed, Mark Cohen and Mary Etherton for their invaluable comments and suggestions. I am, however, solely responsible for the final text.

NOTES

1. Relevant Articles from the UN Convention on the Rights of the Child:

Article 12

1. States Parties shall assure to the child who is capable of forming his or her own views the right to express those views freely in all matters affecting the child, the views of the child being given due weight in accordance with the age and maturity of the child.

2. For this purpose, the child shall in particular be provided the opportunity to be heard in any judicial and administrative proceedings affecting the child, either directly, or through a representative or an appropriate body, in a manner consistent with the procedural rules of national law.

Article 13

1. The child shall have the right to freedom of expression; this right shall include freedom to seek, receive and impart information and ideas of all kinds, regardless of frontiers, either orally, in writing or in print, in the form of art, [or] through any other media of the child's choice.

2. The exercise of this right may be subject to certain restrictions, but these shall only be such as are provided by law and are necessary:
   (a) For respect of the rights of reputations of others; or
   (b) For the protection of national security or of public order (*ordre public*), or of public or morals.

Article 15
1. State Parties recognize the rights of the child to freedom of association and to freedom of peaceful assembly.
2. No restrictions may be placed on the exercise of these rights other than those imposed in conformity with the law and which are necessary in democratic society in the interests of national security or public safety, public order (*ordre public*), the protection of public health or morals or the protection of the rights and freedoms of others.

An excellent independent source of information electronically on Child Rights is the Child Rights Information Network (CRIN) on the Web: http://www.crin.org.

2. Useful documentation on some children's organisations in South Asia includes:

South Asia
Asif Munier et al., *Using Theatre for Development in Child Rights Programming: TfD Training Manual,* Save the Children UK, Office of the South and Central Asia Region, Kathmandu (2001). (Also available on CD-ROM with audio and video clips.) *Training of Facilitators on Children, Citizenship and Governance* (November/December 2000), Save the Children Alliance South and Central Asia Region, Kathmandu.

Bangladesh
John Martin and Sharfuddin Khan, *Shoshur Bari (In-law's House): Street Children in Conflict with the Law* (2000), Save the Children UK in Bangladesh (this records participatory research done

by a group of street children who came into conflict with the law, facilitated by John Martin and Sharfuddin Khan); 'Child Brigade' (an urban street and working children's group directly supported by Save the Children Sweden, on which a review report has also been compiled recently); Children's Congress (supported by a local organisation called Resource Bangladesh, a partner of Save the Children Denmark); and Shishu Parishad (Children's Council) supported by Save the Children Australia. The latter is formed by a replica of adult elections – there are elected bodies at various levels with representatives from more than 40,000 children in the district where Save the Children Australia works, through nine local NGO partners.

India

The Concerned for Working Children (CWC), Bangalore, Karnataka, spearheads support for children's organisations in South India. Its website is very informative: http://www.workingchild.org.

Ladakh (India)

J. H. M. Fewkes and M. S. Bhat, *Our Voices . . . Are you Listening? Children's Committees for Village Development* (2002), Save the Children UK in India.

Nepal

J. Rajbhandary, R. Hart and C. Khatiwada, *The Children's Clubs of Nepal: A Democratic Experiment* (1999), Save the Children Norway and US in Nepal.

Sri Lanka

The Sri Lankan Children's Challenge – Report (November 2001), Save the Children Norway and Save the Children UK in Nepal.

The Save the Children UK's website is http://www.savethechildren.org.uk.

3. At the time of writing, the reports of the UN Special Session on Children are still in preparation, including the child-friendly

version of the outcome document. Consult the Child Rights Information Network (CRIN) website. (I have been involved in the internal evaluation of children's and young people's participation in all the preparatory events that took place around the world in the twelve months before the actual Special Session at the UN in New York.)

Theatre – a space for empowerment: celebrating Jana Sanskriti's experience in India

SANJOY GANGULY

31 May 1985

Dear Naresh,

I hope you are well. You have asked me how I am spending my days. I do not know exactly what to say . . . All kinds of thoughts come to my mind nowadays. I never used to think like this before. I read somewhere that it is not until you reach the top of the hill that you realise yours was not the only path. If only it did not take so long to realise these things. Anyway, let me tell you about some of my thoughts, some of my experiences.

In South Kolkata, near Ballyganj railway station, there is a large slum. A number of us meet there on Sundays and holidays. Except for me all the others work for a Ballyganj-based NGO. The people who live in these slums have come from different villages that fall under the Sunderban Development Authority. They are not alike. Those who come from the vicinities of the Sunderbans [a delta forest] have an intimate relationship with rivers and the jungles that grow on the swamps. Those who come from near the railway tracks have no link with water and marshy land. They are heavily influenced by Kolkata. These diverse people, some from villages near the city, some from remote areas, have come together in this slum, tied together now by a common struggle for daily existence.

In the villages there is not enough work to keep them busy for the whole year. So they are in the city now in search of a living. Some work as domestic labour, some are wage workers on construction sites. A few are hired by pandal [a decorative canopy used in festivals] decorators, some work in small food shops. From multistoried buildings to the metro rail – nothing in Kolkata could have been built without their contribution, yet they live in an area of indescribable filth. If one had not seen this slum, it would have been difficult to imagine that human beings could live in such putrid, foul-smelling and unhygienic circumstances in the twentieth century.

Pashupati is a well-known figure in the slum. He has easy access to everyone – from the important persons in the ruling party to the leadership of the NGO which is implicitly against the party in power. Because of his intelligence Pashupati is recognised as the most reliable person here. How does one explain the source of his intelligence? This was a million-dollar question. Because Pashupati is illiterate. You know how in our party we used to value those who were good in their studies or those who came from aristocratic families. But this man – Pashupati – has neither a certificate from a school nor the stamp of a well-known family. I suppose you can guess the question that naturally comes to me.

The wide world outside is unknown to me, but I had no idea that in the corners of our own familiar city there were patches of such intense darkness. I might have known this in the abstract, but the actual experience was traumatic; it unleashed a flood in my mind. I had always known that in the dialectic between insoluble problems on the one hand and the attempt to surmount them on the other lies the key to human development. But what struck me here is the abundant presence of human qualities among people who are struggling for survival every waking moment of their lives. Poverty does not necessarily erode human values – my experience is fast bringing me to this position. All of you who

*are so involved in economic movements could perhaps think
a little about it . . .*

Sixteen years ago we did not know the answer to that million-dollar question. The closer we came to the people who live here, the more insistent the question became. The answer gradually emerged from our contact with a large number of people. The eighteen-year-old story of my experiences in this slum is not irrelevant, because it contains the pre-history of Jana Sanskriti 'People's Culture'. I must refer to it as I trace the emergence of Jana Sanskriti as perhaps the largest theatre group in West Bengal today.

Pashupati's village, Dahakanda, is seventy kilometres from Kolkata. By train it takes about one and a half hours to reach a small station called Madhabpur – and then one has to walk for another hour and a half. It is a mud path part of the way, but for the rest one has to trudge across the paddy fields. In summer, in spite of the scorching sun, it is easier to cover this distance than in the rainy season when the one-and-a-half-hour walk stretches into three hours. The rains do not only make the field muddy, they make the clayey soil dangerously slippery. There is no electricity in the village and there are no trained doctors. The lanes inside the village are flanked on both sides by human excrement. Children cannot go very far through the slippery fields so they use the roadside regularly for relieving themselves. When it rains this gets mixed with the mud. Walking barefoot along these lanes is an experience I had better not try to describe.

At that time, none of us was involved in theatre. We came from the urban slum to the village to help the people organise themselves. After spending some time with the people who live in the slum near Ballyganj station, we felt the necessity and urgency of going to a village to look at the root of the problem. That is how we came to be in Pashupati's village of Dahakanda.

While narrating our story I constantly feel the need to go back to the source. To lose touch with the source is to me a kind of death. A river, however wide and swift it may be, would begin to dry up as soon as it was disconnected from the source. Yet the source is not the centre; it only pours out the water, it does not control the flow or the direction. Today Jana Sanskriti has spread far and wide, but we hope our link with the source will never be severed.

In our case the source is a concept. In later years the concept has become clearer to us; sometimes its weaknesses have also become apparent, enabling us to think afresh, bring in new ideas and develop them further. It is through interaction and dialogue that ideas evolve. This is why I have come to believe that any dogma is essentially anti-idea. The more we have succeeded in our actual application of the concept of Theatre of the Oppressed in rural areas, the more convinced we have become of the truth of this. Our success encourages us to go back to the source and look closely at our strengths and weaknesses in order to develop an inquiring mind. This spirit of inquiry has enabled us to collect the gems of ideas that lay scattered all around us. But for the moment let me return to the pre-history.

At that time, in the mid 1970s, the entire world was engaged in a major debate. Was it socialism that existed in the Soviet bloc and the east European countries or was a capitalist force operating in the name of state enterprise? Our seniors in the party had taught us to look up to these countries as models. Many others, as well as me, were under the spell of a dream which made us aspire to the conditions that prevailed in these countries. Even after the ideological ground beneath our feet began to shake, it was difficult to come out of this spell. Disillusionment did not happen easily. Dogma or debate? This was the question that agitated my mind the most, and I am sure I was not the only person who worried about it in those days. Even more than economic questions, the most important issue was to decide whether the windows should remain closed or be opened. 'This is the truth because it is scientific' – why did I not realise earlier that such a dogma is actually anti-science?

What is the effect of dogma? I used to ask this question of our seniors in the party. Is it healthy to encourage a plurality of ideas and allow them to interact? If heterogeneous points of view result in confusion, what is the point of talking about dialectical development? We had to wait a long time to get a clear answer. It may not be irrelevant at this point to quote a portion of a letter I wrote to my friend Naresh, with whom I always shared my political thinking:

223

17 August 1987

Dear Naresh,
    . . . Of late I have been frequently meeting people who
are like our leaders. They treat us as autocratic parents treat
their children. They believe that until the children come of
age they should be kept under strict control, and they are
confident that they always know what is best. I feel
disappointed that they do not allow us any space for
discussion. The ability to ask questions would have provided
some relief. So far we have been mute spectators; we have
merely obeyed the orders of leaders in silent submission. The
party system approves of this hierarchy happily. Today it
seems to me this denial of debate had a claustrophobic effect
on us. Unless the political culture of the party can be freed of
this oppressive atmosphere, nothing positive can be achieved.
Meanwhile precious human resources are being wasted.
    Naresh, I must tell you something. The other day I
went to Belur Math, HQ of the Ramakrishna Mission in
Kolkata. I just felt like going there. Religion is the opium of
the people – I do not deny this. As far as institutional religion
is concerned, we experience this every day. This is how a
political perspective considers religion. But when a religious
perspective looks at politics, Christ is born, Buddha, Kabir
and Vivekananda appear among us. It is time to rethink the
truism that religion can only be the ally of reactionary
politics. Religion can also be a form of progressive politics
and progressive political practice can also be religion. I hope
you will not accuse me of abandoning scientific thinking to
escape into a safe haven. So much for today. I will write again.

The realisation of the need to have a space for debate that I
articulated in my letter to Naresh was an important moment of understanding for me. I realised this much later when I began to have free
access to the heart of rural life, and I started interacting with village
people. By becoming a part of a theatre movement from the moment

of its inception, I have had the privilege of sharing my thoughts about theatre and performance not only with the people of Bengal at the grassroots level, but with such people in other parts of India as well. I must thank Jana Sanskriti for that.

It was some time in the mid 1980s. We had our centre at Pashupati's village, Dahakanda. When I stood in the field outside the village, other villages at a distance seemed like clumps of forests, surrounded by tall trees. The landscape was still unfamiliar and created many sensations in me. After sixteen years the newness of the view should have worn off, but I still feel moved by these fields and the sight of the distant villages. This was the beginning of our effort to work outside party politics. We came to the village on our own in order to help the oppressed people organise themselves. The sudden appearance of a handful of English-speaking youth initially created an atmosphere of suspicion in the village. Some thought we were ultra-left extremists, some thought we were foreign spies; others wondered if we were Christian missionaries subtly trying to convert them. Some were more curious than suspicious. We were trying very hard to establish the kind of relationship with them that would enable us to be effective interventionists. It was not easy.

Music was part of the life of the village. From the raised paths crisscrossing the paddy fields, one often heard snatches of *baul* songs. Strains of *bhatiali* or *ujali* (forms of Bengali folk music) wafted in the evening air as people returned home from work or from the weekly market. The magic of these folk tunes cast its spell on me, but it also made me think. I grew up in the nearby colonial city of Kolkata, yet I had never known anything about the richness of our tradition of folk music. This ignorance used to worry me. In later years when I realised that culture is also a weapon of change, I began to see why in the four metropolitan cities developed by the British – Kolkata, Mumbai, Chennai and Delhi – folk culture was never valued. (Chennai in Tamilnadu is an exception that proves the rule, for reasons too complex to go into here.)

On the one hand, we were trying to think of ways to make ourselves acceptable to the village people; on the other hand, I was feeling deeply drawn towards the local forms of music. These two processes continued parallel to each other until the time for harvest drew near. Enacted in every village around March and April, *Gajan* is the most important folk performance in this region. The rehearsals begin just before harvest in December, and (after a break) continue after harvest. By that time I had made friends with a few young men who had natural singing voices and sang lustily without inhibition. I started visiting them in the evenings to listen to their songs, and through them I also earned my right to be present at the *Gajan* rehearsals. I had gained some acceptance by then as a person who enjoys rural music and drama. But I always came back by 7.30 p.m. Everyone in the village slept early to save on the cost of kerosene oil. By 7.30 p.m. or 8.00 p.m. the entire village was dark and silent.

It was during these *Gajan* rehearsals that I came close to village people who were artists – singers, players of musical instruments, actors. I came face to face with the artist dormant in me for the first time. It was like a self-discovery – and it made me graduate to another level of understanding. It was an empowerment, but at that time I did not know the implications of this word. Getting to know the full range of my consciousness – perhaps that is what is called introspection. Augusto Boal has said that theatre is looking at oneself as a spectator, but I did not know this definition then. As long as I was with a political party, I did not have much scope for introspection. Achieving targets was given the most importance there. I felt rejuvenated by the dedication and sincerity I encountered in these *Gajan* rehearsal sessions.

Bimal worked at the loom from morning to evening, weaving rough towels for local use. Jagadish had just returned from Chandannagar where he had gone to work for a decorator to set up a *pandal* for *Jagadhatri puja* (a religious festival). Jagadish's cousins, Jagai and Madhai, were expert *pandal* makers – they had all come back together. Jagadish joined our group now, and so did Sankirtan who had an incredible capacity for physical work. Apart from working as daily wage labour, he went to the Bijoyganj market twice a week to sell rice. He used to pack more than 100 kilograms of rice into two huge sacks and load them on his bicycle. Then he wheeled it and walked along with it for nearly ten kilometres. I remember standing at the edge of the village and watching him push his bicycle away from me. He became smaller and smaller, until he disappeared on the horizon. I looked at this vanishing image and wondered at my own weakness. I used to think the habit of hard work strengthened the body of these people; I did not realise that it is not physical power, but an indomitable will that keeps men like Sankirtan alive and active in their struggle for existence. What is the source of this willpower? None of these questions disturbed my friends or me too much in the initial period. By this time Bhoju had joined the music group, as had Amar and Sujit – all of them had wonderful singing voices. None of them had ever had any musical training, but their songs resonated in the minds of the listeners. Jana Sanskriti began its journey with people like them.

Gradually I was able to put together the first play of my theatre life. The actors were oppressed people, so it was called Theatre of the Oppressed – that is as far as we could think at that point. The first play did not have a continuous storyline from beginning to end. It consisted of many small episodes, apparently not linked with each other, but the episodes were bound together implicitly by the experiences of deprivation and exploitation. This was the unifying theme in the collage. The play was performed in many villages. At that time, women had not joined our group, so men used to enact female roles.

Jana Sanskriti grew out of the initiative of a non-actor like me, who had begun with the intention of becoming a full-time political worker. Before this I had never been involved in theatre or acting. But gradually I found myself being attracted by the entire concept of performance and its rich possibilities. Where did this enthusiasm and ability come from? The answer perhaps lies in a line from Rabindranath Tagore: 'You lay hidden in my own heart/But I did not recognise you.'

About two years after the play was first performed, I invited a noted theatre critic from Kolkata to the village. After watching the play he said it was clearly written by an urban playwright. 'You live in the village. You must be experiencing how people lead their lives here. Why do these actual experiences not get reflected in your play?' I should have realised then that just because the actors belong to the oppressed class the play does not automatically become Theatre of the Oppressed. I had not yet read Augusto Boal's work. Neither had the theatre critic. After this incident I started writing my first play, *Gayer Panchali (The Song of the Village)*, all over again. My friends in the village collaborated with me in this enterprise, enriching the play with their own experience. Thus *Gayer Panchali* was reborn.

It was 1987. Since then *Gayer Panchali* has been performed some 1,500 times, and it remains as relevant today as it was then. It raises questions about the one-sided relationship between the Panchayat (the committee of local government) and the ordinary people, about corruption around the poverty alleviation programme, about the absence of healthcare, about the unavailability of year-round employment. Various laws have been enacted in recent years to make the local government more democratic, but where there is a lack of political will, laws do not change anything.

As Jana Sanskriti emerged as a theatre group, all the doors of the village opened for us, literally and metaphorically. We got to know the minds of the people intimately, something that had seemed impossible at the beginning. A group of young actors from the village were with us who gained confidence from the recognition and appreciation that the village people bestowed on them. They had a new identity now. 'I am not a mere daily wage labour, I am not only a farm hand, I am an actor. My performance inspires hundreds of people urging them to do something. My performance disturbs those who had been enjoying power by exploiting us.' They were proud of their new role in society. Was that not empowerment? I did not know then. My friends, who had come to the village to organise it politically, gained a group of artists who were also political activists. It was theatre which created a group of young men who had conviction and commitment and whose self-esteem was generated by the acclaim of the community. Through writing scripts, directing plays and opening new branches of Jana Sanskriti, I also received my fulfilment as a political worker. Theatre became the medium of our political activity and we became totally involved and busy as the rhythm of work accelerated.

We had performances almost every evening in some village or another. At the end of the play, we discussed various issues with the people of the village. Their views on the different aspects of the play encouraged us and gave us new ideas. By this time women had slowly started to join the group. First one woman came, and then her niece – and men no longer had to perform the women's roles. Some of the villagers came forward when they saw how the young men from villages like theirs, along with some city people, were thinking through theatre about problems that affect rural life. This gave us the opportunity to do organisational work. These enthusiastic people were mobilised to form committees in different villages for protecting the rights of the common people. Theatre made people think, and we discussed in groups the local issues arising out of these plays. The actors in our plays often had a major role in such organisational work because their class solidarity was strengthened by loyalty to the theatre group.

I was losing touch with my urban friends at this time. I was not very happy about this because I felt I needed to interact with them in order to clarify my ideas and give them a distinct shape. I cannot resist quoting from a letter I wrote to Naresh at that time. This letter captures some of my thoughts.

12 October 1988

Dear Naresh,

I have not been home for a long time. I am becoming a villager now. This is quite a different India – without electricity, without telephone. Sometimes I feel rather cut off, especially when I return after a play at midnight after walking for miles in the dark. I eat a little before going to sleep and there are people around me again at daybreak. There are no holidays here because there are no offices, no factories, people are not in the habit of living by the clock.

But Naresh, I seem to have discovered myself anew after coming here. There was an artist in me I was not aware of. This artist returns me to my childhood – arousing in me the wonder and curiosity of the child and the ability to enjoy the simple things of life. You will be glad to know that the child within me is open and free, without any dogma. You will probably see this is as purification of my consciousness, a process of greater humanisation. But I perceive this as an empowerment. In my self-discovery, I must have been through some introspection, but I cannot deny the role of the specific location and the specific people around me who made this introspection possible. Time and place are important in my self-perception. I have learnt so much that was unknown to me. It would not have been possible but for the people around me.

In my last letter I had told you about the actors in our theatre group. They work from sunrise to sunset. But if you see them joking and laughing in the evening you would not guess how backbreaking their day has been. I quite enjoy their lighthearted banter. I have heard that the famous theatre directors of Kolkata impose strict discipline on their rehearsal sessions. If anyone breaks this army-like discipline they are subjected to harsh words and abuse. Perhaps I am not a big enough director yet, so I do not understand the culture of discipline very well. But this does not mean that my actors do not take their rehearsals seriously.

I sometimes think that I had come to the village to empower the people here. But I find myself getting empowered instead. I also realise it would be presumptuous on my part to think of empowering these people who can retain their humour and cheerfulness despite appalling poverty and hard work, and can think of theatre as the most important space in their lives. I am beginning to recognise my own weaknesses when I compare myself with them. All my pride is slowly dissolving in their company. I do not know whether you will agree but I find a great deal of generosity and energy in them. In the words of Vivekananda: 'They are the source of infinite power. With a fistful of gramflour in the stomach they can turn the world upside down.'

Your economism has contributed much to the labour movement in the past. I do not deny the need for that even today. But economics cannot explain why poverty is unable to defeat the spirit of these people. I am continually surprised by the essential generosity of these people, their artistic

*talents, and their ability to laugh and to create. The politics
taught by the party had highlighted their economic
condition, but neglected these human qualities. I had a very
vague idea about empowerment earlier. I am beginning to
think differently now.*

Usually a performance provokes thoughts in the minds of the
audience. The reverse is also true. And this is the reason why it is
important to take this eternal relationship between actor and spectator to a higher and more scientific plane. I remember the experience
of one particular day; it seems as if it was just the other day.

When our theatre group Jana Sanskriti was six years old, a play
called *Sarama* was performed. This was the second play scripted by
me. The central character, Sarama, is an ordinary woman with one
quality that sets her apart from the rest. She has unusual courage and
independence of spirit. When she becomes the victim of the worst
kind of oppression – violation of her body – a new chapter begins
in her life. On the one hand, the man she loved walks out of her
life, and on the other, the newspaper reporters begin to seek her out.
The rapists are part of a well-known anti-social gang nurtured by the
ruling party. She becomes the centre of a political struggle between the
party in power and the opposition. As a victim of the criminalisation
of politics, Sarama receives sympathy and support from a number of
NGOs, something she badly needs at that moment. Sarama survives
these trying times without breaking down. She finds herself pregnant
as a result of the rape but, ignoring the social taboos and the strictures
about the purity of the female body, she decides to have the child and
give it her name.

The entire play was about an ordinary woman who managed to
resist all adversity and social oppression by summoning up a strength
that lay deep within her. What could be a better story for illustrating
empowerment? We were confident about the effectiveness of our play.
It received much acclaim from the cognoscenti, the village people saw
the play with enthusiasm, and the newspapers praised it. What more
could we want? At the end of one performance, we were all basking in
the glow of general applause, and happily talking to the viewers who

came up to give their appreciative comments. Suddenly there was a rude awakening.

'Babu, come here, listen to us!' We looked up to find a group of tribal women calling out to us. In this area of Birbhum district, there is a substantial population of Santhals whose ancestors came from Chhotanagpur plateau in Bihar. I still remember the name of the most articulate of these women. Phulmani said, 'Babu, in your play the woman is strong, very strong. People say you are doing good work. But tell me Babu, what are we to do when the contractor pays us less than our due and asks us to visit him alone? If we don't go to him, he will take away our job. You tell us, shall we give up our work from tomorrow? Tell us Babu, why are you silent?'

I felt that the trees around me were moving and the ground below my feet had suddenly begun to sway. My colleagues realised something was happening, and they gathered around me. Phulmani was still talking and her companions joined her in questioning us. Faced with this tough challenge, we were speechless. Indeed, *Sarama* in our play was shown to be empowered. But behind her was the continuous support of an NGO, which also provided her with economic security. Can organisations like ours really help Phulmani and her companions in reality? Can we say to them confidently, 'Do not be afraid of losing your jobs – you must protest?' Can we advise then on the precise nature of the protest? Should it be a legal challenge or organised workers' action? These questions troubled our minds. Six years earlier, when we began our work in the village, we had wondered whom we were empowering – the village people, or ourselves. I had exactly the same feeling again. Phulmani has to confront a harsh reality every day. She lives in a situation that would have driven us mad. How can we presume to empower her? Despite the adverse conditions of life, the villagers do not seem to lack generosity. If you step into their houses, they will offer you unstinting hospitality. There appears to be no contradiction between poverty and generosity. I am not sure that those who live in affluence are necessarily more generous.

That was a show we were invited to do. We came back to our village with many questions in our minds. It soon became clear to us that if we are touching upon a social problem in a play, it would be a mistake to think that our work is over with the performance. A lot of work remains to be done, or women like Phulmani who have to face oppression will continue to remain helpless. We were lucky that Phulmani and her friends realised that in the context of reality our play has a hollow ring, and they pointed it out to us. After this incident I added a new scene to the play where the actors and actresses raise a question and discuss it among themselves: if an NGO had not come forward to help Sarama, would she have been able to show so much courage against a patriarchal social system, against a weak administration and legal delay? In the new version of the play, we ended by asking the audience to think about these issues.

This was the beginning of our realisation that theatre of empowerment is a long and arduous journey. It does not end with the performance. We could see that it is our responsibility not only to make the people think, but also to mobilise such thoughts towards action. That is why it is sometimes necessary to work in collaboration with other groups who have the same political objective but do not necessarily work through the medium of theatre. We have always tried to collaborate with such groups, and continue to do so today.

At that time, here and there, in an isolated manner, the village people had started getting organised into small groups. But after the Phulmani episode, we saw very clearly that our leadership had influenced these small groups so profoundly that if we were to withdraw from the scene, the existence of these groups would become doubtful. We wondered whether in such a situation of blind dependence our presence could actually be seen as helpful or empowering. Despite remaining outside party politics and electoral games, despite staying far away from state machinery, were we not equating ourselves with the power-hungry political parties by making people dependent on us? There is hardly any political culture in the world which has been able to convince the masses that it is not the people who exist for the party, it is the party that exists for the people. Most political parties exploit people for their profit, as if the relationship is like that between capital and labour – the profit in this case being political power. Yet once in the parliament, the same parties glibly mouth phrases like 'women's empowerment'. Empowerment has suddenly become the buzzword. One wonders where this concern had been earlier.

At this new juncture of Jana Sanskriti's development, I remembered Naresh.

23 February 1991

Dear Naresh,

. . . A new concept enters our thinking and it emerges out of our own accumulated experience. It is new, but not unrelated to what has gone before. It illuminates our existing theories and practice, exposing some of their limitations. It is new because it gives completeness to what was so far incomplete, it frees the old from its limits. I think we cannot recognise the new until we understand the old, and the new cannot exist without the old. I remember Rabindranath Tagore's line, 'You are old but you are forever new.'

Is this what he meant? Don't think we are defensive because for five years what we had considered to be new ideas now appear limited. It does not worry me that these new ideas may seem old tomorrow. Because then one will have to deny the dialectical approach towards development of new ideas.

There was a time when, in spite of our self-image as progressives, we hesitated to go beyond the concepts endorsed by the party. We had no fear in accepting changes in physical sciences. Galileo excited our imagination. But we were not so receptive to developments in social sciences. But let that pass.

I am sure you will be glad to see that I have now finally understood the meaning of the word progress. Perhaps I have written to you about Phulmani and with what dexterity she exposed the stagnation in our ideas. Phulmani's insight came from experience, not from any political institution. Experience constantly teaches us new lessons that institutional education cannot match. Whether

*education should be entirely institutional or not is something
that comes under the purview of the educationist. I am now
thinking of a new play. I will write later with more news.*

Let me return to my narrative. Phulmani's question led us to
become questioners ourselves. How do these people whose daily life is
surrounded by insurmountable difficulties manage to think and laugh?
How can we provide the remedies for every social malady? Will it
not be unscientific to assume that ours is the right position in every
socio-political issue? Can we empower the dispossessed people if we
do not have the humility to acknowledge that we do not know all the
answers?

It was around 1990–91 that I chanced to come across the work
of Augusto Boal. His thinking opened up a new horizon for us. For
me personally, this was the taste of a freedom I had never experienced
before – a liberation not only from the slavery of propaganda, but a
larger liberation. In Jana Sanskriti all the windows began to unlock
themselves, so that breezes from different directions could blow in.
And we began to rediscover what was already around us.

Earlier we used to reach out to the common people with an
unarticulated but inherent assumption of self-importance. We were
artists who were thinking of the masses rather than about ourselves
and our mission was to give direction to their lives. The arena where
we performed the play belonged to us – only to us, the skilled practitioners of this art. Not everyone could possess this skill. However
much we might mingle with the common folk, we were the elite, and
our arena had exclusivity. 'You do not belong here except on conditions of silence and surrender to our way of thinking. We may have
descended from the proscenium to the streets, but we have done so
only to rescue weak, illiterate and backward people like you. You must
listen to us and do what you are told – and that is what will take
you forward and empower you.' This was the message implicit in our
activities. Even though the rural oppressed were participating in this
theatre, it was not Theatre of the Oppressed in the true political sense.
As a result of interaction with Augusto Boal, Jana Sanskriti began to
think differently. We were not doing propaganda theatre any more, nor

were we the fundamentalist representatives of any particular school of thought. We had been able to discard our garb of arrogance and artistic elitism.

I do not know how many times an artist is reborn in a lifetime, but coming into contact with Augusto Boal's thinking was certainly a moment of rebirth for Jana Sanskriti. We could feel that the combined efforts of the local people and those who had come to work for them would help solve social problems. In 1985, when Jana Sanskriti was born and I had just collected some young men of the village in a group, a declaration had been prepared for the new artists. I will quote a section from that here:

> We will not perform on the stage, because that creates inequality. The actors on the stage are situated higher than the audience sitting below. The players are in the light, the audience is in the dark. They are distant from each other. Now think of some of our indigenous art forms – the kind of performances you have been familiar with for a long time. Usually the performers and the spectators sit at the same level – both are equally lighted and they are close to each other. The intimacy between the players and the audience is the main feature here.

In Boal's philosophy of theatre, it was the questions of distance and intimacy, the different levels of location between the players and the audience, which seemed to me the most revolutionary. Not only the performers but the audience were also liberated, because now everybody jointly shared the responsibility of finding answers. Under the influence of Augusto Boal, Jana Sanskriti took the initiative for replacing the earlier monologue by a dialogic process in which the actors and the spectators were collaborators. This was the beginning of Forum Theatre in India.

I will talk about another play that I wrote for Jana Sanskriti called *Shonar Meye* (literally it means 'golden girl', but in Bengali it is an affectionate term for a girl one likes). Before we prepared the play, we had to do a few workshops. It was not an easy task. Because women were involved we could not hold full-time residential workshops. Jana

Sanskriti did not then have so many women's theatre teams. The ratio of women to men in the organisation was not satisfactory then, but today, twelve years later, this ratio is a matter of envy to most theatre groups. In spite of the growth of capital, some feudal values still remain in our villages today. The relationship between men and women is a living example of these feudal remnants. There are other reasons, too, for the extremely unequal relations between men and women in rural families. How patriarchal values coexist with pro-gressivism in so-called progressive political parties is not the subject of this essay. But unfortunately one does not notice any efforts on the part of feminist NGOs in our country to establish democracy at the family level as a way of fighting patriarchy. About the theatre groups, the less said the better.

Initially these women were wives and relatives of the actors of our core team, but even then there were problems. They could join us only in the evenings, and only for about an hour and a half, after housework had been done and the children put to bed. As we would meet for a short while every day, we had to find a workshop space within the village. Some of these women were middle-aged; because they were married early, quite a few were grandmothers already. Some were younger, newly married women, or mothers of small children. This period of one and a half hours in the evening soon became for them a time of freedom and celebration. Even the middle-aged women got into the spirit of the game as if they had travelled back in time. We already knew these women because their families were associated with Jana Sanskriti. They are with us even now and we stay with their families whenever we go to their village.

Normally the women in the village, especially those who are married, do not go outside their homes much. The only occasions when they go out of their enclosed domestic space are when they visit their parents' house to attend the wedding of some relation or during festivals in the village. But even these outings are not without restrictions. Thus the workshops were something entirely new for them. Initially they found it difficult to concentrate or listen to anyone for a period of time. They are used to physical labour; they do some sort of work every minute of their waking hours. The very idea that they would have to sit and listen and think without doing anything with their hands was unfamiliar. I have noticed the same resistance to using the mind among rural men also, but it is especially noticeable among the women because they never sit still at home and they have no exposure at all to the outside world.

Working with the village people helps me understand the structure of our society in general and our own situation. Yet there is a difference in degree and magnitude between the situation of the urban middle class and the rural people who live by physical labour. The men in the village are so totally the victims of a monologic culture that they have rarely any occasion to use their intelligence. It is even more restrictive for the women because no institution is more undemocratic than a rural family. Within the family the relationship between men and women is regulated by feudal values. There is no scope for any dialogue either at home or outside, therefore there is no opportunity for using intelligence. It is as if their role is passively to follow the path laid down by custom. The men at least can look at the blue sky, get a glimpse of the dynamic world teeming with conflicts. That keeps them going, but the women have no such option. Liberation for them is merely a dream.

It was while preparing the play *Shonar Meye* that we first thought of organising an all-woman group. When we did, we found that in such a group those who had earlier seemed shy, docile and reticent began to blossom into vibrantly alive persons in just a few days. The workshops radiated with energy unknown before. Some women turned out to be unusually talented. This was my first workshop with village women and it became a major lesson in understanding the operation of patriarchy at the levels of the family and community in the rural ethos. No feminist could have taught me this lesson. About twenty-two women participated in the workshop. We worked for one and a half hours regularly for ten evenings. The first few evenings were spent in clarifying the concept of an image. Then each person in the workshop created different images representing situations in the family. We eventually had a hundred images deftly incorporating different feelings captured in a nuanced manner. The theme of *Shonar Meye* emerged from these images. The play was scripted by me, but

238

that was the first time I understood that an individual's consciousness can be the aggregate of the consciousness of a collective of people.

'Culture of silence' is a phrase I have heard often. I have never quite understood what it means. Whatever be the lexical root of the word 'culture', its source is in the dynamism of the human spirit. It is a constantly moving and changing concept. I do not know how it can be associated with silence or stillness. Sometimes human beings are silent because for various reasons they are unable to express themselves. Some seek temporary peace through silence, although sometimes in the long run that can become the cause of a greater unhappiness. Some do not express themselves for fear or for lack of conviction, some remain silent because they do not have the habit of self-statement. But human culture is about statement, it is not about silence. While working with the rural women, I never felt that they preferred silence to self-statement. But initially some hurdles seem insurmountable before they gain the confidence to express themselves.

Here I am thankful to Boal because the workshop methodology he devised can change a non-actor into an actor in a remarkably short time. I had learnt – not through theory, but through experience – that everyone has an innate desire to act – if not on the stage, at least in real life. Boal's theatre philosophy highlights this basic human urge and brings out this latent quality by breaking the monologic relationship between the actors and the audience.

In 1992 Boal sent me his book *Games for Actors and Non-actors* as soon as it was published. I noticed that in the Introduction my friend Adrian has written: 'Fundamental to Boal's work [is the belief] that anyone can act and that theatrical performance should not be solely the province of professionals. The dual meaning of the word "act" – to perform and to take action – is also at the heart of the work.'[1]

The play *Shonar Meye* depicts three stages in the lives of women: the period before marriage, the time of marriage and immediately after, and finally life after marriage. The first part highlights gender inequality, the second foregrounds dowry-related problems and the girl's lack of choice in her marriage, and the last part focuses on how violence, duplicity and the centralised character of the family become tools of oppression for women.

Jaipur, the capital of Rajasthan, is also called 'The Pink City' because the palaces and shops in the old part of the city are made of pink sandstone. An invitation to perform in this legendary place was an occasion of great excitement for our artists. After our successful performance at the state government's Jawahar Kala Kendra (a cultural centre for the revival and preservation of the arts) in Jaipur, we decided to do another performance in a slum adjacent to the city where most of the people are Bangla-speaking.

When we performed the full play, we noticed that the audience was silent and totally still. A few women were wiping their tears with the ends of their saris. Empathy? Why not? It is natural that human beings would empathise with each other. Rationalism cannot ignore the demand of emotion, feeling. At this point the Joker said, 'Stop. Today's performance is not like other performances. Today we are not going home after the performance.' The audience was quiet.

JOKER:	Are the problems you saw in the play not problems in your own lives also?
AUDIENCE:	Yes, of course, such problems do exist.
JOKER:	If you do not think about these problems, if you run away from them, will the problems disappear?
AUDIENCE:	No, they will remain. How can they go away?
JOKER:	Will someone else solve these problems for you?
AUDIENCE:	No, no.
JOKER:	Does everyone think so?
EVERYONE IN A CHORUS:	No.
JOKER:	Then, come, let us see how we can find solutions.

The performance began again. This time we started with the third part.

First action

Amba, the central character of the play, is shown busy with her household chores: sweeping the courtyard, cleaning pots and pans, washing clothes, cooking, looking after the children, fetching water, boiling paddy, roasting puffed rice, watering the vegetable garden, serving food to the family, etc. (A housewife in a village works fourteen to fifteen hours on average every day.)

Second action

Enter Amba's husband. He has just returned from the field after a day's work. He wants his food, but Amba has not yet finished cooking. Amba requests him to be patient and wait a little. But there is a simmering anger in him against Amba, because even though they have been married for six months, he has not yet received the entire sum of the promised dowry. Using this delay in serving him food as an excuse, he shouts at her and starts beating her.

Third action

Amba's parents-in-law, who had gone out, return at this point. They hear Amba's screams and see their son beating her. Amba pleads and begs to be spared from this physical torture, but they pay no heed. They encourage their son to throw her out of the house.

Fourth action

A neighbour's wife who has been witness to several such scenes wants to go and protest against this barbaric treatment. But her husband tries to dissuade her. He argues that they have no business getting involved in other people's family affairs.

When the reenactment reached this point, the Joker clapped and called 'STOP!' The actors froze in different postures in an image. The Joker now focused his gaze on the audience. His job was difficult when the audience consisted of men and women. Women in the village are not used to speaking out in front of the men and it would be highly unlikely for them to speak out in public when the issue is the oppression of a woman very much like them. We knew this. But we also knew that if the atmosphere is congenial and sympathetic, and if they feel that the people around are supportive, they can speak very cogently and sensibly. But in this case we did not know. We were in unfamiliar territory. This was Rajasthan, and we come from West Bengal. We did not know what to expect.

The Joker looked at the men in the audience. Quite a few of them seemed ready to come forward, but the first one to enter the arena was a young man of about twenty-two or twenty-three. At the Joker's suggestion the audience and the actors clapped to welcome this young spectactor. The young man said that he would like to change the character of the husband. The Joker's forehead creased in a frown. This is against the rules of Forum Theatre. In any case, if you change the husband – whether you make him better or worse – it would be altering the reality of the situation. But never mind, the Joker thought. Sometimes we have to ignore the rules, it is more important to break the ice.

The spectactor completely humanised the tyrannical husband. Instead of beating the wife or being angry with her over the dowry issue, the spectactor made him sympathetic to her and stood by her, supporting her against traditional patriarchal values. The audience was most amused by this new role and seemed to mock this young man as if he was being hypocritical. The Joker noticed this lack of sympathy, and I also felt surprised because we had never encountered such an attitude in any of our previous performances. There had been attempts to humanise the husband during our earlier performances of the play, but the audience reaction had never been like this. Normally in our familiar environment we know that such an intervention has two positive effects. It dissolves the barrier between men and women, and a congenial atmosphere is created. Sometimes men actually realise what role they could play in their family. Also, women feel freer to speak and participate in this situation.

Anyway, whatever the reason for the strange audience reaction, at least this intervention broke the ice. After thanking the audience the Joker said:

Excellent! If all men and women wanted equality in real life, how much better our lives would be. But do we find such men in families around us? If we did, the play *Shonar Meye* would not have come into being. *Shonar Meye* is not an imaginary story. It is made from the experience of twenty-two women from twenty-two families in a village. We would like to see how you would change this situation. Please come forward. The woman you see in this play – is she a stranger to you? Have you never seen such a woman in your family or among your friends or in your community? In that case, why are you quiet? Please do something. Help us understand your views so that we can help women like Amba, give them courage, offer counsel.

Gradually some women and a few men came up. In the part where Amba's husband is beating her and the neighbour is preventing his wife from going to Amba's rescue, spectactors intervened – sometimes to replace the protagonist Amba and sometimes to replace the neighbour's wife. Responses started coming freely after that. The most interesting was another intervention from the first spectactor, who this time wanted to enact the role of the oppressed woman. As the protagonist, he began behaving in a very submissive and meek manner. He showed Amba obeying her husband, falling at his feet and telling him how much she loves him. At this point, the Joker asked him to stop.

JOKER (*to spectactor*):	You are keeping the oppressed woman's role unchanged. If this kind of behaviour improved her condition, would we have seen this as a problem?
SPECTACTOR:	No.
JOKER:	In that case, what were you trying to tell us by enacting Amba's role like this?

The spectactor was quiet. He stood for a while with his head bent, then looked at the Joker's face and returned to his place. I was watching him from my corner in the audience. He left the place where the performance was being held, and went to a shop near by. He lit a cigarette and sat down to smoke.

When the play was over, we packed our props and walked for about ten minutes to reach the bus stand. While we were waiting for the bus, we suddenly found the young man – our first spectactor – approaching us, with about fifteen men and women and some children following him. They beckoned us to stop. When we turned towards them, the young man suddenly fell at the feet of Sima, our actress who performed the role of Amba, and started crying. He did not say anything. We watched the scene mutely for a while and so did the people who came with him. Then we tried to calm him down. The young man said to Sima, 'Didi, I will not beat my wife again. I beat her quite often. When you were crying after being beaten by your husband in the play, I remembered my wife. She cries exactly like that when I beat her.' The young man burst into tears again. The crowd that came with him confirmed that he was a habitual wife-beater. They were surprised at him today. They said that his behaviour was quite incredible, and hopefully it might mark the beginning of a change. We do not know if he has beaten his wife since then. Two days after that performance, we returned to Kolkata.

But that night, as we walked back in the bitter cold of the Rajasthan winter, we discussed what had just happened. To some of the members of our group, the episode seemed a bit too melodramatic. But to me it brought back memories of an incident that had happened some years ago.

I was walking along the Mridangabhanga River that flows near Digambarpur village in the Sunderbans. Our Mukta Mancha (Open Stage) at Digambarpur is hardly 300 metres away from the river. Whenever I go there for a rehearsal or a workshop, I feel tempted to go for a walk by the river at night. On the banks there are many indigenous trees. On full moon nights the river looks enchanting, but even when there is no moon the rippling waves sparkle like specks of fire.

It was on this river bank that I found Yudhistir in a very distraught condition. He saw me and moved away. This hurt me a little but also got me worried. Yudhistir is a member of our core group. Why was he avoiding me? Had there been some misunderstanding? I returned to the Mukta Mancha and told those who were still there. After discussing the matter they went to the river bank to talk to Yudhistir while I waited. In a while they came back with Yudhistir, who looked repentant and ashamed. 'Dada, how can I do plays with you?' he said. 'I have beaten my wife this morning. I do not know why I lost my patience. My wife said, "You and your *Shonar Meye*, is this what it means to you!"' Yudhistir sounded dejected. Before he joined out theatre group, he used to beat his wife now and then. But that was some five or six years before. We all wondered what had happened suddenly after all these years. We talked to a contrite Yudhistir and later we talked to him and his wife together. The next day we all had lunch together at Mukta Mancha. The fish came from Satya's pond, the vegetables from the gardens of Deepak and Bishwaranjan, the cooking was a joint effort. Yudhistir and his wife remain members of our core group to this day. When we performed *Shonar Meye* near Jaipur, Yudhistir was with us. When the young man fell at Sima's feet at the bus stop, I wondered what was going on in Yudhistir's mind.

Is it not clear that men like Yudhistir have been humanised by theatre? If in a fit of anger he had pushed his wife and hurt her in the morning, what does that have to do with his performing in the evening? He understood instinctively and also from his experience in the group something he would not be able to articulate in words. He had seen that the activities of Jana Sanskriti – Forum Theatre, Image Theatre – were a continuous and evolving process, helping the artist to develop not only his artistic potential but also his social consciousness. It extends his role beyond the arena of the theatre, taking the artist close to the people, making him part of the people, of the greater human self. The artist is then not alienated from the people: he and the people are one and the same.

At one time, I used to do propaganda theatre. The relationship between the actors and the audience did not lack sincerity there. But in that relationship we, the artists, had an implicit sense of superiority, because we thought we understood rural life without being a part of it and believed that we were helping the village people to improve their lot. Even when our intentions were honest, this saviour-like attitude was a barrier to true artistic self-statement. I come across propaganda theatre groups even now who continue to have this attitude. But in Jana Sanskriti we could respond to the criticism of Phulmani or be reborn through the ideas of Augusto Boal, because we had been able to free ourselves from this mindset.

This entire process does not only empower the actors and the spectators, it also humanises them. The movement between artist-I and spectator-I is actually a humanising process. Here the artist on the stage and the artist in real life cannot be different for too long. This is possible in propaganda theatre. I do not know if the young husband in Rajasthan has actually been humanised. Even if the change was temporary, we know that he was touched for a moment by a different kind of consciousness. If the exposure had been longer, he might have been reborn as another Yudhistir. It is such hopes that make us in Jana Sanskriti go on with its attempt to integrate theatre with the real life of the oppressed people.

Anju and her friends live in a slum in Delhi, the capital city of India. Anju, Bhagwandas, Kailash, Kalyani, Ramesh . . . they have all been included in the recent census. Some of them are even voters, some will become voters in the near future. But when it comes to survival, their rights as citizen are different – 'to survive you must fight or else die, and if you survive give us your vote'. The city of Delhi is growing, multistoried buildings are going up, new roads are being built – this is development, isn't it? Anju and her friends are evicted from their homes every now and then. Sometimes, in the name of resettlement, they are sent to live outside the city. As they have to come into the city to work, their travel expenses go up. Anju and her friends work as domestic servants. They are members of an independent workers' mass organisation. This organisation had invited me to conduct a workshop; that is where I met them.

Anju works as a domestic servant in four different houses. She lives with her parents, brothers and sisters. They are Muslims. If it was not for their poverty and desperate need for money, Anju would have been confined within the four walls of her home, not allowed to show her face to any outsider. Her role as a working girl has given her a taste of liberty, but liberation is still a faraway possibility. Anju and her friends have learnt to struggle; they have found within themselves the energy to fight. What other explanation can there be for the way they went about their hard work in middle-class homes and then rushed to attend the workshop with so much enthusiasm and zest?

A Forum Theatre session has begun. The main problem is that the husband of the protagonist has forbidden her from acting in a play organised by a local women's organisation. 'Theatre, dance, music – all this is for men. Women must not do these, it does not look nice. People will say all kinds of things.'

We have seen similar problems in our villages (in West Bengal), too. Many women members of our theatre teams face violence at home when they return from rehearsal. Some husbands do not let them enter the house if they are late. They then spend the night at a friend's house and return home early in the morning. Since we live in the villages and help out families in crisis situations and we are close friends of the men, it is easier for us to deal with problems of this nature there. And besides, women have been participating in discussion and debate on various social problems through theatre. This has imparted a certain self-confidence to these women, which in turn helps them assert their status within the family.

Anju was among the spectators watching the Forum Theatre session. When she raised her hand to say something, I stopped the play. Anju replaced the person who was playing the protagonist.

ANJU (*to her husband*): You work hard for a living and so do I. We do not rest all day. Don't we deserve some entertainment?

HUSBAND: What entertainment for you? I will decide what is good for you.

ANJU: Entertainment is a must if one has to survive. And if even that is unnecessary, then why do you go and

play cards with your friends at the
end of the day?

HUSBAND: That is OK for men. How can women
play cards in public?

ANJU: But I am not playing cards in public. I
am raising awareness among people
about certain social evils. I am doing
a service to society.

HUSBAND: You talk too much, woman! You will
not act in the play. My friends will
make fun of me if you do.

At this point, it was clear to me that the oppressor was imposing his
will through inhuman, patriarchal values. In order to provoke more
interventions, I asked Anju to stop. Anju was irritated. 'But sir, I have
not finished yet.' 'OK, carry on,' I said. The fight for logical victory
between the oppressor and the oppressed continued.

ANJU (to the husband): OK, then tell me, why do you go to
see Hindi films?

HUSBAND: Why? What has all this go to do with
Hindi films?

ANJU: If it has nothing to do with films,
then I shall go to Hindi films
whenever I wish.

HUSBAND: You can go whenever you want, only
take my permission before you go.
All films are not fit for you.

ANJU: That is exactly what I mean. If it is
immoral for women to act in plays
that highlight social issues, then it is
also immoral for men like you to go
and watch scantily dressed women
dancing in the films.

HUSBAND: Those women don't belong to our
families.

ANJU: If it is immoral for women to act in
        plays, then why don't you protest
        when those women dance in the
        films with so few clothes on? Why do
        you buy such expensive tickets to go
        and watch those films?

All the spectators began to applaud. For Anju and her friends, struggle
is an everyday affair. Their struggle is against poverty, against inferiority, against those who make them feel inferior, against orthodox
values. In spite of all that, there is so much life, so much enthusiasm
and confidence in them. There is a proverb in Bangla which says, 'he
who endures, survives'. This proverb can have a reactionary interpretation – that the ability to endure diminishes the will to change. This
used to be my interpretation – until the day I saw Anju performing
in Forum Theatre. I was convinced that the usual interpretation of
the proverb was very typical of middle-class intellectuals, for whom
progress means to destroy all that is old; the more you can demolish
old beliefs and practices, the more revolutionary you are. But if you
do not endure, where will you find the energy to participate actively
in the process of change? To endure means to survive, to live the joy
of life – only then can one become an artist. And, to experience the
joy of life, you have to endure. He who does not have the power to
endure, cannot think of changing the world as it is. Revolution does
not make any sense to him. Frustration and hopelessness become his
companions.

Anju and her friends endure, therefore they survive. And how do
they survive? Through suffering? No. The strength to endure is transformed into the strength to fight for change. The strength to endure is
converted to the energy to change. The mind becomes rational, intelligence develops.

In the play a young man called Bhagwandas was playing Anju's
husband. He is also from the working class – he works in a flour-
mill. He cycles long distances to supply flour to families. People use
this flour to make bread, which is the staple diet in the Hindi belt.
After the Forum Theatre session, I asked Bhagwandas whether he was

really convinced by Anju's argument. Bhagwandas admitted that he had never thought in this way before. But now he thinks that Anju's argument did carry some weight. Anju had escaped the clutches of orthodoxy even though she came from an orthodox family. She had been unable to ignore the urge to change. During the play Bhagwandas had placed himself in the context of his surroundings, therefore the character had become a real character. But when Anju, the spectactor, came up with her irrefutable logic during forum, Bhagwandas found his beliefs crumbling gradually. Now he was his own spectator. He was the spectator of his own reality. 'Anju is right,' he finally admitted. What a wonderful thing. The spectactor's point of view and her feelings had flowed into the actor-character and now the character was the spectator of the actor. Boal says that at such a moment the actor is theatre. This is how humanisation occurs in Forum Theatre. This is where reason and humanism meet, it is a confluence of the two. This gives rise to a consciousness which desires change, which is an expression of empowerment.

The politics I have spoken about for so long is non-party politics. The politics which we use everyday, in our every action. Every human action is a political action. The first political activist of the last millennium was Jesus Christ. Even 500 years before him, there was Gautam Buddha – whose concept of *sangha* is the origin of socialism in our subcontinent.[2]

When Jesus Christ was confined to the church and when Gautam Buddha was dragged into institutionalised religion, it was the beginning of a new kind of politics. A section of people, through their submission to the church, forgot Jesus Christ. In the same way, through their devotion to Buddhism as an institutionalised religion, a section of people forgot Gautam Buddha. The same thing is happening in party politics. Here, too, we see the party becoming larger than the political ideology. The party no longer exists for the people, the people seem to exist for the party. So it is only natural that, like religion, even party politics is resorting to fundamentalism as a strategy for survival. And fundamentalism leaves no space for tolerance. That is why we see a total lack of tolerance even in the case of political parties nowadays. One party splits into many. Like Lakshmi Babu's Jewellery Shop, then the Real Lakshmi Babu's Jewellery Shop, then the New Lakshmi Babu's Jewellery Shop, and so on. Where are the people?

In-party fighting, even violence, is commonplace among party supporters nowadays in our state. For this the party needs violent people – leading inevitably to growing criminalisation within the party. The regular incidents of violence between political parties has brought the underlying truth to light. Not just fundamentalist thinking, this is actually an unholy fight for power.

And this is what my play *Amra Jekhaney Dariye* was all about. This play has been enacted many times by our various Jana Sanskriti teams. In a scene in the play, one sees signboards of four political parties in the four corners of the arena. With each signboard is an actor facing the centre. They are leaders of four political parties. The signboards say, 'Workers Party', 'The Real Worker's Party', 'The Only Original Workers' Party' and 'The Only Workers Party'. At the centre of the stage is a group of hungry, starving people standing frozen in an image, an image that shows various aspects of impoverished life. From the four corners, the four political leaders are calling out to the poor people in the centre; trying to lure them with false promises. What a strategy to demean the people! The image of the hungry people breaks and they begin running here and there, confused by all the promises flying around, unable to understand which party to join.

We were performing this play at one of our centres far away from the city. Among the audience were actors and actresses and representatives of some NGOs. There were some local residents, too, some of whom come to watch Forum Theatre regularly. With such a heterogeneous audience, the forum session would be challenging.

Many spectactors were intervening to replace the hungry people in the play. Forum Theatre was beginning to warm up. Spectactors were facing a challenge. They were bent upon changing the scenario.

As far as I can remember, this is how the first intervention went:

SPECTACTOR *(to the others)*:	See, those four are not people's leaders, they are scoundrels. We must not heed their words.
ONE OF THE OTHERS:	But what else can we do? After all, they are the ones who run the country.
SPECTACTOR:	But can't you see? They are corrupt. They are stealing money, they are . . .
ANOTHER ACTOR:	But what is the alternative *(pointing to the leaders)*? Either it is him, or it is the other or it is the third . . . We have to choose from among them.

The spectactor could not find an answer to this. He kept quiet. The Joker said, 'OK'. The spectactor went back to his place. The actors began to enact the scene again. Another spectactor came up. What he said was something like this:

SPECTACTOR:	Those who do corrupt things in the name of politics should be condemned.
OTHER ACTOR:	We know that. But at least they are promising to do good things.
SPECTACTOR:	All those promises are false. For generations these people have been making promises. If they had kept even one-tenth of all those promises . . .
ANOTHER ACTOR:	But they do keep some promises. I know each is worse than the other, but who else is there?
SPECTACTOR:	But that does not mean you should blindly follow these dishonest hypocrites. The country will go to the dogs.

The Joker asked them to stop. The third spectactor rose from his seat. And this is what he said:

SPECTACTOR: We must show them that we are not paying them any attention.

The spectactor put his fingers in his ears and gestured to the others to do the same. Some of the actors followed him. The political leaders felt they had to do something. They came to the people and tried to explain to them patiently. When that did not work, they threatened to use force. This worked. Some of the people began to follow the leaders. The leaders, with smug expressions, returned to their positions.

Suddenly we heard a woman's voice in the audience. Loud and clear, she shouted 'Stop!' in English. The joker, actors, actresses and spectactor stood still. The woman rose from her place and walked confidently to the arena. She looked hard at the group of hungry people for a few seconds. Then she took out what looked like a small towel from her waistband and went to the centre of the arena and began to wave it like a flag. The actors realised what she was trying to say. They came towards her and sat down in a circle around her, with their fists up in the air. The Joker began to clap and the entire audience followed. Finally, an alternative answer!

The Forum Theatre continued for a long time after that. Someone said to form a new party, another said the people must be aware, yet another said armed struggle, a fourth said non-cooperation. The search for an alternative gave birth to a debate that is relevant in our political context today.

The lady who took out a towel from her waistband and waved it like a flag was called Prabhati. She works hard from dawn to dusk. Tending to the cattle, watering the orchard, sowing paddy seedlings, watering the vegetable garden, cooking for the family . . . and so much more work. The men in her family also work at the same pace. But Prabhati is a very important person in their family. She is at the centre. I have spent a lot of time with Prabhati's family. Her loving and selfless nature has endeared her to everyone around her; she is the nervecentre of the family. At the end of the Forum Theatre session that day, I thought someone who does so much work every day, who is so selfless, who can love so much, who can give so much joy, is no ordinary person. That is why I was not surprised when she took out the towel and waved it like a flag in a call to overthrow the domination of the corrupt political leaders and set up an independent people's organisation. Because those who have scope for empowerment within the family will also be able to find it outside. So which comes first? Family or parliament? Which will give birth to women like Prabhati? We need to answer this question now.

The last time we enacted *Amra Jekhaney Dariye* was about four years ago. I hear that some Jana Sanskriti teams have begun to rehearse it again. But Prabhati and some other spectactors' interventions that day really inspired me. Once again I will present here a section from a letter I had written to my friend Naresh. Perhaps this will also be the conclusion of my piece.

13 May 1999

Dear Naresh,
        . . . every moment there is a new realisation deep within me. Theatre has changed my perspective towards people. As a college student I had once participated in a debate. In a desperate bid to win the prize I had memorised a quotation: 'Education is the manifestation of the perfection already in man.' I did not know then that this was a quotation from Swami Vivekananda. If I had known I would perhaps have dismissed it as reactionary and counter-revolutionary. Now I understand because our theatre imparts an education (in which both the spectators and actors participate equally) which plays an important role in manifesting the perfection within each human being. Theatre is not just a performing art. It is much more. Theatre hides within itself answers to questions such as who am I, what is my strength, etc. Theatre is something with the help of which a new revelation takes place every day, every minute. Boal says theatre is a discovery, from which we learn about ourselves.

In your last letter you said feminism in our country is very United Nations-dependent. I do not know why. But I do see a lot of feminist NGOs nowadays, whose leaders have never really been concerned about the lot of women. Ten years ago they did not use the word 'empowerment'. And even today they see 'empowerment' in very narrow terms. In any party or non-party context that person is considered more empowered who follows orders of the leaders most unquestioningly. Maybe you are right. My work requires me to visit a lot of feminist organisations nowadays. Unfortunately many of these organisations see economic self-reliance as the primary means of empowerment. Economism again! In the present system it is impossible to make each man and woman economically self-reliant. What about those who are deprived of opportunities of economic self-reliance? Will they never be empowered? That is exactly what is happening today on the issue of reservation of seats for women in parliament.

If economism and parliamentary politics were empowering, generations of parliamentary politics would not have kept the ordinary people so resigned to their fate. There would not have been any need for struggle outside parliament for empowering them, people would not die of starvation, and illiteracy would not have been such a widely prevalent phenomenon. But if being empowered means acquiring the courage to dominate and oppress others, then we do not need that empowerment. I think electoral politics is not so much linked to empowerment as it is to the material aspirations of some ambitious women leaders.

Now I understand that the most important step to empowerment is a fundamental change within the human being. I have seen how actors, actresses, spectators, spectactors, everyone involved in theatre finds in this process talents hidden within themselves, identifies the oppressor within themselves, and also recognises the human self. They humanise the oppressor within themselves with their own

*human self. These people are empowered in the true sense.
They can give love, they are not selfish.*

*In my over twenty years of cultural-political activist
life, I have understood the limitations of propaganda theatre.
Of course, its strengths are not to be denied. But through
Theatre of the Oppressed I have seen how the strength of
endurance in the oppressed people gets converted to the
strength to bring about change, a liberation from passivity
and muteness. 'Now I will speak, now I will do. I am no more
a slave to your upper-class arrogance. My intelligence, my
awareness, my empowerment are all linked to each other.'
This, I say, is empowerment. There are so many things that
are integral to this word, 'empowerment' – values, culture,
social norms and so much more. Therefore, at every level in
society a political space is needed where people can question
their social norms, politics, economics, values and culture.
And they will question themselves. And the search begins the
search for an alternative. The courage to embark upon this
search is, to me, empowerment.*

*Perhaps the highest level of empowerment is to go
forward acquiring the ability to win over grief, pain and
adversity. This is the level where each oppressed, deprived
person in the world needs to reach. To tell you the truth, even
today I don't know if I will ever be empowered in that sense.
Write soon.*

NOTES

1. Translator's Introduction to Augusto Boal, *Games for Actors and
Non-Actors* (London: Routledge, 1992), p xix.
2. After Gautam Buddha attained salvation (Absolute Knowledge),
Buddhism spread quickly across Asia largely through the agency
of missionaries called *bhikshus*, who lived on alms and served
the needy. They lived together in groups known as *sanghas*.
Bhikshus believed centrally in three things: i) Buddha, or Absolute Knowledge; ii) *Dhamma*, or that which has human qualities
and iii) the *sangha*, or commune. Gautam Buddha lived and

worked in eastern India; the largest *sangha* was probably in Vaishali, Bihar. It was here that the first *sangha* for women was formed. Initially Gautam Buddha was not in favour of *sanghas* for women. See *Mahamanals Gautam Buddha*, ed. Sukomal Choudhuru (Kolkata: Mahabodhi Book Agency, 1995).

Index

Addis Ababa 12, 125, 128, 129, 131, 132, 144, 149, 151, 152
Adugna Community Dance Theatre 7, 8, 11, 30, 125–53
  Police Training Programme 140, 146–7
  Street Dreams 137–8
Adugna Potentials 149
advocacy 205, 208, 209, 213, 220
Africa 4, 5, 36, 61, 71, 208
African American/s 60, 74, 172, 174
African diaspora 74
African National Congress (ANC) 2, 9, 11, 94–5, 99, 103, 104, 105
  Self-Defence Units (SDUs) 94
  Student Defence Force 94
  Umkhonto we Sizwe 97
Ahmed, Sadia 198, 199, 200, 204
AIDS, *see also* HIV/AIDS 1, 96, 97, 98, 105, 111–16
  counsellors 111, 113
  prevention 111
Alexandra 95, 99, 101, 102–3, 104, 105, 107
America, *see* United States of
American Day of Mourning Parade, The *see* Day of Mourning (DOM) Parade, The
Americans 156, 166, 171, 174, 179
American Indian Movement (AIM) 156, 162, 177, 178

Americanisation Movement 171
Amhara 126, 139
Andrews, Richard 11
apartheid 94, 96
Armstrong, Louis 63
Asia 36, 83
Asian 172
audience/s 8, 10, 14, 22, 23, 24–7, 29, 33, 40, 42, 49, 52, 53, 54, 85, 102–3, 105, 106, 107, 109, 110, 111, 112, 113, 134, 141, 188, 189, 191, 194, 200, 201, 211, 233, 236, 239, 240, 241–4, 245
  adult 195
  black 79, 82
  commercial 104
  involvement 191
  prison 108, 110, 111
  school 112
  target 96, 97, 99, 100, 101, 102, 104, 108, 118
  white 106, 118
autodramma 33, 42, 43, 46, 47, 49, 50, 52, 53, 54, 55, 56

Baldwin, James 80
Balfour Park 101
Bangladesh 1, 189–92, 196–7, 198, 205
Bangladesh Development Programme, The 189
Baraka, Amiri 80
baul songs 225

258

Index

Index

PN 2049 .T39 2004

Theatre and empowerment